S0-AYX-102

Caudillos

Dictators in Spanish America

Caudillos

Dictators in Spanish America

Edited, with an introduction and notes,
by Hugh M. Hamill

University of Oklahoma Press : Norman and London

By Hugh M. Hamill

(editor) *Dictatorship in Spanish America* (New York, 1965)
The Hidalgo Revolt: Prelude to Mexican Independence (Gainesville, 1966, 1970; Westport, 1981)
(editor) *Caudillos: Dictators in Spanish America* (Norman, 1992)

For Sarah and Dan, Molly and Jim, Matthew and Stacey, and Sam

Text design by Cleo Patterson

Jacket design by Bill Cason

Caudillos : dictators in Spanish America / edited with an introduction and notes by Hugh M. Hamill.
     p.   cm.
  Includes bibliographical references (p.   ) and index.
  ISBN 0-8061-2412-1
  1. Caudillos—Latin America—History. 2. Latin America-
-History—1830-   I. Hamill, Hugh M.
F1413.C34   1992
980—dc20   91-50863
                                                              CIP

The paper in this book meets the guidelines for permanence and durability of the Committee on Production Guidelines for Book Longevity of the Council on Library Resources, Inc. ∞

Copyright © 1992 by the University of Oklahoma Press, Norman, Publishing Division of the University. All rights reserved. Manufactured in the U.S.A. First edition.

Contents

Contents

Illustrations

Illustrations

Preface

LEWIS Hanke, as general editor of the Borzoi Books on Latin America for A. A. Knopf, first encouraged me to explore caudillismo. The immediate result was a volume in his series that I edited entitled, *Dictatorship in Spanish America* (New York, 1965). The book prospered for a decade.

Now, a quarter of a century later, I have come back to the subject. What began as a simple updating, however, has turned into a very different book. It could hardly have been otherwise given the continuity of authoritarian rule in such diverse parts of the region as Chile, Cuba, and Paraguay and the rich output of scholarly literature on leadership in the Spanish world.

The students in two seminars at the University of Connecticut deserve the greatest credit for advice on selections in this book. I initially undertook the revision as a teaching device to stimulate discussion. Every week I assigned one or more of the original selections together with several more recent comparable essays. Students wrote criticisms of each before the class met and then debated their value for a new book about caudillos. Votes were cast for and against each potential reading after the discussion. Students were enthusiastic about their involvement in the editorial process. Seminars were exciting events and they convinced me that a new volume would succeed. My own perceptions changed, too, in the course of the debates as well as over time. Eventually I elected to retain twelve of the original pieces and to add fifteen new ones. A new introduction became essential, as did the suggestions for further reading. As in the Knopf volume, the notes from each essay are excluded in the interest of brevity.

My student critics are Tim Alstrum, John Bobko, Peter Caron, Paul Davis, Ann Friedman, Allan Metz, Susanne Muszala, Evelyn O'Connor, Jim Oehrig, Lee Penyak, and Joaquín Santiago. Alfonso

Múnera has been of special help as critic and research assistant. I am also indebted to my most loyal and best critics, Elizabeth Hamill, Paul Goodwin, Charles Hale, and Robert Mead. Leon Campbell encouraged me early to prepare a new book on caudillismo. Georgette Dorn of the Hispanic Foundation of the Library of Congress, Stefan Granito of the Bettmann Archive, Carol Maturo, Jane Rausch of the University of Massachusetts, and Thomas L. Welch of the Columbus Memorial Library of the Organization of American States were crucial in the preparation of the illustrations. Patricia Cutts assisted with the preparation of the map, and Dee Gosline skillfully typed many selections onto disk. Peter Price created the index with sensitivity. Sarah Nestor and Kimberly Wiar, Managing Editor and Acquisitions Editor respectively at the University of Oklahoma Press, helped greatly to complete this book through their interest, high standards, and meticulous attention to detail.

HUGH M. HAMILL

Storrs, Connecticut

Caudillos

Dictators in Spanish America

Introduction

ALL societies have experienced personalist leaders, whether Scottish chieftains, French emperors, Sicilian godfathers, North American frontiersmen, Italian condottieri, Soviet chairmen, Arab sheikhs, Chinese warlords, Indian pacifists, Germanic totalitarians, or Louisiana populists. There is little argument, however, that Spanish American caudillos have been more numerous and more intrusive in history than their counterparts in many other societies. Why has this been so? Do the ingrained values of Hispanic civilization make it more prone to produce this political phenomenon than other societies are, or has a peculiar pattern of historical events encouraged this brand of authoritarian rule to become so visible in a culture no more disposed to it than any other?

Whatever the answer to this fundamental question, historical images of personalist leaders are often the point of departure for studies of the Hispanic tradition. From Reconquest to Conquest we find El Cid in armor on his white horse under the walls of Valencia in the eleventh century; Isabella the Catholic, likewise in armor, as she rode triumphant before the Alhambra in 1492; Fernando Cortés as he and his mistress Malinche played off indigenous factions against each other in the conquest of Mexico in 1519 to 1521; Francisco Pizarro disrupting the Andean power structure by seizing Atahualpa the Inca in 1532; Lautaro, leader of the Araucanians, as he forced the Chilean conquistador Pedro de Valdivia to drink molten gold in 1553—apocryphal but just; and Lope de Aguirre decreeing his own rebellion against the king as he floated down the Amazon in 1560.

More images of powerful people came with the era of independence and its aftermath: Miguel Hidalgo, charismatic man of the cloth, brandishing an emblem of the Virgin of Guadalupe as he incited a mob against the Spaniards in 1810; the Spanish general and hacendado Félix Calleja, Hidalgo's nemesis, leading his triumphant royalist army through the streets of Mexico City in 1812; Simón Bolívar, wielding pen as well as sword in the cause of independence from 1810 to 1825; José de San Martín scaling the Andes to help free Chile in 1817; and the austere Dr. Francia succeeding the Jesuits as master of Paraguay from 1811 to 1840.

Caudillos crowd the aisles of history and legend in the republican nineteenth century: Facundo Quiroga, whose ferocious temperament guaranteed his success at the card table; Antonio López de Santa Anna, famous for losing both his leg and half his country; and "Bloody Rosas," whose obituary said "his greatest happiness [in English exile] seemed to be to sit on his horse and give orders."[1] Then there were Andrés Santa Cruz, who briefly controlled the Confederation of Bolivia and Peru in the 1830s and, along with many others, demonstrated to the creoles that a mestizo could rule; the improbable filibuster William Walker, who proved in the 1850s that a hundred-pound gringo from Nashville could be at least temporarily the caudillo of Nicaragua; and Francisco Solano López, who gained an Irish lover, Eliza Lynch, but lost his life in the carnage called the Paraguayan War.

The last hundred years have been well stocked with authoritarian figures highly conscious of their self-images and media opportunities: Victoriano Huerta reviewing his Mexican troops in resplendent uniform in 1913; Juan Perón speaking grandiloquently from the balcony of the Casa Rosada in Buenos Aires; Fidel Castro stroking his messianic beard before a mass audience of *guajiros,* or country folk, in Cuba; and Manuel Noriega with his fist clenched overhead leering into the camera—and at the United States— before the Bush invasion of Panama in 1989.

How do we explain these dominant figures over such stretches of time and space? One approach is to link caudillos to their countries: Páez and Venezuela, Díaz and Mexico, Perón and Argentina, Castro and Cuba, Pinochet and Chile. Certainly there is no full understanding of the tradition of such leadership and the leaders themselves without close attention to the societies that spawned them. This study has as its focus the caudillo (with all the nuances that word suggests, as we shall see) and does not pretend to explain systematically the histories of the countries that caudillos led nor the processes of economic and social change that they helped promote or forestall. Nevertheless, while the focus will remain on the individual and the phenomenon of caudillismo, the authors of the selections in this book—including some caudillos themselves—serve to a lesser or greater degree to provide a societal and cultural context. Readers will emerge with an aggregate of impressions and interpretations of the countries that produced caudillos. It must be stressed, however, that the caudillo, together with his personal capacity to assume, maintain, and, ultimately, lose power, is at the center of this history.

Definitions and classifications

Caudillo and *caudillismo* are defined in this book as the basic variants of *dictator* and *dictatorship* in the Spanish world. Many writers, including some in this work, would dispute the broad meaning of *caudillo* that I employ. Indeed, *caudillo* is a generic term with its roots in the Latin *capitellum*, the diminutive of *caput* or *head*, and thus is not really more precise than *dictator*. It does, however, have a resonance that suggests the unique milieu and conditioning elements of Spanish America. Only through the use of modifiers or direct application to individual leaders will it be possible to qualify and sharpen the use of *caudillo*. The Bolivian social critic Alcides Argüedas (1878–1946), for example, sought to distinguish between the *barbarous caudillos* and the *cultured caudillos* in two of his books.[2] A nearly endless variety of adjectives will also be found in and out of this volume that range from *gaucho* to *military* and from *frockcoated* to *totalitarian*. The supporters and detractors of particular caudillos have found nicknames for them that are quite as varied as the leaders themselves. Thus Bolívar was "The Liberator," Dr. Francia became "El Supremo," Argentina's Hipólito Yrigoyen was "El Peludo"—"The Armadillo," Venezuela's Juan Vicente Gómez was "El Bagre"— "The Catfish," Rafael Trujillo was "El Benefactor," Mexico's Calles dubbed himself "El Jefe Máximo," Perón was "El Conductor," Castro enjoyed a first-name basis—"Fidel," and Alfredo Stroessner was "El Tiranosauro."

The disrespectful sobriquets in this list suggest the familiar North American pejorative flavor so often given to *caudillismo*.

Such a disparaging nuance obscures its basic meaning and tends to discourage study of the institution except, as Kenneth Grieb suggests, "to condemn [such regimes] by comparison with Yankee-style democracy."[3] As we search for meaning, the question of legitimacy will arise. Certainly there were many caudillos in history whose power was wholly de facto and who fit Argüedas's "barbarous" label. Yet Francisco Franco would never have proudly applied the official title "El Caudillo" to himself during and after the Spanish Civil War (1936–39) had the term been negatively value laden within his society. The task, then, is to arrive at definitions of phenomena that are accurate within the culture that nurtures them. (It should be noted that Franco was loath to share his title with Latin American strong men. Until his death in 1975 Spanish censors attacked any publisher's application of *caudillo* to New World rulers to avoid demeaning the word.[4])

Most of the analytical essays that follow provide working definitions of *caudillo* and related terms, so that readers will have ample choices as they craft their own. In addition, other sensitive writers who know Spanish America will offer their own meanings. Francisco José Moreno, for example, examines caudillismo's emergence in the wake of the wars of independence and distinguishes it from dictatorship:

> Within the Spanish political tradition, caudillismo was an effort to fill the vacuum left by the removal of the symbol of institutional authoritism [i.e., the king]. Caudillismo is an attempt, based upon charisma, to keep political forces under control by promoting allegiance to the person of the leader. Caudillismo, thus, is not to be confused with military control. The former could create legitimacy whereas the latter could not. Allegiance would render the use of violence unnecessary. The employment of force is thus indicative of failure to secure allegiance. Caudillismo is a noninstitutional way of satisfying the authoritistic orientation latent in a country's political culture. Due to its reliance on individual leadership, the caudillistic solution tends to be temporary. The caudillo could be challenged by another charismatic leader, or could be deposed by a militant minority free of his spell. And even if he

were successful in retaining control, his existence was limited. Once he was dead, the legitimacy built upon allegiance to his person would disappear. But despite its temporary nature, caudillismo is more conducive to stability than dictatorial (illegitimate) rule. The caudillistic solution is basically legitimate and thus acceptable. Dictatorial rule rests upon coercion and its mere reliance on force is indicative of its inability to secure allegiance.[5]

The political theorist, José Luis Romero, writing more specifically about caudillos in early republican Argentina, remarks that

> the caudillo received his mandate as leader not from any specific legal enactment, but indirectly, by drawing on the support of elections and plebiscites to legalize his de facto authority. Essentially, it was the people's obedience he had won, given to him in recognition of his innate gifts for command. . . . The caudillos carefully guarded their prestige and made use of their psychological insights to show their superiority. In this fashion, resourceful and wily, the caudillos tightened their grip on the people, only secondarily needing legal confirmation of their right to rule.

Romero does not agree with Moreno over the matter of legitimacy. Rather he argues that "nothing except direct intuition could justify the grant of popular sovereignty to these men, since they belittled the very institutional mechanisms that might have served the people . . . their authority was always de facto and their policies always authoritarian."[6] For example, a classic justification for the concentration of power in oneself is that of Porfirio Díaz. Díaz told the American journalist James Creelman in 1908 that "I received [the Mexican] Government from the hands of a victorious army [in 1876] at a time when the people were divided and unprepared for the exercise of the extreme principles of democratic government. To have thrown upon the masses the whole responsibility of government at once would have produced conditions that might have discredited the cause of free government."[7] Caudillismo was, then, by Díaz's lights the logical vehicle for his country. The selection by Luis González explains what that meant in Don Porfirio's Mexico (chapter 14). The essays by François Chevalier, Peter Smith, and Jane Rausch further explore the question of the legitimacy of a caudillo's power (chapters 1, 5, 9).

One approach in the search for definition is to address the problem of who is a caudillo and who is not. Kalman Silvert, a major interpreter of Latin American politics writing in 1966, emphasizes the "highly personalistic" qualities of caudillos as he remarks on the wide range of circumstances that might produce them. While the military has been a frequent avenue, some caudillos have been civilians; some have been liberals and others conservatives; some have had urban roots and others rural; some have been "modernizing in net influence" and some traditional. Silvert, nevertheless, holds to a more restricted definition by insisting that "the caudillo rules over a situation which is truly primitive, or one which he and his constituency see as primitive and simple. Only the least developed countries in Latin America still have national leaders of the caudillo stripe." As examples he mentions two recently assassinated caudillos, Anastasio Somoza of Nicaragua and Rafael Trujillo of the Dominican Republic, and draws particular attention to their countries as family enterprises.

Silvert defines other leadership categories, including the "ad hoc military amateurs," whom he sets apart from "the traditional caudillo [because they] ally themselves with significant civilian interest groups to obtain complex, institutional, and partially impersonal ends." He has Rojas Pinilla of Colombia, Pérez Jiménez of Venezuela, Pedro Aramburu of Argentina, and Castillo Armas of Guatemala in mind.[8] In this volume, the historian Lyle McAlister further explores the background of civil-military relations and the role of leadership (chapter 16).

A more recent analysis compares the postindependence caudillos with modern military leaders. For Brian Loveman and Thomas Davies, "neither the caudillo nor today's professional soldier is committed to political movements or interests based on traditional ideological questions of liberal or conservative, left or right." For these scholars, "both caudillos and professional soldiers usually justify their rule in nationalist terms of saving and maintaining the fatherland, although this appears more frequently among the latter than the former. Neither the caudillo nor today's professional soldier tolerates dissent, much less formal opposition, and both react quickly to stifle it. Finally, both the caudillo and the professional soldier employ force as the basis for their political rule." Loveman and Davies also stress important differences. Professional soldiers maintain their respect for hierarchical obedience and military education. They submit their own "personal desires to the well-being of the military institution and nation." As we might expect, the individualistic caudillo "hated all laws and authority except his own." Nevertheless, it should come as no surprise that the modern officers respect the "regimes of the great caudillos in their nations' past," because "they alone prevented the national disintegration which would have resulted from 'politics'," the factional morass which, the authors argue, the military hate.[9]

Furthermore, many scholars follow the Brazilian Fernando Henrique Cardoso's warning that in classification of military regimes in recent history we must avoid confusing "family based caudillismo," like the Somoza regime, and "the caudillismo of the old Latin American military," like Stroessner's Paraguay, with the technocratic Bureaucratic Authoritarianism that emerged in full force in the 1970s: "In these regimes it is not a single general or colonel who, like the caudillos of the nineteenth century, imposes a personal order by decrees. Rather, it is the military institution as such which assumes the power in order to restructure society and the state. . . . The armed forces take power not as in the past to maintain a dictator in power (such as Vargas or Perón) but rather to reorganize the nation in accordance with the 'national security' ideology of modern military doctrine."[10] Nevertheless, I find even with the depersonalized aspects of Bureaucratic Authoritarianism taken into account, that a powerful role for an individual officer still exists. General Juan Velasco Alvarado in Peru (1968–75) is one example. Most noteworthy is Augusto Pinochet's extraordinary manipulation of his military base in Chile, which made him a supreme caudillo between 1973 and his electoral defeats in 1988 and 1989 (see chapter 26).

Another intriguing approach to the classification of leaders is what Carlos Rangel, a Venezuelan publicist, calls the *consular* caudillos. He argues that these were products of the growth of U.S. imperialism after the Spanish American War of 1898. He uses the definition of consul as a "person accredited by a foreign state to protect its nationals and interests in the country to which he is accredited." Consular caudillos were those who recognized that they could only acquire and hold power if they enjoyed North American support. As they reciprocated by protecting U.S. nationals and the northern giant's strategic interests, they could confidently expect long-term protection. According to Rangel, "the power of consular caudillos fed on itself. The sale of concessions to foreign investors and the economic activities that directly or indirectly resulted from them brought money to the national treasury; this allowed the consular caudillos to offer their officers better pay, their troops better arms, and their partisans greater spoils." These tidy relationships, of course, had many strains. Franklin Roosevelt voiced his uneasiness about support for Trujillo in his famous quip: "Yes, he is an s.o.b., but he's our s.o.b." Rangel also includes Fidel Castro as a consular caudillo of the Soviet Union for most of his years in power.[11]

The generic term caudillo has a variant or related term: cacique. Though less heralded, the local cacique, the Spanish American political boss, is as compelling a figure in his own jurisdiction as the national caudillo is in his. In the emergence of the national caudillo it may be argued that the cacique is a sine qua non. This argument is implicit, for instance, in Chevalier's essay on the caudillo's personal ties (chapter 1). The term is New World: the Spaniards early encountered it among the Tainos and Arawaks of the Caribbean. The Arawak word kassequa lent itself to Spanish orthography and usage to mean, at first, local Indian chief, and later any regional strong man, regardless of race. Cacique was in such general use by the nineteenth century that it became common even in Spain. Given geographic isolation and the vastness of Spanish America, the scattered power nuclei, controlled by caciques, were fundamental to the emergence of national caudillos. Whereas a cacique is a ruler among men, a caudillo is a ruler among caciques. The Mexican Revolution between 1910 and 1920 produced an extraordinary number of examples of this cacique-to-caudillo elevation. Some writers, like Rangel, have preferred to imagine national "supercaudillos" who dominate and depend upon regional caudillos who are the equivalent of caciques.[12] Other distinctions among the upper levels of leadership include those of *caudillo supremo* and *jefe máximo*. Men like Juan Manuel de Rosas in La Plata, José Antonio Páez in Venezuela, and Díaz in Mexico were particularly adept masters of collections of caciques. The value of the word *cacique* is that it is relatively unambiguous, whereas *caudillo* requires modifiers.

Interpretations and Background

The range of interpretation of caudillismo is extensive. Some students search out theoretical models that have universal application. In his essay on legitimacy Peter Smith employs and expands upon Max Weber's theories (chapter 5); and Jane Rausch evokes Sidney Hook's "eventful" and "event-making" heroes in her analysis of a Colombian caudillo (chapter 9). Howard Wiarda and Michael Kryzanek use Juan Linz's model of authoritarianism as an outgrowth of the collapse of traditional forms of legitimacy in their essay on Trujillo (chapter 20).

Glen Dealy, who poses his controversial cultural argument in chapter 2 that caudillos are the product of societies in which power is based on the accumulation of followers rather than of wealth, has other interpretative approaches worth noting. Among them is his Tradition of Monistic Democracy. *Monistic* refers to Dealy's idea that Latin American society has evolved in a unitary fashion in which potentially competing groups and corporate elements are drawn together and controlled from above by a central authority. This is in contrast to pluralist, laissez-faire, democratic forms, in which competition is encouraged. In his essay Dealy attacks North American social critics of Latin America who see "only hopeless diversity rather than the basic social monism because they have been looking through cultural, i.e., liberal, blinders." The appearance of multiple competing interest groups, Dealy says, is deceptive: "One group tends to be aligned with the government to the exclusion of its natural opposite. With this alignment often comes official proscription or harassment of the competing interest. Unity is achieved by suppression of the opposition and the traditional quest for monolithic control continues." In such a

system, which one may infer favors caudillismo, "it is consistent
. . . that political parties should be monolithic, government should
be centralized, school systems centrally controlled, religious diversity discouraged." Dealy, who is well versed in ancient and
medieval philosophy, invokes St. Thomas Aquinas as well as
Bolívar and, finally, Fidel Castro. He quotes Castro as saying in
1961, "There is only one interest, the collective interest, the interest of all." Under such circumstances individual rights, as Aquinas
put it, "are not absolute but relative." The common good in a
monistic democracy always has primacy over the individual good.
It is obvious, then, that the autocrat may readily determine the
common good with relative ease and extend himself in power, as
Castro has done.[13]

Claudio Véliz's well-known theory of The Centralist Tradition of Latin America is compatible with Dealy's monism. Véliz
builds a centripetal argument based on the historical absence of
feudalism in either Iberia or America. This meant that a powerful
Castilian monarchy, uninhibited by pluralistic barons or permanently autonomous American conquistadores, fashioned an elaborate imperial bureaucracy in which all components depended upon
the central authority of the Crown. By the time of Ferdinand
and Isabella (1474–1516), royal law and royal administration had
become standard while urban and señorial autonomy were reduced. Subsequently Spain's adherence to Catholicism during the
Reformation excluded religious nonconformity and hence another
avenue to pluralism. Véliz argues that, powerful as its influences
were, the French Revolution did not bring about the replacement
of hierarchical and centralized republican governments for very
long after independence. (He calls the nineteenth century "the
liberal pause.") Meanwhile, such industrialization as came to
Latin America was more imposed by the state than developed by
individual bourgeois initiative. In any case, the global depression
of 1929 snuffed out liberal impulses and fostered "authoritarian
recentralization."[14]

The extensive literature on corporatism is intimately related
to Dealy's monism and Véliz's centralism. One succinct effort to
explain corporatism argues that it is an organizational pattern of

state-society relations in which "interest representation [is] based on noncompeting, officially sanctioned, state-supervised groups. In contrast to the pattern of interest politics based on autonomous groups that is posited by the pluralist model, [the corporatist] state encourages the formation of a limited number of officially recognized groups that interact with the state in clearly defined and regularized ways."[15] In *ideal* terms corporatism defines a harmonious society in which well-regulated groups pursue moral objectives under the guidance of the state. The degree to which such a state is authoritarian may vary according to how much autonomy is delegated to the groups and how much freedom to interact among the groups occurs. It is the state, however, that authorizes and licenses the participation by groups and individuals in the business of government. In chapter 4, Richard Morse includes an analysis of the Mexican state by Frank Tannenbaum that provides one example of corporatism at work.

Monistic democracy, the centralist tradition, and state-controlled corporatism all lend themselves well to caudillismo. The problem that all three present, however, is the degree to which theory informs practice. As will become evident throughout this book, caudillos do not easily conform to patterns, nor do they resemble each other any more than countries as disparate as Chile and Cuba resemble each other.

Factionalism: An Alternative Interpretation of the Caudillo
It may be argued that the Spanish background, imperial rule, and colonial conditions were in some ways at odds with the theories just explored. It is possible, for example, to give greater importance to factions in society, the tensions they created, and the means of their control in trying to explain caudillismo. It is well known that there was a powerful tendency toward separatism, regional autonomy, and individual liberty deeply rooted in the Iberian past. These were in part the functions of a divisive geography and of the Reconquest—an eight-hundred-year process of endemic warfare punctuated occasionally by long stretches of peace between Muslim and Christian Spaniards. Those less belligerent times between holy wars left opportunities for petty local grievances to fester and

regionalism to flourish. The twentieth-century Spanish philosopher José Ortega y Gasset referred to this centrifugal phenomenon as "invertebrate Spain." When an occasional major offensive was mounted by the Christian north, as in the great drive across the Sierra Morena in 1212, Spaniards on both sides temporarily suspended their local quarrels and collaborated in the larger encounter. Only exceptional leaders like Ferdinand III of Castile, who captured Córdoba in 1236 and Sevilla in 1248, were able to assemble adequate forces to win irreversible victories in the guise of crusades for the Holy Faith. Thus simultaneous centrifugal and centripetal traditions persisted at the end of the fifteenth century. The coincidental conquest of Granada and first Columbian voyage vastly strengthened Queen Isabella and the institutions of the Castilian monarchy and engendered the power base that would make Spain the dominant European state of the Golden Age. The ten-year contest for the last stronghold of Muslim power in the Iberian Peninsula (1482–92), however, also reenforced the militant values of the ancient *frontera,* or border, ethos. Peasant soldiers and mounted hidalgos learned once again that the sword and the war horse were not only weapons to destroy the infidel but also material instruments that brought them personal advantage through spoils, individual status, and prestige. These lessons were further learned during the next two generations through the unimagined opportunities for military prowess in the Americas.

New World caudillos appeared most dramatically during the Antillean and circum-Caribbean explorations and, especially, the epic conquests of Mexico and Peru. Cortés, Pizarro, and a host of lesser leaders were, first of all, adept at attracting support for their explorations. Recruitment and funding were largely private affairs sanctioned by a state willing to wait for individual initiative, capital, and management to deliver, relatively risk free, new subjects, new souls, new territories, and new tax bases to the Crown. The soldiers of fortune who became conquistadors were bound together by a complex set of material, spiritual, and psychological goals. As Bernal Díaz del Castillo, Cortés's foot soldier turned chronicler, put it, "We came here to serve God, but also to get rich."[16] A caudillo quickly learned, however, that, as J. H. Elliott has written, at one and the same time [he had] to meet the requirements of his backers, and to satisfy the demands of the no less individualistic body of men who had placed themselves temporarily under his command. Tension was therefore built into every conquering expedition—tension about aims and objectives and about the distribution of the spoils. The discipline, such as it was, came on the one hand from the capacity of the leader to impose himself on his men and, on the other, from the collective sense of commitment to a common enterprise.[17]

Early on, then, the proto-caudillos of Spanish America established traditions of military personnel management and the nurture of loyalty that would surface again centuries later.

Meanwhile, factionalism erupted almost simultaneously with successful conquest. Iberians, who had traditionally defined themselves as Castilians, Gallegos, Basques, Murcians rather than "Spaniards," gravitated to regionalist cliques. Order of arrival also determined other groups. Before the dust had settled over the ruins of the Aztec capital of Tenochtitlán, rivalry between the followers of Cortés and Pánfilo de Narváez broke out. By 1524 Cortés "himself epitomized the conquistador-become-settler attitude toward more recent immigrants when . . . he reported that the majority of new arrivals were vice-ridden sinners of low birth, and that he would trust Indians sooner than such Spaniards."[18] The bitter civil wars between the followers of Pizarro and Diego de Almagro in Peru revealed another bloody example of factional disarray.

The Castilian Crown's imposition of authority over these bickering subjects took a shape that would be profoundly important for our understanding of the emergence of caudillismo. The monarch very quickly emerged as the focus of appeal for resolution of factional wrangles. Not only did royal officials move in to exercise sovereignty, but they also became the channels through which mediation and judgment could be available to New World subjects. In short, the Crown made itself indispensable as the referee of disputes. Far from emerging as a harmonious colonial state, the king presided over endless quarrels in a faction-ridden society and indeed even deliberately encouraged them through overlapping jurisdictions and ambiguous decrees.[19]

To make clear the Crown's role and the colonial response I prefer to employ a radically different conceptual scheme for imperial rule than that of the familiar but unrealistic administrative flow chart that places king and Council of the Indies at the top and local officials such as corregidores at the bottom. My scheme is a wheel, the Crown in the center, the rim composed of an infinite variety of viceroys, judges, intendants, prelates, monopoly officials, corporate representatives, Indian municipalities, hacendados, mine operators, and merchants united as common subjects and creatures of the king. Dependent upon the hub of the wheel for jobs, privileges, and corporate charters, the component parts of the rim sought arbitration of their endless disputes through the spokes of open communication in appeals to the corpus of monarch-based law.

As long as the moral authority of the Crown was vested in the hub, the medieval Thomistic order, which Morse discusses in chapter 4, prevailed and sustained the empire through difficult times—even when, as occurred between 1665 and 1700, the monarch was insane. Although a dynastic shift from Hapsburg to Bourbon rulers in 1700 ushered in an era of drastic reforms and created enormous resentments among colonials, the empire survived until the hub was destroyed by the French invasion of Spain in 1808 and Napoleon's seizure of the legitimate monarch, Ferdinand VII. Only then did the rim of the wheel crumble into its component factions. With no recourse to the legitimate judgments and moral imperatives of the hub, the fragments sought to resolve their quarrels by resort to violence. The disastrous years of the independence wars were not only struggles to establish new states free of Spanish control; they were also civil conflicts to establish dominance of one faction over another. A dynamic tension that had balanced centrifugal factionalism with centripetal authority suddenly broke.

Into this chaotic scene—different in intensity, of course, from region to region—moved the caudillos. As Chevalier and I demonstrate in chapters 1 and 6 respectively, the fabric of colonial society had already created personalist networks and resources to which the earliest caudillos—including, for example, Padre Hidalgo and his archenemy, royalist general Calleja—could resort to build their armies. The leadership qualities of Peninsular Reconquest and New World Conquest, so long subliminal, quickly reappeared.

The Collection

Consideration of the Peninsular and colonial background leads to the selections that compose this book. They were culled from an immense literature on caudillismo. My object is to represent as broad a spectrum of interpretation and substance as possible. The often brutal essence of caudillismo is such that objectivity about the institution, and particularly its exemplars, is rare. The majority of the pieces in this collection are therefore biased and have been included to challenge readers to achieve their own unique definitions and views.

In making the selection I have sought provocative essays that combine narrative development and theoretical underpinnings. The writers include cultural, political, social, and intellectual historians as well as anthropologists, political scientists, sociologists, journalists, and practitioners. They come from many places, including Argentina, Canada, Chile, Colombia, Cuba, the Dominican Republic, France, Mexico, Spain, and the United States. Among these authors are revisionists, sycophants, bitter enemies of dictators, apologists for caudillismo, a turn-of-the-century racist, and three caudillos who speak for themselves. On the other hand, while breadth is important, it is not my purpose to compile a historical encyclopedia of caudillismo. Many famous leaders are not considered, while some obscure caudillos receive ample attention. Some major countries with rich histories of caudillismo are not included, while a small country like the Dominican Republic is examined from three perspectives. The intent is to represent a range of leadership styles across a varied landscape and to encourage debate over the nature of a historic phenomenon that has approached universality in Spanish America at one time or another.

Some of the essays are paired because of their contrasting or related approaches to a problem of interpretation or to an individual caudillo, as in the case of Fidel Castro. The first five are grouped together in Part One because they stress theoretical arguments. The collection begins with an essay by François Chevalier that explores the ancient personal ties that have bound Iberians to leaders and propelled those leaders to prominent positions throughout Spanish and Spanish American history (chapter 1). In the next essay, Glen Dealy, whose work on monistic democracy was discussed earlier, argues that a personalist leader or Public Man in a Spanish Catholic society finds his way to power through the accumulation of friends rather than through material wealth (chapter 2). The essay by Eric Wolf and E. C. Hansen is in sharp contrast to those by Chevalier and, especially, Dealy. Wolf and Hansen argue that systems of material rewards—together with a dose of *machismo*—were essential if caudillos were to build and sustain their power (chapter 3). Richard Morse, in a classic essay in political theory, sees two major traditions in Iberian history that have important implications for the study of caudillismo. He polarizes medieval Thomism, exemplified by Queen Isabella of Castile, against Renaissance Machiavellianism, personalized by Isabella's husband, King Ferdinand of Aragón, and demonstrates that these philosophies became dominant and recessive forces at different intervals in the unfolding of Spanish America over the last half-millennium (chapter 4). Peter Smith concludes this theoretical part of the book with his search for an authentic treatment of caudillos within Hispanic political culture. He focuses most of his attention on the problem of legitimacy (chapter 5).

It is often maintained that "the nineteenth century" in Spanish America began in the 1820s with the achievement of independence and the establishment of republics. It is logical, however, for students of caudillismo to examine the immediate origins of those leaders in the earliest days of the independence wars during and after 1810 and the subsequent proliferation of caudillos who would dominate politics into mid-century. My essay on proto-caudillo antagonists, the Mexican priest Hidalgo and the Spanish brigadier Calleja, which opens Part Two, demonstrates the links between colonial networks and the subsequent struggles for power (chapter 6). It is followed by two conflicting views of the crude regional caudillos who flourished during the general political instability of the early republics. Facundo Quiroga from La Rioja in western Argentina owed his notoriety, among a large and anonymous collection of *caciques* to the pen of Domingo Sarmiento, the famous Europeanized liberal promoter of civilization over barbarism. The essay by Sarmiento comes from his influential book, *Life in the Argentine Republic in the Days of the Tyrants* (chapter 7). A modern historian, E. Bradford Burns, presents caudillos such as Quiroga, and especially Rafael Carrera of Guatemala, in a very different light. Burns sees Carrera as a "folk caudillo" who used his leadership to protect for a time the indigenous cultures of Guatemala from the negative impact of progress and modernization (chapter 8).

Other new approaches to the study of leadership are found in the next two essays; both treat caudillos who, for different reasons, were frustrated in their ambitions. Jane Rausch tells the fascinating story of political ineptitude and elite distrust of a former lieutenant of Bolívar, Juan Moreno, who came from the eastern Llanos, or grasslands, of Colombia in a vain effort to dominate the country from Bogotá (chapter 9). Martín Güemes, the wartime caudillo of Salta in northwestern Argentina, was likewise made and broken by an elite. In his case, as Roger Haigh demonstrates, it was Güemes's own local extended family that successfully destroyed him when he ceased to serve their interests (chapter 10). These essays undercut the myth of the all-powerful caudillo and demonstrate that even successful leaders were dependent upon favorable backers.

Two contemporary nineteenth-century liberals, both much influenced by their years in Europe, are authors of the next two essays. They contrast profoundly, however, both in what they wrote and in the political directions they ultimately took. Francisco Bilbao was a Chilean radical and anticleric who railed against the persistence of colonial institutions and values and attacked those caudillos who cynically manipulated the law to their own benefit. He died in exile in 1865 soon after he wrote this blistering attack (chapter 11). Rafael Núñez of Colombia might have been in sympathy with Bilbao in the 1860s, but by the 1880s he had abandoned his liberal federalist views in favor of a more conservative centralism. In the process, as president of his country, Núñez illegally abrogated the liberal constitution, imposed a centralized one, and gradually became dictatorial. Núñez was one of several sophisticated nineteenth-century politicians who, like Benito Juárez, reluctantly assumed autocratic powers for what they considered to be the most noble of reasons (chapter 12).

The next three essays illustrate and capture the mood of the transition from the nineteenth century. The ideology of that period was heavily influenced by French Positivism, Social Darwinism, and various theories of racial superiority and inferiority. These theories helped to establish a climate in which authoritarians like Porfirio Díaz could flourish. Carlos Octavio Bunge was an Argentine sociologist who used what we would now consider outrageously racist theories to condemn what he held to be the weaknesses of Latin American civilization. His influence was widespread among readers sharing his admiration for leaders like Don Porfirio, who knew how to take advantage of "incurable native indolence," (chapter 13). No contemporaneous caudillo was better known or more successful—up to a point—than Díaz. In the next essay Luis González, one of Mexico's most distinguished historians, demonstrates how skillfully Díaz was able to exploit the "orthodoxy among the people" and to feed the popular need for nationalism (chapter 14). John Johnson offers yet another perspective on the era with his innovative essay on foreign factors that played into the hands of caudillos, including everything from bank loans to railroads, from Positivism to the militant menace of political "outs" operating from neighboring states (chapter 15).

Many of Johnson's observations concerning the nineteenth century continue to apply in the post-World War I era and even, in some cases, for many decades after the Wall Street crash of 1929 (which is often taken as a watershed in caudillo studies because of the militarist coups that economic disaster provoked). This raises the question of when the twentieth century really began in Spanish America. My decision to provide a final division in the book called "Twentieth-Century Dynamics" was made to allow a consideration of both modern computer-age autocrats and vestigial caudillos whose personal styles belong to ancient traditions.

The first two essays in Part Three help set the institutional context for twentieth-century caudillos. In a particularly enduring essay Lyle McAlister establishes a classification scheme for civil-military relations that helps to illumine many of the subsequent selections (chapter 16). Russell Fitzgibbon adds another dimension to our understanding of caudillismo with his essay on *continuismo*, which is the clever use of constitutions, legal systems, and rigged elections to perpetuate oneself in power while pretending to do so legitimately (chapter 17).

Rafael Trujillo (1930–61) came as close as anyone to being the quintessential caudillo. It is for that reason that I have included three essays that help explain "The Benefactor" in some depth. The first is by Trujillo himself and is, ironically, a speech about "democracy" (chapter 18). This is followed by an amusing but scathing report on the Dominican Republic by Jesús de Galíndez, who lived and worked there for six years in the early 1940s. Galíndez was a refugee from the Spanish Civil War. Trujillo took revenge for this essay and other publications by abducting Galíndez from the streets of New York City and later murdering him (chapter 19). The final essay on Trujillo is by Howard Wiarda and Michael Kryzanek, two political scientists who have closely studied the Dominican Republic. While they accept the standard treatment of Trujillo as a bloody dictator, Wiarda and Kryzanek contribute a dispassionate analysis of the regime from a developmental perspective, with close attention to the historical changes that took place during three crucial decades (chapter 20).

In the next essay, Alain Rouquié, a French scholar, diplomat, and expert on military history, focuses his attention on an extended family in Nicaragua and considers how it was able to sustain its power base by co-opting the armed forces. The National Guard was the creature of Anastasio Somoza. Through it he established a dynasty that endured from 1933 until his son's overthrow in the Sandinista Revolution of 1979 (chapter 21).

Although Juan Perón was president of Argentina for less than ten years (from his election in 1946 to his ouster in 1954, and again from his reelection in 1973 to his death in 1974), he cast as long a shadow as any modern caudillo. Fifteen years after he died, for example, the presidential election was won by the Peronist Party candidate, Carlos Menem. Two essays can only begin to explore the substance of Peronismo. Nevertheless, these selections do help to illuminate the man by indirection. The first concerns his wife, Eva Duarte de Perón, the unforgettable "Evita." Marysa Navarro examines her career with special attention to the question of the extent of Evita's power. Readers may decide for themselves whether she was a caudilla (chapter 22). Fernando Cuevillas, a sociologist trained in Franco's Spain and a faculty member at the University of Buenos Aires in the early 1950s, was among the intellectual sycophants who became apologists for Perón. Calling caudillaje a "new form of monarchy," Cuevillas argues that it is a kind of "leadership which must surely be a reaction against the depersonalization of power associated with liberal rationalism." His praise for the system not only helps explain Peronismo but also how caudillo supporters more generally justify their position (chapter 23).

Fidel Castro has created a greater volume of words about his country, his revolution, and himself than any other major caudillo in history. Among the multitude of interviews Castro has granted to foreign journalists, none has come closer to producing a frank self-assessment of Castro as a charismatic leader than the one conducted by Lee Lockwood in 1965. In the excerpt in this book Castro deals candidly with the sources and nature of his power (chapter 24). Maurice Halperin, a Canadian scholar with long experience in Cuba, offers a contrasting view of Castro's leadership in the next essay. Impressed by the optimistic facet of Fidel's personality, Halperin nevertheless discovers a major weakness in the Cuban's failure to delegate authority and to make his bureaucracy function creatively. Halperin calls this Castro's "power to disrupt" (chapter 25). The two pieces together provide some insight into the mind of the most visible and audible caudillo of modern Spanish America.

The final essays in this collection have to do with two military caudillos who brilliantly exploited their understanding of their respective societies. Augusto Pinochet of Chile and Alfredo Stroessner of Paraguay both used the military as avenues to autocratic rule. They did so in very different ways. As Genaro Arriagada, a keen observer of modern Chilean politics, makes clear, Pinochet shrewdly found his way to power by manipulating the hierarchical nature of his country's military establishment and by co-opting the rich tradition of Chilean legitimacy for his own benefit as "President of the Republic." Along the way he ruthlessly repressed any opposition (chapter 26). In his essay on Paraguay,

James Cockcroft shows how army commander-in-chief Stroessner used a classic coup d'etat to overthrow his boss, the president, in 1954. Once in power he developed and sustained his authority for thirty-five years by a clever combination of factional provocation in the ancient Hapsburg fashion, encouragement of a single Colorado party to give him a popular base, extensive graft and political patronage, and a secret police with all the apparatus of late twentieth-century electronic torture devices. When the end of his rule came abruptly in 1989, it was the result of a coup d'etat staged by his right-hand man, Andrés Rodríguez. Caudillismo had come full circle (chapter 27).

Have we seen the last of the caudillos? As Stroessner, Noriega, Pinochet, and Castro move off stage, will there be no more? Is the apparent trend toward more pluralist democratic systems inexorable? This historical collection was not designed to answer these questions. Instead, the volume explores the rich variety of caudillos over the past two centuries and makes its readers aware of the complex nature of leadership in Spanish America.

Notes

1. Obituary of Juan Manuel de Rosas, *The Times* (London), 15 March 1877, 5, quoted in John Lynch, *Argentine Dictator: Juan Manuel de Rosas* (New York: Oxford University Press, 1981), 358.

2. Alcides Argüedas, *Los caudillos bárbaros* (Barcelona, 1929), and *Los caudillos letrados* (Barcelona, 1923).

3. Kenneth J. Grieb, *Guatemalan Caudillo, the Regime of Jorge Ubico: Guatemala, 1931–1944* (Athens: Ohio University Press, 1979), 526.

4. Stanley G. Payne, *The Franco Regime, 1936–1975* (Madison: University of Wisconsin Press, 1987), 625.

5. F. J. Moreno, "Caudillismo: An Interpretation of its Origins in Chile," in *Conflict and Violence in Latin American Politics*, ed. F. J. Moreno and B. Mitriani (New York: Crowell, 1971), 38–39.

6. José Luis Romero, *A History of Argentine Political Thought* (Stanford: Stanford University Press, 1963), 110, 111.

7. James Creelman, "President Diaz: Hero of the Americas," in *History of Latin American Civilization*, ed. Lewis Hanke, vol. 2 (Boston: Little, Brown & Co., 1967), 259.

8. Kalman H. Silvert, "Leadership Formation and Modernization in Latin America," *Journal of International Affairs* 20 (1966): 326, 327.

9. Brian Loveman and Thomas M. Davies, Jr., eds., *The Politics of Antipolitics:*

The Military in Latin America, 2d ed. (Lincoln: University of Nebraska Press, 1989), 19–21.

10. Fernando Henrique Cardoso, "On the Characterization of Authoritarian Regimes in Latin America," in *The New Authoritarianism in Latin America*, ed. David Collier (Princeton: Princeton University Press, 1979), 35–36.

11. Carlos Rangel, *The Latin Americans: Their Love-Hate Relationship with the United States*, rev. ed. (New Brunswick, N.J.: Transaction Books, 1987), 224–27. For a discussion of whether or not Roosevelt said this of Trujillo and also, perhaps, of Anastasio Somoza, see Robert A. Pastor, *Condemned to Repetition: The United States and Nicaragua* (Princeton: Princeton University Press, 1987), 3–4, 322nn. Pastor argues that "son of a bitch" was not FDR's style and that it was therefore apocryphal. Without documentary evidence of his bon mot I can only conjecture that "s.o.b." is more likely. See also Bernard Diederich, *Somoza and the Legacy of U.S. Involvement in Central America* (New York: Dutton, 1981), 21.

12. Rangel, 223.

13. Glen Caudill Dealy, "The Tradition of Monistic Democracy in Latin America," in *Politics and Social Change in Latin America: The Distinct Tradition*, ed. Howard J. Wiarda, 2d ed. rev. (Amherst: University of Massachusetts Press, 1982), 83, 86, 88, 90.

14. Claudio Véliz, *The Centralist Tradition of Latin America* (Princeton: Princeton University Press, 1980).

15. David Collier and Ruth Berins Collier, "Who Does What, to Whom, and How: Toward a Comparative Analysis of Latin American Corporatism," in *Authoritarianism and Corporatism in Latin America*, ed. David Collier (Pittsburgh: University of Pittsburgh Press, 1977), 493.

16. Quoted by Lewis Hanke, *The Spanish Struggle for Justice in the Conquest of America* (Philadelphia: University of Pennsylvania Press, 1949), 7.

17. J. H. Elliott, "The Spanish Conquest," in *Colonial Spanish America*, ed. Leslie Bethell (Cambridge: Cambridge University Press, 1987), 8.

18. Peggy K. Liss, *Mexico Under Spain, 1521–1556: Society and the Origins of Nationalism* (Chicago: University of Chicago Press, 1975), 103.

19. John L. Phelan, "Authority and Flexibility in the Spanish Imperial Bureaucracy," *Administrative Science Quarterly* 5 (1960): 47–65.

Part One
Theories and Background

1

François Chevalier
The Roots of Caudillismo

Best known for his monumental and controversial study of
the creation of the great haciendas in New Spain during the
sixteenth and seventeenth centuries, *Land and Society in
Colonial Mexico: the Great Hacienda* (1963), François Chevalier is among the most influential of French Latin Americanists in the twentieth century. He has directed historical
research centers in Madrid, Mexico, Bordeaux, and the Sorbonne in Paris. Chevalier uses his familiarity with the entire
region to explain how local caciques and national caudillos
have relied on personal ties for their success throughout the
Iberian and colonial past as well as the nineteenth and twentieth centuries. The author demonstrates how strong men have
sustained themselves in power through complex systems of
military prowess, accumulated wealth—especially in land,
rewards to their followers, extended families, godparenthood
(*compadrazgo*), nepotism, personality cults, and, finally, international economic ties. In concluding, Chevalier suggests
ways by which caudillos may adjust to modern conditions
and remain significant players in Spanish American societies.

IT has been observed that in many countries of Central and South
America the local and even national government has often been
monopolized by "strong men," "caudillos," and "caciques" who
perpetuate themselves in power, sometimes even under cover of
constitutional or judicial fictions. There is, also, nothing new in
emphasizing the exceptional importance that "personal relations"
have had in these countries for the conduct of business affairs and
the function of institutions in general. But rarely have these two

From François Chevalier, " 'Caudillos' et 'caciques' en Amérique: contribution à
l'étude des liens personnels," *Mélanges offerts à Marcel Bataillon par les Hispan-
istes Français*, a special issue of *Bulletin Hispanique* 64 (1962): 30–47. Reprinted
with permission.

phenomena been linked so as to delve deeply into their causes and to reveal their mechanisms. . . .

Origins

In times or in countries where life is difficult, where man is placed in a hostile environment constantly menaced by enemies or famine, where a state, if it exists at all, is too weak or too far away to insure the security of individuals, these individuals associate and naturally coalesce into firm groups: at first, into groups of relatives because the ties of blood are fundamental; then into groups of the most faithful, of clients, of friends . . . around an elder, a chief, a powerful man, around a man who has more experience, more initiative, or a man of more material means than the others. Ties of blood and personal bonds are the only ones which have a real importance in societies where written contracts, if they exist at all, play a limited role; where the typical relations of modern societies, and even of certain traditional communities, are found only in the embryonic state.

There are countless examples. In Rome itself the *gens* and the *clientes* survived in spite of the development of a central power having a relatively complex administration and in spite of the birth of the personal property concept under Roman Law, which favors the autonomy of the individual capable of operating independently of a group. With the Germanic invasions, the clientes and the group reappear with new vigor, not because of a peculiarly Germanic influence . . . but because of the fact that the newcomers were simply more primitive socially. . . .

In the West during the Middle Ages, the chiefs were surrounded by relatives and retainers who lived and ate with them, who helped them in time of peace as well as in time of war. While in a large part of Europe these faithful received land, at first temporarily and later on in a hereditary manner according to the classic feudal system, in Castile, on the contrary, . . . the *criados*, or retainers, continued to be rewarded ordinarily by sustenance and by presents, for reasons which doubtless have something to do with the Reconquest of the Peninsula from the Moors and the possible distribution of important spoils of war.

No matter what the causes may be . . . it is noteworthy that in the sixteenth and seventeenth centuries groups of criados around powerful men and high royal functionaries persisted in Spain. They might be hidalgos and nobles; and when it was a question of men of high rank, they did not always live permanently under the same roof as their protector, all the more because they were often charged with missions of confidence, even to foreign countries. Thus Hernán Cortés was a criado of Diego Velázquez. The obligations were clear for each party: protection, help, favors, and presents for one side; faithfulness and help from the other.

The institution went to America with the conquerors, and it found new forces in the immensity of a continent where the king of Spain had difficulty in making his authority felt in all places. In a case in Mexico in 1602, Guadalajara had only 160 households, but the president of the Audiencia there was surrounded by forty-six relatives and by a quantity of "dependents" who monopolized the offices and the most lucrative jobs of a huge region called New Galicia. Similar cases are by no means rare in the New World. [The Crown], however, reacted against these practices and sought to prohibit the distribution of administrative positions or other advantages to the retainers of royal bureaucrats. . . . Above all, the latter changed posts and could therefore take root in one place with difficulty.

On the other hand, there were few obstacles for the private citizens who had the means, whether Spaniard, creole, or mestizo, to have permanently the kind of personal following that poverty, insecurity, or the hostility of the environment often rendered natural, and even necessary in many regions of the vast Spanish Empire. . . . Incapable of extending its administration everywhere, at least before the end of the eighteenth century, . . . the government of Madrid sometimes found it advantageous to use powerful men so that order might be kept, even at the cost of abandoning to them a little of its sovereignty. Sometimes contracts of this kind were made with rich proprietors of lands or mines, who took it upon themselves to maintain private armies in exchange for honorary titles. . . . Nevertheless, in a time of monarchic centralization, the king avoided as much as possible the creation of judicial precedents lest his rights be alienated, especially if they were to be hereditarily alienated. There were, therefore, more frequently de facto situations, especially in dangerous areas or in troubled times.

It is clear that the mentality of the great proprietors encouraged the proliferation of personal bonds. If they received only a small income from their haciendas, which were, by the way, heavily mortgaged to the Church, they found compensation in the quasi-seignorial prestige that a crowd of men attached to their land and to their person could give to their masters. . . . Employing the authority of their military titles, they occasionally led these followers to fight nomadic Indians and bandits or, during the wars of independence, the party opposed to the one they themselves had chosen. Finally, the haciendas were often entailed estates which belonged to dynasties rather than to individuals; these family lines thus insured the importance and the primitive force of blood ties.

In fact, certain proprietors reigned on their estates somewhat in the manner of lords and seigneurs of ancient time, at least before the reforms of the eighteenth century. Sure of themselves in a world where the hierarchy seemed immutable, their psychology was simple and their authority a tradition. It would not always be so after the earthquakes of independence which seriously shook the established order.

The National Period

In renouncing the presidency of Gran Colombia, Bolívar, in a disillusioned address, foresaw the coming of cruel petty tyrants "of all races and colors" who would divide the continent among themselves. In fact, caudillos, big and small, sprang everywhere from the wars of emancipation. The disappearance of the Spanish state left a void made larger by the retreat of the traditional aristocracy and soon that of the Church.

When a precarious peace returned, the new men often kept the power which audacity and chance had given them. The most energetic, sometimes the most violent, became "the first of his village or the republic, the one who has more authority or power and who because of his pride wants to make himself feared and obeyed by all his inferiors," to employ the definition for *cacique* used by the first Spanish dictionary of the Academy published in 1729.

Where did these chiefs come from? Sometimes, they emerged from the old landed aristocracy, but more often from the petite bourgeoisie or from the people. Because it is usually not in his tradition . . . that he commands others, the new man does not feel sure of himself. Therefore he is in urgent need to affirm his power, if necessary by force, and at the same time to distinguish himself from the common man. Thereby we see a new style among these dictators, these caudillos and caciques of the national era, whether they sprang directly or not from the wars of independence.

The Horsemen

In countries where "mounted barbarism" of the gauchos or of the llaneros still ruled, in rural areas of little population, these all-powerful caudillos were often primitive beings whose power seemed to be tied to physical force and virility *(hombre macho)*. In Argentina the Spanish state abandoned the region to these "kings of the big spurs," to use Sarmiento's expression: a Facundo "courageous almost to boldness, gifted with Herculean strength," an extraordinary knight who imposed himself by violence, and even by terror; a Rosas so overflowing with energy and with life that . . . he could ride a horse almost to death; . . . in Venezuela a Páez, who became civilized later; Monagas; Zaraza . . . exalted in the popular . . . *corrido* [ballad]; and also a fictional character taken from life, like Rómulo Gallegos's Doña Bárbara, the terrible female cacique of the boundless wild llano. . . .

It would be easy to make this list of names longer, because in those regions of extensive animal raising which cover vast spaces in almost all the countries of the American continent, it is or was almost impossible to conceive of the chief as other than a man physically stronger than his rivals, a better horseman and a better shot, . . . (which, however, did not always prevent him from meeting a violent death . . .).

The Military Men

In general, the easiest means for an ambitious man . . . to secure power is, naturally, through a military career. This is true whether he be a man raised by revolution or war to leadership, or whether he be a professional soldier, the latter being of particular value in one of the numerous countries where the army is, with the Church, one of the only two solidly organized forces. . . . In fact, almost all dictators have been military men. Those who were not so originally have usually taken the title of "general." . . .

Even in Mexico, a country which has long passed the stage of *pronunciamientos*, and where politics is entirely in the hands of civilians, it is only rather recently that a general changes posts without including in his transfer all those officers who were personally attached to him. This situation, outmoded under the government of Porfirio Díaz, was recreated by the revolution of 1910–17. Thus, in 1919 the psychology of the caudillo and the resort to purely personal ties were still expressed in a manifesto of General Obregón: "I declare myself a candidate for the presidency of the republic, backed by my own pistols without ties with any parties nor offers of any platform. My background as a soldier of the revolution is sufficient guarantee that I know how to insure the well-being of the people and the happiness of the country. He who loves me follow me!"

Other Styles

In the old days the powerful men were great landlords and sometimes captains of private armies. Some of them, who had chosen the party of independence, kept their local power. In Mexico this was reinforced by the renewed incursions of nomadic Indians and by the climate of insecurity which existed in the whole country. The land being the essential source of income and prestige, the generals, caudillos, and caciques had to own haciendas or to acquire some if they had none to start with. Later Porfirio Díaz, who favored large holdings . . . integrated the proprietors into his system because they seemed to him the most able to control local governments.

During the nineteenth century, however, ideals changed while pressures of the haciendas on the rural communities increased. This brought about an uneasiness among the peasants which was expressed by uprisings of Indians and of village people or peons all anxious to recuperate their land. In Mexico this tendency was clear fifty or eighty years before the agrarian revolution began in 1910–11. . . . So it was that caudillos of the new style appeared here and there, sensitive to the aspirations of the most humble rural groups from which they sometimes came.

Thus in Mexico General Juan Alvarez emerged all-powerful in the southwest and the state of Guerrero during the decades which followed independence. He was the type of the "good cacique," who lived very simply on his hacienda, and defended the Indian communities and the poor people in these vast regions of arid sierras. . . . In a series of neglected pamphlets, "the patriarch of the south" described the misery of the natives in dramatic fashion, with precise examples, and the methods which the proprietors used in order to despoil them of their water and their lands. . . . He himself quelled uprisings by extending justice to the peasants who were very deeply attached to him at the same time that they expressed their defiance toward the aloof government of the capital. . . .

Quite different, certainly, was the famous Manuel Lozada, absolute ruler of Nayarit, a little further north, which he dominated through fear and terror for several decades, first as a bandit chief and then as military commander supported by the conservatives, before his death in 1873. He was even decorated by order of Napoleon III! This man, once a shepherd on a hacienda and of Cora Indian origin, was a born chief who enjoyed great prestige among all the natives and who did not hesitate, on occasion, to distribute the lands of a hacienda among his soldiers. Finally taken by treason and sent to the firing squad, fifty of Lozada's principal adherents accepted invitations to a great banquet of reconciliation where, at a signal—the host raising his glass—they were all assassinated.

But the chief who wants to stay in power forever—which is the essence of caciquismo—must be able to count on the collaboration and unconditional support of forces which he permanently attaches to his person. The popularity, the ascendancy, and the prestige, absolutely necessary to start with, are never sufficient for a prolonged retention of power. To rule by fear or by terror does not last if it is impossible to create a stable community of interest with the men and the groups on which the chief leans.

Then, how to succeed? In countries where resources are few, the *primum vivere* is an unavoidable imperative: the chief must first be able to feed his relatives, his dependents, . . . and the soldiers who support him. He must be rich.

To Be Rich

For the caudillo time is pressing. If he is not rich, he must become rich as soon as possible. . . .

Sarmiento in the last century described how Facundo Quiroga, the Argentine caudillo, gathered a large fortune; the means are numerous, from the collection of the tithe to gambling, but the terror he inspires is at the base of all gain. Who would dare bid above the ridiculously small sum which Facundo offers in order to get the right to collect the tithe? Who would dare break up a card game after having won the gold of this frightful chief? It is he alone who can decide when to end the game and it is he who, having unlimited resources at his disposal, will win.

Facundo was, certainly, a kind of a barbarian. Later, in other places, the means may have been more discreet but, especially for those who have nothing to start with, influence peddling is a way to acquire some early capital, after which a fortune increases more easily by itself: monopolies on imports or manufacturing, extremely lucrative contracts obtained from the state for public works, contraband, . . . and above all the acquisition through intimidation of the best land . . . are but a few of the ways to wealth. . . .

For the ambitious officer or politician during the nineteenth century, all kinds of financial arrangements allowed him to take a cut from the sums borrowed from England or other countries, sums which were generally guaranteed by the income from customs. During the second half of the nineteenth century, the Venezuelan dictator Guzmán Blanco became rich in such a way. . . . Later the increasing commercial relations and the development of foreign capitalistic enterprise in a large part of the continent offered increasing possibilities to the new man thirsty for power and money, a few of whom have made huge fortunes in the twentieth century. The guarantees that the men offered to powerful financial groups were compensated by effective support, thanks to which they maintained themselves in power. . . .

There are chiefs of state who still [or until recently] posssess large fortunes. For instance, in [Nicaragua in 1956 Luis Somoza had] properties . . . inherited from his low-born father who had governed the country as an absolute master. The list makes quite an impression with its fifty-one stock-raising haciendas, forty-six coffee plantations, and eight of sugarcane; thirteen industries; his daily newspaper; his shipping, aviation, trucking, and import-export companies; and finally his interests in almost everything from the monopoly of firearms to gold exports. . . .

If modern capitalism did not color such a system, one would tend to think about the retainers who served their chief, making war or working for him, in exchange for food, presents, and protection. One might even recall the ancient concept of the personal patrimonial state. . . .

The Dependents

The men whom caudillos call upon first will naturally be their relatives, because the ties of blood are the surest and the strongest. Familial solidarity often remains very strong in rural and provincial environments, and is sometimes revealed in the form of extreme "vendettas." Spontaneously the relatives, even those living far away, take the side of that member of the family who occupies an important position or who wants to occupy it, and consequently they find themselves fighting with rival factions. These family rivalries, made so famous in the old days in Italy, divided many regions of the American continent, such as the Argentine Rioja at the time of Sarmiento. . . .

The relatives of the strong man expect from him positions, favors, or simply their daily bread. This reaction is so natural that any person receiving a fixed income of any importance would usually feed at his home his cousins and supporters who render him little services in return. For example, in Spain a successful torero may see his whole familial clan move into his house, expecting him to insure their subsistance. By the same token, the caudillo cannot refuse assistance in the form of positions and favors to relatives who, after all, are his surest support. Even the most personally disinterested men sometimes practice nepotism, which seemed natural enough in the old days. Now such practices are severly censured, at least in Mexico, where the governor of [Michoacán] had to resign [in 1959] under pressure of public opinion. Newspaper readers were shocked to learn that his relatives occupied all the important positions of the state, ranging from treasury and tax collection offices to that of attorney general, including along the way the director of public works, the mayor of the only important city, and the state liquor inspector.

At a much higher level, [Anastasio Somoza of Nicaragua] placed his sons or near relatives at the head of the high command of the army, of the presidential guard, of the bank of issue, and of the presidency of the national assembly. . . . Another and most typical example would be [Trujillo], whose brothers, legitimate and illegitimate sons (the latter in impressive numbers), nephews, relatives, and allies divided among themselves the principal positions of the country in such a manner as to deal with it as with a big business or . . . a patrimony.

One cannot help but think of the groups of relatives and dependents of ancient Europe when one sees in such Latin American countries the parade of people who accompany, surround, and assist certain chiefs of state, politicians, or important figures when they move from one place to another or even when they are in their own homes.

To the ties of blood can be added those which create a religious relationship between the *compadres,* or godfathers . . . and the relatives of the baptized as well as the child himself. These ties often remain powerful enough to oblige the partners to help each other in all circumstances. Thus [Trujillo] systematically agreed, and even used pressure to become the godfather of thousands of children, obviously in order to create a tie of fidelity toward him with a large number of families, belonging by the way to all social classes, including the most humble. There is no doubt that this practice gained [Trujillo] the support of a considerable part of the population, who became thus linked to him as if by a blood relationship. . . .

The local caciques lean so much on these *compadrazgos* that the word itself often takes on a political shade. Among the rural people, the mestizos, and the more advanced [sic] Indians, the extraordinary proliferation of these religious relationships even appear, in a spontaneous fashion, to replace and to recreate personal bonds . . . where solidarity among the clan has softened or lost its control. It has been noted that in Maya communities, where ancient clannish organizations exist, there are neither compadres nor *comadres*. Everywhere else, however, compadrazgo plays an essential role which is perhaps similar to that of the religious brotherhoods of Spain in creating reciprocal obligations of assistance which were, and still are, sometimes necessary in isolated regions where law has little influence and . . . the individual lacks personal guarantees. Furthermore, the ties of compadrazgo multiply even outside baptism: in some villages this occurs through the acquisition of a religious image to which sponsors or "godfathers" are assigned or through an important event in the life of a child . . . and in other places because all the ancestors and descendants of compadres assume the same title. . . .

The word *amigo* itself implies, especially in the countryside, a solidarity and reciprocal duties which are not evoked to the same degree by the word "friend." . . .

Personality Cults

In the political and military phase of the conquest of power, the caudillo lived in a state of quasi-permanent alert. [An Argentine chief] "always had a harnessed horse ready at the door for fighting or for flight at the least sign of attack from his domestic enemies." For the caudillo who has taken power and who retains it for profit, the state of alert, like that of war, leads to a double state of insecurity. First, physical, because of the enemy whom he has not been able to eliminate or who rekindles the ambitions of faithless partners. And second, that [derived from the] internal sense of insecurity of someone who needs to justify to others, perhaps even to his own kin, the exercise of an unlimited power which has neither the social prestige nor the legitimacy, and certainly not the majesty of an ancient absolute monarchy. Consciously or not, the new chief of state seeks, therefore, to provide a moral and intellectual base for the loyalty of his subjects, for he is well aware that without traditional foundations for fidelity he cannot depend solely either on economic interests or on coercive force.

From this stems the caudillo's propensity to exalt and magnify his personality beyond all limits, especially if his humble origin and total absence of family tradition make him believe in the necessity of convincing others of the transcendental and exceptional character of his own person. From this, also, comes the taste for all which can strike the popular imagination: the theatrical gesture, the sumptuous uniform, the impressive monument, the spectacular performance . . . to engrave the ideal of a superman in the minds of the citizens.

In the Mexico of the first half of the last century a president, Santa Anna, showed such inclinations when he organized the solemn burial of his leg shot away by a cannonball, or when, after having arranged that he be made dictator for life, he organized a whole etiquette according to which his ministers had the obligation to travel in yellow coaches with valets in green livery, while His Most Serene Highness—himself—was escorted by lancers in red uniforms and plumed hats.

Here, too, it would be easy to give more examples, from the regional cacique who gives the name of his father, of his mother, of himself to markets, to schools, or to avenues of the *pueblos* which he dominates to the dictator or president with overly ornate and bemedaled uniforms whom it has become such a pleasure to caricature in Mexican newspapers and elsewhere. . . .

The Caudillo as Unifier

If the power of the national dictator is of the same nature as that of the local cacique and they both use similar means, then between them the only difference is one of station; on the other hand, the two authorities may sometimes be at odds, and even at war. According to circumstances and his personal temperament, the caudillo either will want to destroy the provincial caciques who limit his power, or else he will cooperate with them by drawing them into his system of government.

In this regard the Mexican economist Germán Parra sees in certain Latin American dictatorships a state of social development comparable to that which the emergence of absolute monarchy in

Europe represents. In fact, certain chiefs of state have succeeded in centralizing the government and in unifying under their authority badly organized nations which were being exploited to different degrees by local caciques. Thus, in Argentina, Facundo Quiroga broke the spirit of independence in eight provinces which he dominated as a semibarbaric gaucho. He and other tyrants were in turn destroyed by one of their own, the "federalist" caudillo Rosas, who by violence and trickery succeeded in what the "unitarian" parliamentary governments of Buenos Aires had not been able to obtain: the fusion of the entire country into one compact unit. . . .

In the same way that the railroad, in replacing the horse, widened and strengthened the sphere of influence of the provincial chief, so, too, the national dictator tends to replace the local cacique. But because the roots of personal power were so deep in some more or less isolated rural areas, it could not be destroyed in a complete and definitive fashion with one blow. In short, other caudillos, who were not able [to] or who did not want to choose military means as brutal as those of Rosas, tried to integrate into their system of government those caciques judged useful and assimilable. Such was the approach of Porfirio Díaz in Mexico. . . .

What General Díaz did was to counteract existing threats to centralized power and to reinforce the authority and prestige of the state everywhere, which before him had only little influence beyond the central plateau, except for a small portion of the Atlantic coast. In most other places "the supreme law was the will of one man—a cacique." [As Luis Chávez Orozco has written,] "in order to centralize this power absolutely General Díaz did not destroy caciquismo, because this would have been impossible even if he had wanted to. What he did, was to give to caciquismo more vigor by placing it under official protection. The result was that all the caciques recognized him as the supreme political authority (the Great Cacique) in exchange for certain economic advantages which he deigned to let them enjoy."

Perhaps geographical reasons obliged Díaz to compromise with certain caciques instead of trying to suppress them. The topography of Mexico presented obstacles to the unification of the country which did not exist in the Argentine pampa: it is only [since the 1930s] that the influence of the Mexican capital has been able to penetrate everywhere through the sierras. This has been due to an important road system, completing on a large scale the work of centralization begun by the Porfirian railways. Moreover, Díaz did not support himself with the army, which never was very large, and he never tried to enrich himself personally.

In a large country with complex structures such as Mexico, no amount of money, distributed as presents, would have been sufficient to win over enough dependents and friends to form solid bases for personal power, which was, as we know, so often managed in isolated provinces or countries with rudimentary economies . . . elsewhere on the American continent. But Díaz let the caciques, governors, and *jefes políticos* get rich under his protective wing, while keeping public opinion opposed to possible rivals and convinced of the advantages and prestige resulting from his personal honesty.

This system, carefully perfected over more than thirty years of rule, left neither perspective nor room for political parties, because everything rested on personal power from the top to the bottom of the ladder. But Díaz felt the need to give to his government the ideological bases which it lacked.

Quite naturally he found these bases in Auguste Comte's Positivism which had been adapted by Mexican thinkers and educators of the second half of the nineteenth century. From a political standpoint, the ideals suited the Porfirian system admirably because they advocated the establishment of an authoritarian regime to fight against any tendency toward anarchy or disintegration, and to maintain social unity at all costs during the transitional phase when theological beliefs were fast disappearing yet before the doctrine of Positivism had definitely triumphed in the minds of the people. This "Order," closely linked as it was to economic "Progress," also represented the goal of the "Científicos," those technocratic friends of Porfirio Díaz. The Científicos and Díaz, however, did not know how to add "Love" for the peasants who had been despoiled of their land, as Comte had finally done. It was this failure which was a fundamental cause of the powerful social revolution of 1910–11 that caused his downfall.

Especially since the beginning of the century, the influence of powerful economic interests has been and often still is important. Large private companies, most of them foreign, which exploit or sell oil, tropical fruits, sugar, and other export products, are proprietors of large enterprises and huge estates with enormous incomes. Naturally they have feared the demands of their employees, the requests for land from the peasants, the nationalistic and xenophobic tendencies of the mob, and they have also feared popular troubles which might compromise the success of their businesses. Thus, their representatives have sometimes shown certain preferences for authoritarian government which seemed to them more capable of insuring order and better disposed to support their interests in exchange for financial and even political support.

The importance of personal and familial ties as a caudillo's means of government may now be somewhat archaic. But as with other American institutions, caudillismo and caciquismo still bear the marks of a long history: the prestige of physical force, of the proud horseman, of the best shot; the semipatriarchal authority of the landed proprietor, once lord and master of extensive domains; the prowess of the military man who encounters no obstacles . . . ; the ostentation of the new man, who is not quite sure of himself; and, finally, the power of the businessman who succeeds in controlling the principal means of production.

Today this boss or that dictator may be maintained and propelled by economic interests in an environment where money retains all the strength and vitality of youth. At the same time he is more and more questioned and threatened; he is often eliminated by societies which have achieved self-awareness and no longer allow themselves to be guided blindly as once they were. However, when the strong man learns how to adapt himself to this new situation, when, instead of representing personal interests and of leaning on clans or families, he becomes the representative of the rural people and the "leader" of masses, then he still may enjoy a long career.

2

Glen Caudill Dealy
The Public Man

Many writers have sought to characterize the culture and psychology of a society in their works. This absorbing quest for cultural character has ranged from Alexis de Tocqueville's *Democracy in America* to E. M. Forster's *A Passage to India* and from José Martí's essays "inside the monster" of North America to Salvador de Madariaga's *Englishmen, Frenchmen, Spaniards.* These and a multitude of other writers have provoked endless controversy. Critics have invariably argued that gross culture-wide generalizations about a people, especially if they come from the pen of a foreigner, smack of ethnocentrism and fail to perceive the universals which apply to all of humankind and which transcend nationalism.

Glen Dealy is a critic of those whom he believes have misunderstood Latin American values. This is evident in his work on monistic democracy discussed in the Introduction. He has, however, been sharply criticized himself for the application of new stereotypes in his book, *The Public Man.* It is Dealy's fundamental argument that as Protestant Man accumulates wealth as a means to capitalist power, so Catholic Man accumulates friends as a means to public power. The author identifies what he calls "the spirit of caudillaje," which is a life-style as fully rational in deeply Catholic societies (Mediterranean as well as Latin American) as anything in Protestant-based societies. For their part, his critics believe that he overdraws the dichotomy between Catholic/Public Man and Protestant/Capitalist Man and presents caudillismo as an immutable cultural feature. It is that very polarization, however, which puts the caudillo phenomenon in relief and engenders controversy over its relation to Spanish American culture.

From Glen Caudill Dealy, *The Public Man: An Interpretation of Latin American and Other Catholic Countries* (Amherst: University of Massachusetts Press, 1977), 3–32. Reprinted with permission.

The Public Man

The selection which follows is from the first chapter of *The Public Man*. Admirers and detractors alike will find valuable debate material in the balance of Dealy's volume.

OUT of the Renaissance era arose a style of life which I have labeled *caudillaje* . . .—from the Spanish word *caudillo*. Caudillaje designated in ideal-typical fashion a life-style oriented toward values of public leadership. It embraces a concept of man personified as a leader in a public setting. The word itself may be defined as the "domination *(mando)* or government of a caudillo." But we are not here speaking of political leaders per se, but of a style of life according to which everyman attempts to be a leader or caudillo: a caudillo in the sense given the word by the *Diccionario enciclopédico ilustrado de la lengua española* (1953) as "one who, as head (chief) and superior, guides and commands people." The word itself is unimportant other than as a means of discussing the life-style of a people—a life-style oriented toward the goals and values of public leadership.

What must be insisted upon is the rational quality of activity in caudillaje society. Caudillaje man, or the "public man" as I shall alternately call him, lives a life of rule-bound behavior. His acts contribute to his goals, and it is this which sets caudillaje society apart from other, more primitive patterns of behavior. History as sometimes written is little more than a struggle of men for public power. Yet what has usually been lacking in such struggles is an internalized code guiding personal behavior: a value frame directed toward the goal of becoming a public man. Historically men have sought public power through class prerogatives, heredity, force, wealth, divine intervention, or a combination of these features. But in the Western world since the Renaissance we have seen the development of what might be termed, to parallel Weber, a "spirit" of caudillaje. That is, we are considering a rational culturewide ethos propelling men in an unending, insatiable quest for public influence. Seldom, if ever, have whole nations followed an ethos of leadership where everyman aspires to public power; where the logic of the ethos produces a nation of leaders without any followers.

This spirit of caudillaje pervades those areas of Western Christendom that have remained monolithically Catholic in culture since the Renaissance. Most obvious in fitting that description are Spain, Portugal, Italy, Spanish and Portuguese America, and to a lesser extent Hungary, Ireland, France, French Canada, Austria, Romania, and Poland. Caudillaje is not a phenomenon reserved to a particular time period in a nation's history, for example, Renaissance Italy with its condottieri or nineteenth-century Latin America with its colorful caudillo presidents. Nor is caudillaje related to specific groups within these geographical units, for example, Renaissance princes or Latin American gauchos. No culture of poverty or of affluence separate from the larger society can be found. Rather, there lives a pervasive culturewide phenomenon of caudillaje which dominates every level of these societies and every facet of human behavior. One thinks, then, of "everyman" when referring to a "spirit of caudillaje." My thesis is that from the lowly cobbler to the caudillo-president there exists a common uniting value frame—that it would be as egregious an error to separate the values of political followers in those areas of the world as it would be to sever the world outlook of nineteenth-century robber barons in the United States from the Horatio Alger values of the "common man" in this country at that time. Caudillaje men are public men, men who may or may not become leaders in fact. . . .

Observation of these monolithic Catholic societies shows that they are characterized by a value structure that supports the goal of becoming caudillos or leaders. Catholic man is public man. He defines himself in terms of a code of excellence that derives (originally) from the public or political sphere. He thinks, acts, and has his being within a framework of public values. . . .

But while these men take their orientation from public values, they may often shy away from public participation in a formal sense. In many a town or village across the caudillaje landscape, political offices go begging for want of candidates. This is because real power may be only slightly related to the holding of designated formal positions. In such cases it is possible to have "massive indifference to public life, and a mobilization of egos and ambitions" exist side by side. By definition, then, a public man is a leader. We are defining a mode of behavior that is elitist. While asserting that Catholic culture exhibits a pervasive value system extending to all levels of society, it is not contradictory to also contend that in a qualitative sense we are examining an elitist value system and code of ethics which is at once democratic in its pervasiveness and indifference to class barriers and elitist in content. . . . To see the Catholic world as grounded in a haphazard struggle for power among contending opponents would miss the unique character of caudillaje society. Catholic man has been extremely rational and his behavior highly ordered with regard to achieving his end of public power. . . .

Catholic man pursues public power the way Protestant man strives for private wealth. In the one context there is a political referent for life's activities, in the other an economic referent. Both world views generate extremely rational worldly activity. One might ask, for example, what are the functional equivalents within caudillaje society for capitalist man's economic virtues of hard work, frugality, and reinvestment of capital? Immediately come to mind the virtues of leisure, ostentation, and instant gratification through the spending of one's capital. In short, I will argue that the latter virtues are equally as rational for caudillaje society as the former are for capitalistic society.

We are focusing here upon the accepted rational means for gaining public power and for gaining wealth: in the case of caudillaje man certain agreed-upon, essentially public or political virtues are demanded; for capitalist man, certain agreed-upon virtues emerge. Both fulfill the function of personal self-realization. And each carries its own "signs" or "indicators" of individual excellence which are readily recognizable by both pretenders and observers within their respective social orders. While not all capitalists who aspire to become millionaires act with equal talent, so too not every would-be caudillo aspiring to become a Machiavellian "New Man" possesses equal ability. Yet all participate inside the ethical boundaries of their respective cultures. Caudillaje man seeks public acclaim for public deeds. The feats which he attempts are calculated to bring this approval every bit as much as the bourgeois-capitalist calculates his entrepreneurial dealings in such a way as to produce economic profit. . . .

Public power like economic wealth is rooted in rational accumulation. Capitalism measures excellence in terms of accumulated wealth; caudillaje measures one's virtue in terms of accumulated public power. While capitalistic man thus seeks to ensure his economic credit, "to secure my credit and character as a tradesman," as Ben Franklin said, caudillaje man moves to secure his base of political credit, a "credit with the people," as Machiavelli phrased it. It is certainly an unfounded prejudice that only liberal democracy rests upon this "credit" of the people. Machiavelli's *Il principe* attests on every page to the significance of such popular support. The importance of power as a currency has been sketched within the larger social-political order by Karl Deutsch:

> Power cannot be counted exactly, but it can be estimated in proportion to the power resources or capabilities that are visibly available, such as the numbers of countable supporters, voters, or soldiers available or required in a particular political context. Levels of intensity of support, or morale, of skills and resourcefulness, insofar as any or all of these can be estimated, may also be taken into account by appropriate weighing, much as manpower budgets or estimates of military forces can be at least roughly calculated. . . . Prestige is then to power as credit is to cash. And physical force—enforcement in the narrow sense—is to power as gold is to paper money or to savings accounts and checks. . . .

"Rational" friendships provide the roots from which springs public power. However acquired, one becomes rich in terms of public power by the number and quality (power) of one's friends:

> He weakened himself by casting off his friends . . .
>
> Not having friends in the country . . . he was forced to accept what friendships he could find . . .
>
> Consider how little difficulty the king would have had in maintaining his reputation in Italy if he had observed the aforesaid rules, and kept a firm and sure hold over all those friends of his . . .
>
> He abolished the old militia, raised a new one, abandoned his old friendships and formed others; and as he had thus friends and soldiers of his own choosing, he was able on this foundation to build securely. . . .

> I will only say ... that it is necessary for a prince to possess the friendship of the people; otherwise he has no resource in times of adversity. ...
>
> One ... who becomes prince by favor of the populace, must maintain its friendship, which he will find easy, the people asking nothing but not to be oppressed.

In these phrases of Niccolò Machiavelli, the Ben Franklin of Catholicism, we see an already developed ethos of a world view according to which the goal of public power finds a rational means in the acquisition of friends. The currency of public power is friendship. For the public man friends are used as currency in the identical sense in which capitalists speak of money and currency as synonymous terms. Capitalism and the exploitation of man by man only became feasible with the introduction of currency. ...

The public man is dominated by a need to acquire friends. He undertakes this acquisition as the ultimate purpose of his life. The common man of caudillaje society knows that power depends upon friendship, that there are certain means of acquiring, holding, and losing friendship, and that without it one is lost. By contrast, the capitalist has no need for such interpersonal connections. The marketplace reduced his relationships to a cash nexus, as Marx said, where not friendship but alienation would predominate. Adam Smith in *The Theory of Moral Sentiments* characterized this appropriate "go it alone" attitude of capitalists:

> It is a sedate but steady and faithful attachment to a few well-tried and well-chosen companions, in the choice of whom he is not guided by the giddy admiration of shining accomplishments, but by the sober esteem of modesty, discretion, and good conduct. But, though capable of friendship, he is not always much disposed to general sociality. He rarely figures in those convivial societies which are distinguished for the jollity and gaiety of their conversation. Their way of life might too often interfere with the regularity of his temperance, might interrupt the steadiness of his industry, or break in upon the strictness of his frugality ...

For the public man worldly success is directly correlated with his public power. And the test of public power is found in the extent of his friendships. Friendship, or *amicitia* as here used, does not pertain to sentiments of private congeniality but functions as a weapon of power. Personal relationships therefore must be cultivated, the circle of friendship extended. "Playing the friendship game" thus becomes a necessary way of life—as all-consuming as playing the money game within capitalistic cultures. As one Venezuelan is recorded to have said, "I believe that the correct and exemplary life of the individual depends on the friends he chooses . . . on the opportune exchange of ideas and advice on both sides. . . . One often has friends whom one serves. At other times one demands to be served and is satisfied. I . . . have made a cult of friendship."

Public power readily grows for those who already possess a sizable capital. "It takes money to make money" is a well-known truism of the bourgeoisie. So too for caudillaje man. His slogan becomes, "It takes friends to acquire friends." Success breeds success. Followers go to the followed the way money and credit gravitate toward the rich. Public men know this and therefore endeavor to demonstrate to one and all the extensive nature of their existing friendships. It is necessary for one to appear successful. Hence, he must surround himself with friends, visible and invisible, in order to assist himself in still further accumulation. J. A. Pitt-Rivers observes,

> It is a commonplace that you can get nothing done in Andalusia save through friendship. It follows then that the more friends a man can claim the greater his sphere of influence; the more influential his friends are the more influence he has. Friendship is thereby connected with prestige, and boastful characters like to assert how many friends they have, how extensive is the range of their friendships. . . .

The public man strives to become the "surrounded man." To be surrounded with friends accomplishes for the common man of caudillaje society what a new car furnishes for the common man of capitalistic society. It is an objective sign of success. And the means of aggregating these persons no more enters the picture at the moment of this demonstration of importance and achievement than does the means of acquiring a new house or car for the capitalist. Both may indicate a lack of "good sense," a final exhaustion of effort. Friends, like cars, may be repossessed, will return to another power center tomorrow. But on the other hand, the show of added friends may contribute to yet other quite tangible gains of public power.

Caudillaje man can best convey the impression of being a successful public man by becoming the surrounded man. Everywhere one sees this surrounded man in caudillaje countries. From the extended family to the sidewalk coffee shops; from the sports palace to the national palace, one observes the phenomenon. Most of life is lived in a public forum and most of life is deliberately social. In caudillaje culture men consciously seek out the center of activity as a desirable place to live, work, and enjoy oneself. . . .

Unlike the capitalists, caudillaje men actively endeavor to aggregate friends. Life is organic rather than atomistic, as the medievalists would say. Indeed, one finds that caudillaje man avoids appearing alone in public as capitalist man avoids being idle in public. Friendship thus has the connotation of the Roman *clientes.* The number of hangers-on, the size of one's entourage, becomes an indication of one's public power. Miguel Asturias in his novel, *El señor presidente,* demonstrates what it means to be at the pinnacle of power: "All those who recognize that you are worthy to be First Citizen of the Nation and who therefore surrounded you at that terrible moment, . . . surround you now and will continue to do so as long as it is necessary." Being surrounded in no way implies a communitarian ethos. An aggregation in caudillaje society almost invariably indicates a degree of organization and hierarchy. One day caudillaje man may pay deference to a friend who has invited him to dinner, and the next week that friend may in turn pay deference to him at a similar function which he in turn has arranged. What is important is that outside of the family, nay, even within the family, persons seldom meet as equals. Someone clearly takes the role of the surrounded man and the others assume the role of surrounders. By playing this game from an early age, caudillaje persons learn much about domination, subservience, and role-playing in general. . . .

Timeworn procedures exist whereby the public man can surround himself. . . . Caudillaje cultures are ordered, hierarchical,

and "proper" in the sense of conveying deference to whom deference is due. Such a quality lends itself to maintenance of structures (after first establishing the institutional base) for gaining
status through waiting numbers. By illustration, one of the more
effective means a lawyer, professor, businessman, civil servant, or
military person may utilize for building a constant aggregation
around his person and/or office is to (1) refuse to delegate any
responsibility, and then (2) become "inaccessible." One sees this
game played out in a hundred variations throughout caudillaje
countries in the smallest village as well as in the largest cities.
Whether it be a long line of *indígenas* waiting to see a *juez de paz*
[justice of the peace] in an Ecuadorian provincial *aldea* [village],
angry numbers seeking opera tickets in Milan, or an American
tourist endeavoring to settle a traffic violation in Madrid—the
same logic is being pursued by the jefe. His importance increases
as the number of persons seeking his assistance, approval, help,
or mercy grows. . . . [An] observant writer summarizes the theme:

> It is almost recognized as good form that a public official keep
> subordinates and clients waiting far beyond their appoint-
> ment time. Indeed, power is treated almost as if it were a kind
> of quality which needs to be displayed in order to validate it.
> Part of the style of politics is behavior that displays this qual-
> ity; it can be used at any bureaucratic level. No matter where
> you stand there will be someone sometime over whom you
> have power—whether you are the minister of state who casu-
> ally keeps a waiting room perpetually full of petitioners, or
> the janitor who slams the gate just before closing time and
> opens it tardily in the morning.

Such behavior is wholly rational given the goal of the public
man. That is, it achieves the end of surrounding one's office and
person with large numbers of people who in fact need him. Love
for bureaucratic procedures, elaborate hierarchies, inefficient secretaries, stamps, and seals, all attest to the public man's desire to
give the appearance of possessing special qualities by prolonging
the matter at hand. Behaviorally, then, one finds that it is not the
"efficient" man who through hard work has cleared his desk and
seen all of his clients who is perceived as the man of excellence.

In fact, efficiency is counterproductive in terms of caudillaje values. It constitutes a public confession of one's lack of importance.

If one looks hard enough, in almost any office in caudillaje society one will find an unassuming man usually dressed in black who in fact understands how things are done and runs the day-to-day business of the office. His longevity in office is proverbial— in Guatemala he seems to survive all administrations from Communists to right-wing militarists. These men are, in short, unexpendable as, almost like the eunuchs of Roman bureaucracy, they appear to uniquely operate upon other than the values of the society in which they live. That is, at first glance they seem not to be "public men." Yet . . . their hold upon true power places them well within the value frame of caudillaje society. Like Machiavelli, they are advisers to the power holders and by supplying continuity make governance possible.

It is, consequently, the surrounded man who is beheld as the man of virtue. Clients, therefore, are not persons to be taken care of and expedited on their way. Clients are to be savored, preserved about one's person. Thus, the later one arrives for an appointment, the more people who await one's entrance, then the more excellent one must be. And this kind of public virtue can be successfully sought and exercised in any size community. For example, professors in caudillaje society are usually late for class and often do not show up at all. When they do arrive tardily, their rage knows no end if the students have left. It is as if the knights would not await the king. His purpose in being late has backfired. Whence emerges the picture of a society wherein the conduct of each individual is minutely attuned to the disposition and behavior of others. . . .

Some men in caudillaje society are born to a wealth of public power while most must strive for it. For the fortunate few, servants, chauffeurs, gardeners abound from childhood. Their parents have many friends—a life of power is secured, barring some unforeseen catastrophe or a great squandering of the public credit they have inherited. But for most the struggle for influence is real, pervasive, vicious, and all-consuming. Their resources of power are marshaled, saved, and spent in such manner as to enlarge their capital of public power.

The endeavor to surround himself occupies most of Catholic

man's waking hours. Such efforts are necessary not merely for ego fulfillment but also to achieve real ends. The surrounded man has at his fingertips vast resources of power and influence through his "connections." Those who are alone have very little to bank upon.

One of the prime methods by which these friends can be of help is through the phenomenon of intercession. Friends can intercede on one's behalf to accomplish almost anything. Without such intermediaries very little could be achieved. Catholic societies since medieval times have relied upon these agents to expedite one's interest. Today personalistic mediation constitutes one of the hallmarks of caudillaje culture and distinguishes it from the impersonal mediation of the marketplace economy and world view of capitalism. For Protestants intermediaries between God and man have tended to be economic due to the default of organized churches to fill the void of intercession thrown off at the Reformation. By contrast, caudillaje culture carries into societal life the notion of personal mediation found within its religious tradition. . . . Men appeal to saints for religious intercession the way they appeal to "friends" to intercede upon their behalf for the accomplishment of this-worldy goals. . . . Here one sees the advantage of being surrounded with multiple and overlapping friendships. "God" is usually inaccessible, taking a day off, short of money, and so on. But ask one of his saintly acquaintances who over the years has become your good friend—one who has presided over your wedding, birth of your children, one to whom you have made many offerings and sacrifices—and anything becomes possible.

The systemization of supplication has created what a Spanish author calls "the mendicancy of influence." Today, he says,

> everything in Spain—access to employment, the concession for a business, the leasing of a flat, the installation of a telephone, the resolution of the most common bureaucratic requirement—is obtained because one has a friend. Of course, the immense majority of people don't have those friends who take care of things, but they can ask to borrow some from those who have mountains of them. With this a veritable traffic in favors has been unleashed upon us, a new and curious

form of mendicancy, the mendicancy of influence, which . . . brings, to those well endowed with contacts, a large clientele of hopeful or grateful supplicants. . . .

What merits emphasis in the phenomenon of personal intercession . . . is that "individuals forming the chain are anxious to oblige the person who was the last link, not the actual applicant who is unknown to them." Caudillaje culture thus spins upon these letters of credit. The rational quality of the system overwhelms the social analyst. To function within such a culture, "living successfully," is contingent upon the influence of others. Certain worn and prescribed methods exist for gaining their accommodation.

The first means to power available to the public man is his family. An orphan indeed presents a pathetic figure in this culture, as he is bankrupt at birth. All others begin life "surrounded," if only by a mother. Those who have father, mother, and many brothers and sisters are almost assured of some success in life: they already have at least minimal power because they are surrounded by "natural" human resources which may be exploited. Additional power will come easier. Strength of family ties does not appear to be some quaint holdover from traditional times that disappears in Catholic societies with modernization. There are many indications that this institution continues to dominate the life of caudillaje man after a degree of industrialization has taken place. One can with confidence predict that the strong family system will survive as long as caudillaje values prevail.

Consider the extended family: that network of second cousins, godparents, and close friends of blood relationships. It surely survives because it rests upon the felt needs of everyone within the group. Family relationships and the *compadre* [godfather] system of Catholic culture serve as a power base for each participant—it is his one constant and "free" aggregation. Others must be earned. Interchangeable, each member of the family helps each other member toward the personal achievement of power. This in contrast to the capitalistic loose family relationship according to which an endeavor to accumulate wealth may serve as a divisive rather than a unifying factor, particularly among the middle class.

The closeness of families in caudillaje culture can therefore be explained in part as surviving out of individual self-interest while capitalistic families disintegrate for the same reason. In North America upper-class families often function as a unit while middle-class families do not. This may well be because the father in middle-class families can be of much less "use" to his children in their struggle for selfhood, status, and economic power than in the case of the upper-class family. Also, it should be noted that within Catholic society children are useful to their parents in that a new child can bring in a new compadre. The circle of power thus broadens for the parents.

The extended family as the cornerstone of public power has most frequently been commented upon in relation to dictators. "The men whom caudillos call upon first will naturally be their relatives, because the ties of blood are the surest and the strongest." "To the ties of blood can be added those which create a religious relationship between the compadres or godfathers . . . and the relatives of the baptized as well as the child himself. These ties often remain powerful enough to oblige the partners to help each other in all circumstances." What must be recognized, however, is that nepotism at the highest ranks of political power only reflects culturewide behavior. The nepotism of a Castro, a Batista, a Perón, or a Trujillo does not simply represent the corruption of an economic, money-oriented behavior, as is so often assumed. Rather, their actions are typical of previous reliance upon friends and relatives and of an accepted mode of behavior that can be traced back to the very foundation of the society itself. For example, in Francisco Pizarro's tiny conquering army in Peru, men from Trujillo, Spain, occupied the first thirty-seven positions while the top five were held by Pizarro, his two bastard brothers, a half-brother, and a legitimate brother. . . .

It is outside of the extended family that the attempt to surround oneself takes on a competitive nature. Schools, political parties, bureaucracies, barracks become battlegrounds in this endeavor. Caudillaje man enters into competition to surround himself with friends. By analogy, capitalistic societies have long been organized in such manner as to expedite the making of money. Wealth being the capitalist's prime goal, one finds societal and political arrangements so constructed that many may efficiently achieve their common end. This same efficiency in structured goal achievement is visible within caudillaje societies. Thus, while capitalistic countries established their stock markets to assist men in the accumulation of money, so caudillaje nations have institutionalized the means for the accumulation of friends.

For example, formal educational institutions do not exist to convey technical knowledge that will be economically useful, as in capitalistic cultures, but to provide a place where young men may begin to sort out and establish hierarchies of power. They prepare the youth for a lifetime of such activity. . . . Consistent with the ethos, education furnishes "the verbal and intellectual skills that are useful to *gente buena* ["good people," hence elite] activities," not something as relatively worthless as improved knowledge of planting and harvesting. Students thus do not study so much as prepare a following, consolidate a power base. Often their instructors become pawns to be manipulated or discarded according to the dictates of political exigency. From the professor's standpoint it is not the goal of teaching that determines behavior so much as aggregating followers to support his ends of public power whether that be in the form of a deanship, rectorship, or political party post. University clubs, elections, and protest movements in caudillaje culture are thus a microcosm of national life. Not only do they reflect a pervasive set of cultural values, they embody a process of socialization into the values of these societies. A student's ideology may overtly shift from Communism to Fascism between his university years and age thirty. But his goals of public power remain constant, and the process of aggregating friends, of becoming the surrounded man, goes on unabated. And . . . the code of ethics which he has early embraced will probably not change with his shift of political allegiance from the Left to the Right. . . .

National politics in caudillaje society is almost constantly in the hands of university graduates or the military. This has much less to do with a monopoly of coercive force than usually supposed. Rather, it follows from the fact that both university and barracks provide an ideal setting for the aggregation of a following which may sooner or later prove useful. Most personalized political parties in these areas can be traced back either to coteries of friends within the university and professional *colegios* or to military cliques. For this reason, the ambitious young man in caudillaje society does not begin his career by hawking newspapers or going "West." Instead he dons a tie and goes off to school aspiring to become a lawyer or a general—either may lead to the pinnacles of public power.

The public man's values are reflected in the type of organization he joins. Throughout caudillaje society "brotherhoods" exists. While animal clubs (Elks, Lions, Eagles, etc.) with their atomistic, businessman, egalitarian, service-oriented nature characterize capitalistic society, so brotherhoods characterize caudillaje culture. They are often religiously oriented (for example, Opus Dei in Spain) . . . and are always organic, elitist, and exclusive. Their unity derives from effective ties of brotherhood which have little to do with public "service" and much to do with building and appropriately displaying one's public image. Thus, since the Renaissance, literary *tertulias* [circles], aristocratic clubs, and military cliques have existed in abundance wherein individual excellences might be appropriately displayed and aggregations solidified. There is not, however, any of the fanatical joining of multiple groups which Tocqueville found in the United States. One who seeks power based on an individualized following cannot afford either to spread himself too thin or to align himself with groups whose membership might possible conflict with his clientele in another public setting. As a consequence, the public man tends to concentrate on one organization, and very often this will be an informal "power behind the scenes" aggregation.

One of the settings wherein individual qualities may be properly exhibited is the barracks. Universal to caudillaje society is a love for those attributes of the public man derivative of military life and organization: formalism in etiquette, speech, and dress. Deference can be secured through rank itself. The public man thus finds military existence very compatible once he removes himself from the bottom rung of the hierarchy; he then always has someone below to wait upon his needs. Hierarchy allows him to assume the role of public man. Naturally, then, an affinity for militaristic values can be seen everywhere within caudillaje society. Uniforms are worn by maids, school children, street sweepers, and guards as well as presidents, generals, and clergymen; deference is shown by everyone to his superior in the realm of physical, linguistic, and ideological posturing.

What better organization could the mind of man contrive for the surrounding of oneself with "friends"? Martial life consists of advancement based upon an individual's performance before his fellowman as well as friendship, influence, and family. Opportunities for one to aggregate a following through the sole exercise of his public virtue are excellent. Bolstered by the hierarchy of rank, the man of aspirations can assure himself of a mass public and a mass following by concentrating upon the few: his fellow officers. No doubt this explains the affinity for military life of the ambitious enlisted men from the middle and lower classes. In the barracks they find that execution of public virtue provides opportunities for success which energetic young capitalists have traditionally found in the marketplace. Thus barracks revolts, coups, and countercoups often typify caudillaje society. The successes and failures of those revolts are the functional equivalents of the ups and downs of the capitalistic marketplace: they signal the building of empires and the periodic bankruptcies of these empires. Behind each "disturbance" lies a clash of two or more aggregations of men. Hence, while caudillaje nations traditionally fight few wars and tend to lack international bellicosity, they have singular emphasis upon the military order. What has been said of Machiavelli might be extended to the public man in general: "One suspects that he wants all the glory of arms without the sufferings of actual war. . . ."

Ideology is of secondary importance. Doctrinal content tends to be of less significance than the person espousing it throughout caudillaje society. Such propagandistic activity reflects within an organizational framework the values of a whole society. For example, a Venezuelan labor leader said in an interview:

> What attracts one is the attention of a leader, the quality of the leader that wins over masses. Well, I was an admirer of (name) and if (name) had gone into the Communist Party perhaps I would now be a Communist or if he were from

(party) I would also be in that party . . . because it is only later that one begins to know party doctrine . . . philosophy, programs, objectives. But first one is drawn by a man, and it is this same attraction that a labor leader may also have. (Workers) join a union out of sympathy and fondness for a leader who listens to them, who calls them. . . .

National bureaucracy is another setting that furnishes structure for the aggregation of followers. The "goals" of the organization are usually secondary. For the participant it provides, rather, a vehicle for aggregating friends, making "connections," and serving to enlarge his power base. In all likelihood the very utility of the civil service accounts for the fact that within caudillaje countries, even in an age of organization, there exist disproportionately big bureaucracies, just as the military organizations and especially the officer corps within these nations are inordinately large. The bureaucracy necessarily operates as a catering service to caudillaje man's pursuit and demonstration of his ability *tener muñeca* ("to have connections"), *tener palanca* ("to have leverage"), or *tener cuello* ("to have pull"). In performing their function, correctly understood, these organizations move faultlessly.

Bureaucracy within caudillaje culture functions with supreme rationality. Given the public man's goals of deference and respect based upon control over other persons, the interminable delays, stamps, "procedures," giant logbooks, and so forth, become perfectly logical. Capitalists see nothing but "backwardness," "inefficiency" in such procedures. Yet on an individual basis the bureaucrat of caudillaje culture is achieving in the same sense that the impatient capitalist is achieving. From the psychological aspect, the capitalist's abrasiveness and impatience says, "I have self-worth because I represent such and such a company and I am entitled to service." The caudillaje person says, "I have self-worth because I am in charge of these stamps and forms and I will exact your deference on that basis the way you would exact deference on the basis of your wealth and economic position. . . ."

Common errors of capitalistic man arise from a mistaken impression of what he is seeing when he looks upon caudillaje society. Consider for example the statement of a Uruguayan, trained in the language and concepts of Talcott Parsons, writing about his own country:

> It is clear that particularism is a very important phenomenon in Uruguayan society and it prevails over universalism. A great number of facts support this. It is well known that the prevailing system of selection for government employees is based on kinship, on membership in a certain club or political faction, on friendship, etc. These are all particularistic criteria. A similar phenomenon is present in private enterprise where selection of personnel on the basis of particularistic relations is very common. The use of universalistic criteria, such as the use of standardized examinations, is exceptional. Quite frequently when such universalistic criteria seem operative, they are applied to candidates who have been previously selected on the basis of personal relationships.

The average person from capitalistic society who reads these words will at least unconsciously reject the Uruguayan system as being tied to an intolerable randomness under which one's life chances are inexorably related to the power and position of his economic heritage; a society in which not only individual merit but graft, corruption, nepotism determine all. In short, it appears to be a situation in which "equality of opportunity" is denied, and as this phrase is part of our holy of holies, then words that describe the doors through which pass the achievers must be sacred. "Universalism" and "standardized examinations" are in truth distressingly neglected or rigged in caudillaje culture.

Yet for someone within caudillaje culture a very different interpretation emerges. According to the above statement at least five criteria are available for possible entrance to government service: (1) kinship; (2) membership in a certain club; (3) membership in a political faction; (4) friendship; (5) etc.

Except for number 1, these will depend upon one's aggregative skills. True, the first will often determine the level at which one begins, but certainly, once begun and skillfully played, the game has infinite possibilities. In fact, the public man will scan requirements for a position, and nothing will discourage him so much as a standardized examination. For many these exams, if rigidly adhered to, would mean the end of the road in terms of upward social mobility. Only the educated would have access to such jobs because education more than any other qualification demands affluence. Friendship, membership in a club or political faction, and those wonderful possibilities embodied in "etc." mean that everyman can perceive the probability of some success. Particularistic selection within the bureaucracy becomes in this sense as rational as universalism. That obvious truism prevents caudillaje society from adopting a merit system as we know it in other than name—they already have their own merit system. Anonymously graded competitive examinations make no sense where public power is the goal. Friends and relatives can contribute to that goal, but followership can hardly be tied to answering a civil service examination or doing geometry.

Examples of the unimportance of examinations for advancement in caudillaje society amplify the point. In his study of the Guatemalan bureaucracy Jerry Weaver found that "most Guatemalan bureaucrats see themselves being evaluated and promoted on the basis of criteria other than manifest skill, training, or experience. Only 20 percent of the sample thought that specific skills, technical training or on-the-job experience was most important for promotion. . . ."

Behavior may or may not accord with legal procedures of selection but tends to be extremely routinized. The public man depends upon his family and friends for access to position the way private capitalist men put faith in education as a vehicle for meeting entrance requirements to gain position. To believe that there is not a rational procedure for the acquiring of friends belies the facts. . . . At times even family has been "created" where none existed. All of this requires enormous skill and competence, albeit of a nontechnological, nonbureaucratic, noncapitalistic nature. In short, the procedure fails to be legal but passes the test for rationality.

Finally, while one would be foolish to downplay the importance of family within caudillaje society, still, the matter must be kept within perspective. Obviously to be born to wealth anywhere in capitalistic society means that one's life chances are significantly different from those who are not. Yet in some version the

Horatio Alger myth remains a culture belief for capitalistic man even among the poor. One finds here the essence of the situation within caudillaje culture. Certain individuals begin much higher up on the scale of public influence than others, yet this does not guarantee them success or absolutely prohibit the rise of those born to parents who lack status: it simply means fewer obstacles for them to overcome. . . .

Setting also is in part determined by the spirit of caudillaje. While one could easily claim too much here, urbanization in caudillaje culture appears to stem in some measure from the individual's desire to surround himself. An urban setting contributes the most ideal conditions for exercising a code of public virtue and the aggregation of friends. One's extended family may suffice for a beginning, but ultimately one must seek a broader constituency. Here lies a partial explanation for the persistence with which caudillaje societies continue to urbanize even when conditions in rural areas are improved: opportunity for aggregating followers becomes greatly augmented within cities. . . .

In short, the business of aggregation is taken seriously in caudillaje culture. While their counterparts in Protestant bourgeois culture are out selling newspapers, young people in these areas of the world . . . are already sitting in cafes beginning to accumulate their fortunes via the coinage system of public power. Here lies the unity of theory and practice. Caudillaje youth in their coffeehouses are not engaging in idle chatter. They are learning the criteria of public activity and beginning to apply their knowledge through the aggregation of friends, some of whom will be useful for a lifetime.

3

Eric R. Wolf and Edward C. Hansen

Caudillo Politics: A Structural Analysis

A materialist exploration of the nature of caudillismo is one facet of the collective effort to understand the phenomenon. Eric Wolf, an anthropologist best known to students of Latin America for his classic *The Sons of the Shaking Earth* (1959), and Edward Hansen stress economic factors to explain the emergence of caudillos in the nineteenth century. In the full essay the authors examine the waning years of the empire and the processes of independence that engendered an uncomfortable alliance of criollo and mestizo elements in the society. The selections included here emphasize how the system of gifts and rewards for loyalty from subordinates combined with such personal qualities as *machismo,* a variant of masculinity, to sustain caudillos in the discordant decades after independence. Wolf and Hansen take pains to show that there were serious flaws in the system including the problem of succession. They also argue that by the 1870s and 1880s "the dictators of 'order and progress' " had superseded the cruder caudillos and that new political alignments diverted mestizos away from caudillaje into mass politics at the turn of the century. Readers, however, may find ample evidence in recent history of certain echos of the times Wolf and Hansen describe. The overthrow of Alfredo Stroessner in Paraguay in 1989 in a coup engineered by his right hand man General Andrés Rodríguez is more than a vestige of the past.

THE Latin American Wars of Independence realized the long-standing hope of the criollo gentry to rid themselves of Spanish limitations on their economic and political activities. [Before that happened and] in spite of the decline of Spanish power, however,

From Eric R. Wolf and Edward C. Hansen, "*Caudillo* Politics: A Structural Analysis," *Comparative Studies in Society and History* 9 (1967): 168–79. Reprinted with permission of Cambridge University Press.

the New World planter class proved too weak numerically and too lacking in cohesion to oust the Peninsular forces by its own unaided efforts. To gain their own independence they were therefore forced into political alliances with the numerically strong and highly mobile—yet at the same time economically, socially, and politically disprivileged—social strata of the population which are designated collectively as mestizos. Not without trepidation, criollo leaders armed elements derived from these propertyless strata and sent them to do battle against the Spaniards. Success in maintaining the continuing loyalties of these elements depended largely upon the ability of leaders in building personal ties of loyalty with their following and in leading them in ventures of successful pillage.

The emerging pattern had colonial prototypes. Landowners had long maintained armed retainers on their own estates. The creation of a colonial army had underwritten the creation of such localized militia. In Mexico, for instance, "the viceroy and the military authorities found it convenient that a militia captain be at one and the same time the landlord of the men who served under his command." The Spanish government had thus contributed paradoxically to the diminution of its own power and to the formation of many local power centers. Yet the additional step of granting independent armament both to retainers and to other potential military elements in the population entailed further risks. Although the alliance of criollos and mestizos was instrumental in winning the Wars of Independence, granting arms to the mestizo elements freed these to create their own armed bands. The mestizos in turn were thus enabled to compete with the criollos for available wealth. . . . In granting independent armament to the mestizos, therefore, the criollo gentry also sacrificed any chance it might have had to establish a monopoly of power.

The beneficiaries of this distribution of weaponry were the leaders on horseback, the caudillos, the resultant political system, caudillaje. It came to be marked by four salient characteristics: (1) the repeated emergence of armed patron-client sets, cemented by personal ties of dominance and submission, and by a common desire to obtain wealth by force of arms; (2) the lack of institutionalized means for succession to offices; (3) the use of violence in political competition; and (4) the repeated failures of incumbent leaders to guarantee their tenures as chieftains. This paper is concerned with an analysis of this political system, and with a search for its causes and consequences. It also wishes to suggest that this is best accomplished by an understanding of the system in Latin American terms, rather than in terms of concepts derived from events in Europe. . . .

The Caudillo and His Organization

In our discussion, we shall employ the ethnographic present. The aim of the caudillo band is to gain wealth; the tactic employed is essentially pillage. For the retainers, correct selection of a leader is paramount. No retainer can guarantee that he will receive recompense from his leader in advance, because the band seeks to obtain wealth which is not yet in its possession. All know that the wealth sought after is finite; only certain resources are "safe game." The band cannot attack with impunity the basic sources of criollo wealth, such as land; and it cannot sequester, without international complications, the property of foreign firms operating in the area. Hence there is not only intense competition for movable resources, but great skill is required in diagnosing which resources are currently "available" and which taboo. The exercise of power therefore gives rise to a code which regulates the mode of access to resources. The code refers to two basic attributes of leadership: first, the interpersonal skills needed to keep the band together; second, the acumen required to cement these relationships through the correct distribution of wealth. Possession of interpersonal skills is the initial prerequisite; it suggests to the retainers that the second attribute will also be fulfilled.

The social idiom in which the first of these attributes is discussed is that of "masculinity": the social assertion of masculinity constitutes what has come to be known as *machismo* (from *macho*, masculine). According to the idiom, masculinity is demonstrated in two ways: by the capacity to dominate females, and by the readiness to use violence. These two capacities are closely related; both point to antagonistic relations between men. The capacity to dominate women implies the further capacity to best other men in the competition over females. But the vocabulary of sexual relations, focusing on the interplay between active and aggressive males and passive, suffering females, also covers situations in which one dominant and aggressive male bests another whose defeat thereby casts him in the role of the submissive and passive sufferer. Assertion of masculinity in interpersonal relations thus implies a social ordering between a dominant leader and a following which suffers his dominance and admires his prowess. The theme of sexual competition should also be read against the wider social background, in which female seclusion on the part of the gentry symbolizes their hold on property and status. The assertion of masculinity on the part of the caudillo threatens that monopoly; like the possession of arms [as Richard Morse says], it "threatens to derange the predictable interplay of hierarchical class relations."

Assertions of dominance are tested in numerous encounters, in which the potential leader must test himself against other potential claimants. . . . Such situations are charged with potential violence, for in such antagonistic confrontations, the claimants to victory must be prepared to kill their rivals and to demonstrate this willingness publicly. For the loser there is no middle ground; he must submit to the winner, or be killed. Willingness to risk all in such encounters is further proof of masculinity. The drama involved in such tests of leadership is illustrated by the following episode in the rise of a Bolivian caudillo:

> Mariano Melgarejo, an ignorant and drunken murderer given to the wildest sexual orgies . . . ran the country from 1864 to 1871. Melgarejo got into power by killing the country's dictator, Belzú, in the presidential palace. The shooting took place before a great crowd which had gathered in the plaza to see the meeting of the two rivals. When Belzú fell dead into the arms of one of his escorts, Melgarejo strode to the window and exclaimed: 'Belzú is dead. Now who are you shouting for?' The mob, thus prompted, threw off its fear and gave a bestial cry: 'Viva Melgarejo!'

Personal leadership may thus create a successful band; by the same token, however, the personal nature of leadership also threatens band maintenance. If the caudillo is killed or dies of natural causes, the band will disintegrate because there can be no institutionalized successor. The qualities of leadership reside in his person, not in the office. . . .

Proof of masculinity does not yet make a man a caudillo. Men will not flock to his banner unless he also proves himself capable of organizing a number of minimal bands into a maximal faction, and demonstrates his ability to hold the faction together. To this end, the caudillo must weld a number of lieutenants into a core of "right-hand men" *(hombres de confianza)*. Important in this creation of a core of devoted followers is not merely assertion of dominance, but also calculated gift-giving to favored individuals who are expected to reciprocate with loyalty. Such gifts may consist of movable goods, money, or perquisites such as the right to pillage a given area or social group. The importance of such gifts is best understood as a prestation of favors defined not merely as objects, but also as attributes of the giver. Where the receiver cannot respond with a countergift which would partake equally of his own personal attributes, he is expected to respond with loyalty, that is, he makes a gift of his person for a more or less limited period of time. The existence of such a core of right-hand men produces its own demonstration effect. They are living testimony to the largesse of the caudillo aspirant and to his commitment to grant riches in return for personal support.

To satisfy this desire for riches, the caudillo must exhibit further abilities. We have already discussed some of the limitations under which the caudillo labors in acquiring wealth: there are certain groups he may not attack with impunity. To cast about in quest of riches may stir resistance; resistance may imply defeat. To be successful, therefore, a caudillo needs what we may call "access vision," capabilities closely related to the "business acumen" of the North American entrepreneur. He must be able to diagnose resources which are available for seizure with a minimum of resistance on the part of their present owners. He must estimate how much wealth is needed to satisfy his retainers. He must also control the free-lance activities of his followers, such as cattle rustling and robbery, lest they mobilize the resistance of effective veto groups. He must be able to estimate correctly the force at the disposal of those presently in control of resources; and he must be able to predict the behavior and power of potential competitors in the seizure of wealth. Nor can he rest content with initial success in his endeavors. He must continuously find new sources of wealth which can be distributed to his following, or he must attach resources which replenish themselves. Initial successes are therefore frequently followed by sudden failures; many caudillo ventures end as "one-shot" undertakings. The caudillo may be successful in seizing the government treasury or the receipts of a customhouse; then no other source of wealth is found, and the faction disintegrates. The more limited the supply of ready wealth, the more rapid the turnover of caudillos. Thus Bolivia, one of the most impoverished countries during this period, averaged more than one violent change of government every year.

It follows from this that the caudillo with ties to the criollo gentry possesses advantages denied to his mestizo counterpart. The criollo may be able to draw on his own wealth at the beginning of his undertaking; when liquid wealth grows scarce, he can retrench to provide booty from his own estate. However much of a burden this may put on own resources, it can enable him to weather a period of scarcity, while the mestizo caudillo requires continuing abundance.

Such considerations affected even the most successful caudillos, such as José A. Páez and Juan Manuel Rosas. Páez held sway in Venezuela for thirty-three years (1830–63); Rosas dominated Argentina for twenty years (1829–31, 1835–52). Both owned enormous cattle ranches which furnished large quantities of beef, the staple of the countryside. Both drew their retainers from the ranks of the fierce cowpunchers of the tall grass prairie, the gauchos in Argentina and the llaneros of Venezuela, whose mode of livelihood provided ideal preparation for caudillo warfare. Time and again, both men defeated the attempts of rivals to set up centralized forms of government. Despite the initial advantages of abundant wealth, their control of "natural" military forces, and their ability to neutralize a large number of competitors, however, both men had to beat off numerous armed uprisings, and both ultimately met defeat. Their cases illustrate the difficulties which beset caudillos operating even under optimal conditions.

Eric Wolf and Edward C. Hansen

Salient Weaknesses of the Caudillo Organization

The caudillo organization must thus face always the threat of insufficient "pay-off." At the same time, it is also threatened from within, by the very nature of the social ties which hold it together. There are, at any one time, always more men qualified to become caudillos, or aspiring to demonstrate their capabilities as potential chieftains, than there are caudillos. Such competition necessarily encourages rivalry within the band for the position of chieftainship. Usually the salient rival is one of the caudillo's own "men of confidence," a person who is himself a leader of men within the framework of the maximal band. Latin America's political history during this period is therefore expectably rife with examples of treachery by influential underlings. Thus Páez was betrayed by Monagas, to whom he had granted titular control over the government, and Rosas by his own General Urquiza. In the absence of institutional controls, the caudillo himself can only guess whether his subordinates are loyal or disloyal. The classic loyalty test occurs when rivals meet head on in violent encounter, in a situation of public confrontation. Such a situation demands that retainers take a stand; they must "declare themselves" *(declararse)* for or against one of the protagonists. If they stand by their leader, their support constitutes a kind of vote of confidence; if they desert him, his career will come to an end. Such votes of confidence take various forms. Rosas's gaucho retainers deserted him on the field of battle. García Moreno, theocratic caudillo of Ecuador, was assassinated in plain view of his followers; Mexico's Santa Anna was declared "for" and "against" repeatedly, during the many crises of his government in its relations with France and the United States. A farsighted caudillo is well advised to plan his route of escape from the country in advance of the moment when his retainers transfer their loyalty to another, if he wishes to live to fight another day in an attempt to return to power.

Caudillaje and Modern Latin America

This paper has presented a model of caudillo organization, and has explored the causes underlying this political phenomenon. We have seen the reasons for its emergence in the inability of any socio-economic class to monopolize sufficiently both wealth and power in order to organize a centralized political apparatus. Criollos, while endowed with wealth, lacked the economic and social cohesion to develop the wide-mesh coalitions necessary to control government. The mestizos, on the other hand, lacked the permanent and replenishable sources of wealth necessary to support wide-ranging political activity. In the absence of a framework for institutional politics, Latin American politics became personalized.

In spite of its chaotic appearance, caudillaje was a true political system, an organized effort on the part of competing groups to determine who got what, when and where. For the criollo caudillo, possession of control often guaranteed a temporary position of preference in dealings with foreign trade interests; for the mestizo it meant access to a new arena in which to seek wealth. Given the terms of competition, violence constitutes a predictable aspect of the system. Leadership can be achieved only through violence; resources claimed only through violence; and the balance of power between criollos, mestizos, and foreign traders only maintained by veto group violence against a caudillo who overstepped his bounds. While the endemic threat of violence rendered uncertain the tenure of any one caudillo, however, in the end it served to stabilize the system of caudillaje as a whole. We have argued that the system depended upon a particular balance between criollos, mestizos, and foreign interests. We are thus arguing implicitly that the caudillo system could persist only as long as this balance of interests prevailed. We would thus take issue with investigators who continue to see in caudillaje the dominant political system in Latin America down to the present day. While much of the code of caudillo behavior survives—in a continuing idiom of machismo, readiness to use violence, gift-giving, personalized loyalties—by the 1870s the caudillo system was giving way to a new political system, the dictatorships of "order and progress." While these dictatorships exhibited some caudillo features, the dictator functioned with an increasingly centralized governmental machinery, predicated upon a very different balance of social forces.

The cycle of change from caudillaje to these new dictatorships was triggered by the great European depression of 1873–86, which marked the onset of protectionism at home and of imperialist expansion abroad. Where overseas expansion before this time had been largely characterized by the simple extraction of goods from the dependent countries and the conversion of these goods into commodities on the home market, the new imperialists began to invest heavily in the transformation of certain sectors of production in the dependent areas. In Latin America, this signaled major changes in the production of cash crops; it also resulted in the growth of some light industry, primarily in urban areas. Most significantly, the hacienda—with its built-in defenses against the laissez-faire market—became a thing of the past. Large landed criollo-owned estates might remain intact, but they witnessed a wholesale transformation of their plant from labor-intensive hacienda to the mechanized and capital-intensive plantation, complete with railroad spur leading to the nearest port.

This transformation required the development of credit institutions, the stabilization of currencies, the improvement and widening of the network of transportation. In turn, these requirements demanded a modicum of political stability and an end to anarchic pillage. This need was met by the forging of alliances between foreign interests and native criollo oligarchies of landowners and merchants. The stability of such alliances for order and progress could be guaranteed by the use of foreign armed forces. The local representative of such an alliance was typically the new dictator, often a caudillo in origin, but no longer a caudillo in function. His recompense no longer derived from the systematic pillage of "free" resources; it was furnished by the alliance. In turn, he functioned as head of an alliance police force, neutralizing forcibly all threats to the alliance. The prototypical dictator of this type was Porfirio Díaz, who ruled Mexico between 1876 and 1911. His expressive slogan *pan o palo* (bread or club) symbolizes the twin functions of his government: wealth (pan) to the beneficiaries of the alliance, the use of force (palo) against potential challengers. Thus while harbors were dredged, industry built, commerce expanded, and foreign capital poured into the country, Mexico's prisons were filled to capacity.

The new balance of power represented by the alliances of order and progress spelled the end of the caudillo on horseback. On the national level, they produced dictatorships underwritten by foreign guarantees. At the same time, they drove the mestizos, deprived of resources which would have enabled them to participate in the alliance, to seek countervailing coalitions with groups not hitherto represented in the political process. They turned to the rural population of the hinterland. Everywhere they raised the slogans of land reform, popular education, and mass participation in politics. In countries with strong Indian components, these countervailing alliances formed under the ideological banner of Indianism, a utopian ideology that envisaged a synthesis of the industrial age with the glorious Indian past; elsewhere they groped towards one form or another of populism. Cast in the organizational form of mass parties like the Peruvian APRA, the Mexican PRI, or the Bolivian NNR, they substituted for the insurrectionary caudillo a very different type of leadership, skilled in the management of the "organizational weapon" employed to synchronize divergent group interests. Thus politics in modern Latin America is no longer caudillo politics; it is a many-sided conflict between alliances of order and progress ranged against populist coalitions.

4
Richard M. Morse
Political Theory and the Caudillo

In the preceding chapters the authors have stressed personal bonds and the societal relationships of caudillaje. We turn now to a provocative and original examination of political theory within the framework of early modern Spain and Spanish America. The author of this classic piece, Richard M. Morse, is best known for his work on the history of Latin American urbanization and for a series of trenchant essays. His distinguished academic career has included positions at Yale, Stanford, and the Smithsonian. His examination here of European philosophies that "might be correlated with Spanish American political history" has produced a working polarization of Thomistic medieval values and Machiavellian Renaissance values. He associates these with the personal models of Isabella of Castile and Ferdinand of Aragón, respectively. The interplay of the concepts of the medieval world order and Renaissance statecraft underlies Morse's 1954 reconstruction of the Spanish Empire in America and has important implications for an understanding of caudillismo.

The Viceregal Period and Its Antecedents

THE purpose of this essay is neither fully to analyze the political experience of Spanish America nor to construct a mature theory which will comprehensively illuminate it. The histories of these eighteen countries are, taken singly, too fragmentary and, taken jointly, too uncorrelated to permit of so systematic a project. In this as in most areas of New World studies the elements for conclusive synthesis are still unavailable. Therefore [let us] examine certain formal European notions in the hope, not that they will concisely epitomize Spanish American political experience,

From Richard M. Morse, "Toward a Theory of Spanish American Government," *Journal of the History of Ideas* 15 (January 1954): 71–93. Reprinted with permission.

but that they may be "played off against" that experience—contrapuntally, perhaps—in a way to evoke corresponding themes. . . .

Spanish American preceded British colonization by more than a century, and thus belongs to an era that antedates not only the Lockean rights of man but also the Bosseut- and Hobbes-type apology for the absolutist national state. It is the Catholic kings, Ferdinand and Isabella, who symbolize Spanish America's political heritage.

Isabella in a sense prefigures the divine-right monarch. Her thwarting of the nobles and of the Cortes wherein they formed an estate; her royal agents and administrative reforms that centralized the government; her replacement of feudal levies with a modern army; her use of the faith to further political unity—all have been cited to identify her as a precursor of the Hobbesian autocrat. Yet it must be remembered that for three centuries after Isabella's death the Spanish Empire retained, in comparison at least with the burgeoning capitalist countries, many hallmarks of the medieval, hierarchical state. The "common law" of Isabella's Castile was the Siete Partidas, drawn up ca. 1260 and promulgated in 1348 [which] assumed the nuclear element of society to be, not Lockean atomistic man, but religious, societal man: man with a salvable soul (i.e., in relationship with God) and man in a station of life (i.e., having mutual obligations with fellow humans, determinable by principles of Christian justice). The ruler, though not procedurally responsible to the people or the estates, was bound, through his conscience, to be the instrument of God's immutable, publicly ascertainable law. The Partidas, in fact, specifically excoriated the tyrant who strove to keep his people poor, ignorant, and timorous and to forbid their fellowship and assemblies.

As mistress of the hierarchical Castilian state whose governance was largely by immanent justice and specially ceded privileges *(fueros)*, Isabella found constant occasion to make inter- as well as intranational assertion of her spiritual authority. Unlike Aragón—from whose border the Moorish menace had been lifted in the thirteenth century and whose rulers were therefore indifferent to the Reconquest—Castile directly confronted Moorish Granada until 1492. Furthermore, it was Cisneros, the Queen's confessor, who largely animated the African campaigns against the infidel Turks and Moslems. And it was with the Castilian sovereign that the expeditions which claimed dominion over millions of pagan Amerinds were initially associated. In her major foreign ventures, therefore, Isabella's policy reflected not only politico-military vicissitudes of statecraft but also spiritual responsibilities in the face of non-Christian multitudes. After Columbus had assigned three hundred Indians to forced labor, it was as the imperious agent of the Church Universal that Isabella demanded: "By what authority does the Admiral give my vassals away?"

If Isabella, in her enterprises to the south and overseas to the west, symbolizes the spiritualist, medieval component of the emergent Spanish Empire, then Ferdinand, whose Aragón was engaged to the east and north, represents a secular, Renaissance counterpart. His holdings (the Balearics, Sardinia, Sicily, Naples) and his Italian and Navarrese campaigns confined his problems of rule, alliance, and warfare to the European, Christian community. Isabella presented the unity of spiritually intransigent Christendom to infidel and pagan. Ferdinand was committed to the shifting, amoral statecraft of competing Christian princes in maintenance and expansion of a domain which, within its Christian context, was diversely composed. Ferdinand ruled under transitional conditions which precluded resorting for authority to Isabella's Thomistic sanction or to statist apologetics. Managing with sheer personal verve and cunning, he was, in the fullest sense, Machiavellian. . . .

Spanish conquistadors, colonizers, and catechizers, then, carried with them to American shores this dual heritage: medieval and Renaissance, Thomistic and Machiavellian. . . . For half a century after Isabella's death in 1504 Spanish New World administration hovered between medieval and Renaissance orientations. . . . [After Philip II came to power in 1556,] the structure of the Spanish American Empire assumed the cast which, for purposes of this essay, it kept until ca. 1810. That cast I describe as dominantly Thomistic with recessive Machiavellian characteristics. . . .

In the 1570s, by extending the Inquisition to America and by declaring Church patronage inalienable from the Crown, Philip set his governance definitively within a larger framework of divine law, imbuing his own and his agents' directives with spiritual purpose. No entry was left for the atomistic tolerance that England, despite its state religion, had already begun to evince.

The Crown considered the political and social hierarchy to be energized at every level and in every department. As Indian peoples were absorbed, for example, they were not indiscriminately reduced to a common stratum. Certain of their leaders retained prestige in the post-Conquest society, and many lowborn Spaniards raised their own status by marrying caciques' daughters. . . .

To be sure, the social hierarchy had its anomalies. Creoles (American-born whites or near-whites) rarely received the prestige and the economic and political opportunities that were officially assured them. Mestizos, mulattos, Indians, and Negroes, on the contrary, occasionally found a social fluidity that they could not officially have expected. Broadly speaking, however, a man's status was defined somewhat fixedly by his occupation and by his place and condition of birth. Transferral from one status to another (e.g., an Indian who passed from mission to *encomienda,* a Negro from slave to free status, or a mestizo to the creole nobility) generally entailed official sanction and registration.

The multiplicity of judicial systems underscored the static, functionally compartmented nature of society. The fact that they—like the several hierarchies of lay and clerical administrators—constantly disputed each other's spheres of influence only served to reaffirm the king's authority as ultimate reconciler. Nuclear elements—such as municipalities or even individual Indians—as well as highly placed officers could appeal directly to the king, or to his proxy, the viceroy, for redress of certain grievances. The king, even though he might be an inarticulate near-imbecile like Charles II, was symbolic throughout his realm as the guarantor of status. In Thomistic idiom, all parts of society were ordered to the whole as the imperfect to the perfect. This ordering, inherently the responsibility of the whole multitude, devolved upon the king as a public person acting in their behalf, for the task of ordering to a given end fell to the agent best placed and fitted for the specific function. . . .

The Spanish Empire, to be sure, could scarcely avert contagion from the post-medieval world in which it existed and for which it was in part responsible. The Jesuits, who had received extensive privileges overseas for the very purpose of bolstering the empire's moral and religious base, were outstandingly versed in modernism. An "enlightened" Bourbon regime expelled them in 1767 less for their reactionary perversity than for their shrewd, disciplined commercial activities and their faith-defying "probabilist" dialectics.

Spanish American bullion was a lodestar for foreign merchants. Introduced as contraband or else covertly within the Spanish system itself, the wares of Dutch, French, and English were temptingly cheap, well-made and abundant. They, like the fiscal demands of the mother country, were a constant incentive for creoles to organize local economies from which bullion and exportable surplus might readily be factored out. The calculating acquisitiveness of capitalism, if not its institutions for unlimited accrual, was frequently in evidence.

Moreover, Indian and Negro burden-bearers were, unlike the medieval serf, never fully identified with the historical and cultural ethos of their masters. For this reason they suffered more from the emergent exploitative psychology than, perhaps, postmedieval peasants who remained bound to the land. The African received no comprehensive protective code until 1789. And the very laws that assured the Indian status in return for fixed services could in practice be perverted, rendering him servile to an encomendero or a royal agent (corregidor). Indeed, the existence of Thomistic guarantees for the common man can be confirmed only by examining Spain's New World experience in selected eras and locales, or by comparing it en bloc with other European ventures in the Antilles and North America.

Yet however strongly such "recessive" Machiavellian protocapitalist or secularistic traits might erupt, the underpinning of the empire—social, economic, political, intellectual—bore a rubric of the earlier era. Eighteenth-century Bourbon reforms (the notable ones being those of Charles III, 1759–88) did little to alter this generalization. Some reforms—like the intendant system— . . . superimposed on the old structure, caused added confusion. . . . Others—like the Caracas Company, a more modern and enterprising trade monopoly—found harsh opposition because their services entailed strict enforcement of regulations which a more adaptive, personalistic regime of local control had traditionally winked at. The hierarchical, multiform, precapitalist Spanish America of 1800 was ill prepared for the ways of enlightened despotism, still less for those of Lockean constitutionalism.

The Republican Period

That the heterogeneous Spanish American realm was for three centuries relatively free from civil strife and separatist outbreaks must largely be explained by a steadfast loyalty to the politico-spiritual symbol of the Crown. Even the sporadic Indian revolts of the eighteenth century were directed not against the Catholic sovereign and imperium but against malfeasance of local agents. . . .

Not until 1809, during Spain's Napoleonic interregnum, did local juntas appear overseas. Yet even then their autonomy, in expectation of a legitimist restoration, was provisional. Only when the ad hoc "liberal" Cortes, established in unoccupied Spain, tried to reduce Spanish America from viceregal to colonial status did the independence campaign, championed by a few firebrands, gather momentum.

Ferdinand VII was restored in 1814. But in the face of the independence movement, his character and policy discredited both himself and the Church, whose support he retained. For Spanish America the Thomistic keystone had been withdrawn. Efforts to supplant it, on a continental basis or even within regional blocs, were vain. No creole caudillo and no prince of European or Inca lineage could command universal fealty or age-old spiritual sanction. A Thomistic sovereign could not be created ex nihilo, and Spanish America's centrifugal separatism was for the first time unleashed.

Another idiom than the Thomistic is therefore needed to be played off against the republican experience. Hitherto the most satisfying analyses have been those that attribute Spanish American instability to the imposition of French-, British- and American-type constitutions upon peoples whose illiteracy, poverty, provincialism, political inexperience, and social inequalities rendered ineffectual the mechanisms of constitutional democracy. This somewhat negative view, however, does not fully draw one into the fabric of Spanish American politics. If postulates of the Enlightenment were not relevant to that milieu, how, in a positive sense, [can] . . . we comprehend it?

The answer this essay proposes is that at the moment when the Thomistic component became "recessive," the Machiavellian component, latent since the sixteenth century, became "dominant." . . .

Machiavelli was born into an "Age of Despots." Italian city-states had lost their moral base; they no longer shared a common Christian ethos. The pope had become one of many competing temporal rulers, Machiavelli perceived that the mercenary "companies of adventure" of his time, unlike national militias, were undependable since they lacked any larger loyalty. They could be used to further intrigues of statecraft, but not to wage open and steady warfare. The Italian was effective only in dueling and individual combat.

Like Machiavelli, the Spanish American nation-builder of ca. 1825 had to contend with nucleated "city states," the rural masses being passive and inarticulate. The absence of any communities intermediate between such nuclei and the erstwhile imperium had been revealed by the autonomous urban juntas of 1809–10. Only the somewhat arbitrary boundaries of colonial administration defined the new nations territorially. Only virulent sectionalism could define them operatively. The Church, once coterminous with the State, had become the intruding handmaiden of a hostile sovereign power (Spain). For lack of a politico-spiritual commonalty, sources and directions of leadership were wholly fortuitous. The consequent emergence of opportunist caudillos—as of Italy's city tyrants—deranged the predictable interplay of hierarchical class interests.

The Spanish American who held to constitutionalism and avowed the existence in fact of a state-community was swept away before winds of personalism. Mexico's Gómez Farías, vice-president under Santa Anna, was a statesman who, despite his energy and dedication, would not infract "the principles of public and private morality" before which, wrote his contemporary, Mora, vanished "his indomitable force of character." Why did he not cast out the treacherous Santa Anna? "Because the step was unconstitutional: . . . a famous reason which has kept the reputation of Señor Farías in a very secondary place at best and caused the nation to retrogress half a century."

A similar case was Rivadavia, Argentina's first president and proponent of bourgeois democracy and economic liberalism. His plans and principles had been no match for provincial caudillismo. The exiled statesman wrote sadly from Paris in 1830 (shortly before the personalist tyranny of Rosas):

> In my opinion what retards regular and stable advance in those republics stems from the vacillations and doubts that deprive all institutions of that moral force which is indispensable to them and can be given only by conviction and decision. It is evident to me, and would be easy to demonstrate, that the upheavals of our country spring much more immediately from lack of public spirit and of cooperation among responsible men in sustaining order and laws than from attacks of ungovernable, ambitious persons without merit or fitness and of indolent coveters.

Machiavelli's writings are the handbook par excellence for the leader who could cope with "lack of public spirit and of cooperation among responsible men." . . .

On nearly every page of Machiavelli appears practical advice which almost seems distilled from the careers of scores of Spanish American caudillos. Of crucial importance is the leader's commanding physical presence. In time of sedition he should: ". . . present himself before the multitude with all possible grace and dignity, and attired with all the insignia of his rank, so as to inspire more respect. . . . [For] there is no better or safer way of appeasing an excited mob than the presence of some man of imposing appearance and highly respected. . . ." [*Discourses*, I, liv]

The personalist leader must be physically disciplined, skilled in warfare, and "learn the nature of the land, how steep the mountains are, how the valleys debouch, where the plains lie, and understand the nature of rivers and swamps" (*Prince*, XIV; see also *Discourses*, III, xxxix). This is almost a page from the autobiography of Páez, who knew Venezuela's vast *llanos* (inland plains) like the palm of his hand, a knowledge that confounded the royalists in 1817 and later earned respect for him as caudillo of the new republic. Writing of an assault against the Spaniards, Páez recalled:

> Necessity obliged us not only to fight men but to challenge the obstacles opposed by nature. Counting on these, we proposed to turn to our advantage the impediments that gave the enemy surety and trust in his position, for to no one would it occur that in that season cavalry troops could sortie from the lower Apure to cross so much inundated terrain and especially the many streams and five rivers, all at the period of overflow.

This telluric, earthbound quality so vital to Spanish American leaders was matched in Argentina's Quiroga and San Martín, Uruguay's Artigas, Mexico's Pancho Villa, Venezuela's Bolívar, Peru's Santa Cruz, and innumerable others. Their guerrilla warfare was a far cry from the chessboard strategy and diplomatic power alignments of Europe. . . .

[But] how is it . . . that Spanish American caudillos or governments have in certain countries and eras, achieved political stability in the face of [the New World's] brand of social and moral centrifugalism? I define three essential modes of stability, which are categorized here merely for schematic purposes and with the understanding that the "pure" type never occurs. By way of further analogy I suggest a correspondence between these types and the three "legitimations of domination" which Max Weber distinguishes in his essay, "Politics as a Vocation."

The first mode of stability is furnished by the Machiavellian leader who asserts himself by dynamic personalism and shrewd self-identification with local "original principles," though without ever relinquishing government, as Machiavelli would have wished, "to the charge of many." The system remains subordinate to the man and unless a suitable "heir" is available, which happens infrequently, it falls with him. Here we perhaps have Weber's charismatic leader with the personal gift of grace, who flouts patriarchal traditionalism and the stable economy, whose justice is Solomonic rather than statutory, who maintains authority "solely by proving his strength in life." One recent writer, Blanksten, holds that the caudillo and charismatic types correspond. George S. Wise, on the other hand, claims that the "stratagem and chicanery" of at least one caudillo (Venezuela's Guzmán Blanco) revealed an insecurity and lack of purpose precluding the oracular prophetic qualities that he attributes to charismatic legitimacy. Weber's specific consideration of the condottiere type leads me to feel, however, that charisma need not invariably imply "anointment."

The charismatic leader may be dedicated to molding the self-perpetuating traditions of a state-community—for example, Bolívar's vision of federated Andean republics, Morazán's Central American union, the constitutionalism of Mexico's Juárez, and perhaps the quasi-theocracy of Ecuador's García Moreno. Or, which is more usual, he may set about exploiting the country as his private fief. In the decades after independence such a caudillo would win the army's allegiance (or create his own plebeian militia), then assert control over the several classes by blandishment, personal magnetism, or threat of force—the method depending, in the case of each segment of society, on "original principles" and the leader's own antecedents. Examples are Argentina's Rosas, Mexico's Santa Anna, Guatemala's Carrera, Paraguay's Francia.

Toward the end of the century the exploitation of new sources of mineral and agricultural wealth, together with a strong influx of foreign investments, gave caudillos more dependable leverage for control. Though force and personalism did not go in the discard, financial resources and the protective favor of foreigners allowed the leader to govern by "remote control." He adopted bourgeois bon ton and even paid lip service to constitutionalism. Such men were Venezuela's Guzmán Blanco, Mexico's Porfirio Díaz, Guatemala's Barrios.

Intensified economic activity might also give rise to a second type of state: a modified version of laissez-faire democracy. This development, which Weber calls legitimation through bureaucratic competence and public respect for rational legal statutes, has been rare in Latin America, even in hybrid form. Argentina affords an example. In that country after 1860, and especially after 1880, the pampas experienced a torrential land rush, occasioned by a world demand for meat and grains and by improved methods of husbandry, transportation, and refrigeration. Though the lion's share of the benefits accrued to an oligarchy of large proprietors, many immigrants took small homesteads in the northern provinces; moreover, the expanding economy created niches for articulate, middle-class city dwellers. Argentines were, relative to Latin America, homogeneous and white. A growing nucleus identified its interests with the stability and prosperity of the nation-community, even though the positions of highest socio-economic authority were already preempted.

Given Argentina's economic direction and momentum, it remained for a series of statesmen-presidents merely to encourage and guide its development, in tolerable conformance with the Lockean Constitution of 1853. Eventual malfeasance in high office led, not back to tyranny, but to the emergence in 1890 of the Radical (liberal, middle-class) Party, to free suffrage and the secret ballot, and finally to Radical control of the presidency. Twentieth-century Radical leaders, however, reined back certain socio-economic forces from a natural course by acquiescing in the continued entrenchment of the landowning oligarchy. Only then did thwarted urban classes fall prey to demagoguery of an ominous breed—and to Juan Domingo Perón.

A third solution for anarchy has been a full-scale implementing of the Machiavellian blueprint. A personalist leader emerges (as in the first case), but goes on successfully to create a system, larger than himself, that is faithful to "original principles." In Spanish America such a system is larger than the leader, to frame a paradox, only when it *recognizes* the leader to be larger than itself. This statement has Thomistic implications, and the more successful Spanish American constitutions have translated into modern idiom certain principles under which the viceroyalties enjoyed three centuries of relative stability.

This solution, insofar as it reinvigorates the body social by setting its classes, or "estates," into centrally stabilized equilibrium, is a neo-traditionalism reminiscent of Weber's third category: "the authority of the eternal yesterday." Of Mexico's present Constitution—brought into being in 1917 by Carranza, a shrewd, opportunist caudillo—Frank Tannenbaum has written:

By implication, the Constitution recognizes that contemporary Mexican society is divided into classes, and that it is the function of the State to protect one class against another. The Constitution is therefore not merely a body of rules equally applicable to all citizens, but also a body of rules specially designed to benefit and protect given groups. The community is not made up of citizens only; it is also made up of classes with special rights within the law. What has in fact happened is that the old idea of the "estates" has been recreated in Mexican law. The pattern of the older Spanish State, divided into clergy, nobility, and commons, has been re-created in modern dress, with peasants, workers, and capitalists replacing the ancient model. This is not done formally, but it is done sufficiently well to make it evident that a very different kind of social structure is envisioned in the law, even if only by implicit commitment, than that in a liberal democracy.
. . .

The Revolution has certainly increased effective democracy in Mexico. It has also increased, both legally and economically, the dependence of the people and of the communities upon the federal government and the president. The older tradition that the king rules has survived in modern dress: the president rules. He rules rather than governs, and must do so if he is to survive in office and keep the country at peace.

I have reserved any mention of Chile until now because its history usefully illustrates our three political types as well as a twentieth-century variant which has yet to be considered. Like its sister nations, Chile fell after independence into anarchic factionalism. A revolution of 1829–30, however, brought the conservatives into power; at their head was Diego Portales, who, as a business man, was atypical among Spanish American nation-builders. Portales appreciated more keenly than most the need for disciplined, predictable conditions of life and was more empirical in perceiving that liberal slogans and mechanisms were meaningless within an aristocratic, agrarian society. His views were reflected in the centralized, quasi-monarchic Constitution of 1833, which, by recognizing Chile's hierarchic social anatomy and at the same time guaranteeing status and justice for the component members, lent the government a suprapersonalist sanction. Portales himself did not become president, but wisely designated a military hero, General Prieto, whose prestige, aristocratic bearing and benevolence, traditionalism, and religiosity further enhanced the office with an aura of legitimacy. None of Chile's presidents was overthrown for sixty years, while the Constitution lasted nearly a century.

Portales, alone among his Spanish American contemporaries, brought to fulfillment the policy of "the compleat Machiavellian." As the century advanced, however, a leavening took place within the system he had fathered. A law of 1852 abolished primogeniture, infusing new blood and interests into the landed oligarchy. Mineral exploitation in the north and the activities of German immigrants in the south posted new directions for economic change and opportunity. The consequent desire for more effective economic competition provided a rallying cry for enthused liberals emerging from the new (1842) University. So too did growing dissatisfaction with the constitutional ban on public exercise of non-Catholic religions.

At length the Chilean élite, larger and more diversely composed than in 1833, revolted against centralized, one-man rule by ejecting President Balmaceda from office in 1891. This élite then governed through its congressional representatives, and the fitfulness of public policy for the next thirty years reflected the jostling of private economic interests.

As in Argentina, however, the modified laissez-faire state could not indefinitely subsist if it was to victimize the increasingly self-aware lower classes, such as, in Chile's case, the copper and nitrate workers. The little man eventually found his champion in President Arturo Alessandri (1920–25, 1932–38).

The dictatorial interregnum of Carlos Ibáñez (1925–31) can be considered [as of 1954] as Chile's nearest approach to the first, or pure caudillo type of rule. His advent is partially explained by the post-World War I collapse of the world nitrate market, which impaired the mainspring of parliamentary, laissez-faire government and left Chile (since Alessandri had not yet given shape and momentum to his social democracy) in its primordial anarchy.

Ibáñez, though sometimes referred to as a "man on horseback," effectively used modern technocratic methods and was not a caudillo of the old stamp—to which his reelection in 1952 bears witness.

Alessandri's and subsequent administrations represent an attitude toward government that has in this century become universal throughout Spanish America. It has in varying degrees infiltrated the three earlier systems, or combinations thereof, wherever they exist. Essentially, it is a recognition of need to build into public policies a dynamics for socio-economic change. This need stems from two interrelated phenomena: first, the urbanization and industrialization of hitherto extractive economies; second, the growing self-awareness and articulateness of the citizenry at large.

[From the perspective of mid-twentieth century] the Spanish American leader, whether dictator or democrat, is fast adopting a broader, more sophisticated view of how modern political power must be won, maintained, and exercised. Hc also knows that, regardless of any nationalistic rhetoric to which he may be committed, he must import more and more blueprints and technical solutions from abroad. Such solutions, however—whether socialism, fascism, exchange control, or river valley authorities—take on a new complexion as they flash into amalgam with conditions of life wholly different from those by which they were engendered. Not only is the receiving ethos broadly speaking sui generis, but in a strictly technological sense the particular juxtapositions of ancient and modern in Spanish America are quite beyond the experience of any of the capitalist countries. Therefore slogans of foreign systems ring far differently upon Spanish American ears than their originators imagine.

In fact, Peru's Aprista movement and Mexico's . . . "Revolution" attest that Spanish America is starting to generate its own credos. Sometimes, as with Perón's *justicialismo*, they are heartlessly cynical rhetoric. At best they designate, as did our own New Deal, a piecemeal pragmatism, uncommitted to the mysticism or fixed morality prescribed for the New World by Hegel. Yet the fact that Spanish America is by tradition accustomed and by economic necessity forced to rely heavily on official planning, intervention, and protection has on occasion led its statesmen to a "total view" (to be distinguished carefully in nature and intent from a totalitarian view). From such views flow social, economic, and cultural agendas which, however imperfect of execution, uniquely contribute to an understanding of man-in-community.

Coexistent, indeed, with Spanish America's atomism . . . is a sense of commonalty, however latent, deriving in large part from its Catholicity (in the ingrained, cultural sense) and from its agrarian, Negro and Indian heritage. Native to this commonalty is an ethic upon which the hyper-rationalist logos of the industrial world seems able to make only limited and conditional encroachments. The prediction is sometimes heard among Spanish Americans that this logos will in the long run exhaust itself; that their descendants will be freer to weave certain principles of a pre-Machiavellian age into the new patterns of an entering one; that the promise which erratically flashes in the travail of twentieth-century Mexican democracy is yet to be realized.

5

Peter H. Smith

The Search for Legitimacy

In this essay Peter Smith asks his readers to consider dictatorships in Spanish America not as aberrations but as phenomena
that may be explicable within the region's political culture
over a long historical continuum. He eschews the often ethno-
centric North American penchant for treating Latin authoritarian regimes as failures to achieve democracy and, at the
same time, he avoids any rigid cultural determinism. His
inquiry, for example, includes an exposition of Glen Dealy's
study of the authoritarian features of early independent Spanish American constitutions. Smith, a historian who has written extensively about Argentine, Ecuadorian, and Mexican
power politics, goes on to examine the nature of legitimacy
and the multiple ways caudillos were often able to achieve it.
As have many other students of Spain's former possessions in
America, Smith finds Max Weber's "traditional," "legal," and
"charismatic" classifications of legitimacy valuable. Smith,
however, adds two other criteria, "dominance" and "achievement-expertise," which he believes are necessary in the
unique context of Spanish America.

It should be noted that Smith published this piece in
1974, at a time when military bureaucratic-authoritarian regimes were increasing in number and influence. Readers
should weigh the more recent resurgence of democratic governments in the 1980s, a process which has raised questions
about a socio-cultural addiction to authoritarian regimes. As
is true of the approach of this book in general, however, Smith
brings a historical perspective to his assessment as he looks
at the problem of understanding political legitimacy in the
past.

From Peter H. Smith, "Political Legitimacy in Spanish America," in *New Approaches to Latin American History*, edited by Richard Graham and Peter H.
Smith. Austin: University of Texas Press (1974), 225–55. By permission of the
author and the publisher.

ONE of the most critical dimensions in any political culture involves the notion of *political legitimacy*, that is, the set of beliefs that lead people to regard the distribution of political power as just and appropriate for their own society. Legitimacy provides the rationale for voluntary submission to political authority. Obviously, concepts of legitimacy can vary greatly from culture to culture: a political order that is morally acceptable for members of one society might be totally abhorrent for members of another.

My basic proposition is that authoritarian polities have dominated Spanish American history because they have been to some degree "legitimate." No doubt some people have accepted dictatorship as a matter of self-serving convenience; other people, possibly large sectors of the population, have been too frightened to resist; others have been indifferent. Still others have resisted authoritarian rule because of democratic convictions, though this does not mean that all opponents of dictatorship have acted for the same reason. But I maintain that, over time, politically relevant segments of Latin American society have considered authoritarian structures as legitimate and therefore worthy of acceptance or support.

The immediate task is to identify strains in the political culture that have given rise to this situation. For this purpose, and as a heuristic device, I shall examine the content of claims to legitimacy that have been made by political leaders in Spanish America. This practice involves some intrinsic distortion, since claims made by leaders may well differ from the beliefs and attitudes of the community at large; and, as emphasized below, not all rulers are legitimate.

To begin, all modern analysis of political legitimacy must come to terms with Max Weber. In his famous treatment of "imperative coordination," Weber posited three modal categories or "ideal types" of political legitimacy: traditional, legal, and charismatic.

Traditional authority, in Weber's usage, rests on "an established belief in the sanctity of immemorial traditions and the legitimacy of the status of those exercising authority under them." A political order is here viewed as proper simply because of its immutability over time: since the rules for allocating authority "have always been this way," they should therefore continue to exist. Under these conditions obedience is typically owed to the person of the traditionally anointed leader, who has considerable discretion in authority but who must also stay within the bounds of tradition itself. Thus precedent, as both custom and law, assumes paramount importance.

Traditional claims to authority have occupied a prominent place in Spanish American history, particularly during the colonial period. Obedience had *always* been due to the Crown, which demanded—and for centuries received—recognition on precisely these grounds. Noting the extensive networks of personal loyalty, some writers have emphasized the "patrimonial" qualities of traditional authority under the empire. . . .

Almost by definition, separation from Spain nullified the possibility of relying explicitly on traditional authority. With new polities to govern, leaders in the postindependence period would have to present new, or at least different, claims to authority.

Some of these demands fit Weber's category of *legal* authority, which rests upon "a belief in the 'legality' of patterns of normative rules and the right of those elevated to authority under such rules to issue commands." In contrast to the traditional case, obedience is here owed to the legally established order itself, instead of to the persons who occupy the special offices. Typically, legal legitimacy derives from the generalized acceptance of rational rules for distributing power. The rules are consistent, unambiguous, and universally applied.

The most obvious evidence of legal claims to legitimacy in Spanish American history lies, of course, in the many constitutions that have proliferated since independence. Such documents represent a clear effort to codify and promulgate rules for the allocation and acceptance of authority. Standard interpretations have long asserted that constitutional rule, inspired by French and North American models, evinced persistent attempts to implant democracy in Spanish America. By this same logic, illegal seizures of power thrust the continent into a "legitimacy vacuum," and defiance of the constitutions signaled the weakness of democracy.

While this view may be partially true, at least in some specific instances, there is no inherent reason for legal legitimacy to be necessarily democratic. (Weber's own example of the archetypal legal system was a corporate bureaucracy, in many ways an anti-democratic structure.) As Glen Dealy has argued, Spanish American constitutions have contained a large number of authoritarian features. Rejecting the notion that constitutional ideals were imported from the United States and France, Dealy asserts: "Eighteenth-century political liberalism was almost uniformly and overwhelmingly rejected by Spanish America's first statesmen. Though there is wide variety in the form and content of the early charters, not one could be construed as embodying constitutional liberalism, however loosely that term may be defined."

According to Dealy's analysis, most constitutions placed power in the state and not in the people. In explicitly elitist fashion, they defined the major requirement for holding political office as moral superiority rather than popular support. And they put virtually no restrictions on governmental authority. Civil rights existed at the tolerance of the state and could readily be set aside, usually by the chief executive. At all times the collective interest reigned supreme. "Politics is the achievement of the public good, which is in constant opposition to private interest."

Without presenting traditional grounds for authority in Weber's sense of the term, Spanish American constitutions have thus drawn upon time-honored canons of medieval and Hispanic political philosophy. There persist, in constitutional form, the Thomist notions of divine, natural, and human law. The purpose of political organization is to rise above the innate fallibility of its mortal constituency and, through moral purification and leadership, attain a social order that complies with natural (and ultimately divine) prescription. Since human judgment is erroneous, so are election results. The true political leader must respond not to his constituency but to the imperatives of higher morality. Insofar as he follows that precept, he commands, and deserves, absolute power.

Thus legal claims to legitimacy have often been made, but not necessarily in democratic fashion. In fact one might well construe these constitutions as efforts to legalize dictatorship rather than to implant democracy. Moreover, the acceptability of the resulting political order has depended entirely upon the moral quality of its leaders. An inferior leader betrays an inferior constitution, which, being the product of fallible men, should therefore be overthrown. In this sense Spanish American constitutions have contained implicit provision for their own abandonment. Coups thus become part of the cultural pattern, rather than a deviation from it.

A third kind of legitimacy consists of *charisma*, which Weber defines as "devotion to the specific and exceptional sanctity, heroism or exemplary character of an individual person, and of the normative patterns or order revealed or ordained by him." Literally, charisma means "the gift of grace." The exceptional powers of the charismatic leaders are not available to the ordinary persons, and they are held to be either exemplary or of divine origin. The charismatic leader typically represents a movement, a cause, or some higher truth. His followers, out of their commitment to the ultimate mission, obey the leader from a sense of moral duty.

Charismatic leaders have played prominent parts in Spanish American history, and political missionaries have pursued a wide range of varied goals: collective redemption, national salvation, social justice, and so on. Fidel Castro and Juan Perón offer classic instances of charismatic types, and there have been many others too. As Dealy has shown, constitutions were often designed to bring men with a kind of "gift of grace" to power—and to this extent, Spanish American constitutions can be understood as efforts to "routinize" charisma. For reasons spelled out below, however, I think the concept of charisma has often been misused.

Most writers who have dealt with the problem of political legitimacy have stayed within the Weberian framework. According to the standard logic, if a leader cannot make effective claims to a traditional, legal, or charismatic authority or a proper combination of the three, his rule is ipso facto illegitimate. The absence of legitimacy means there is a legitimacy vacuum. A legitimacy vacuum begets instability. Ergo, the absence of traditional or legal or charismatic authority means there must be instability.

What this reasoning fails to consider is the possibility that, at least in Spanish America, there might be additional types of legitimacy. This oversight is particularly unfortunate in view of the thoroughly relativistic quality of the concept of legitimacy. Weber himself recognized the limits of his ideal construct and introduced his own typology with a clear disclaimer: "the idea that the whole of concrete historical reality can be exhausted in the conceptual scheme about to be developed," he wrote, "is as far from the author's thoughts as anything could be." It is my intention to propose two additional categories of political legitimacy that, in my judgment, have appeared in Spanish American history. Whether or not they have existed elsewhere is a question that far transcends the narrow limits of my own expertise. But even if my analysis of Spanish American political culture is wrong, the methodological lesson remains: we should try to explore political legitimacy in terms that derive from the immediate culture.

The first of my categories, which could be called *dominance*, rests on a somewhat tautological assertion that those in power ought to rule because they are in power. By gaining power, people demonstrate their suitability for it. In a sense, this precept simply inverts a traditional canon of Hispanic philosophy, which holds that the law of the prince loses force "if the majority has already ceased to obey it." The principle of dominance maintains that the law of the prince acquires force if the majority (or at least a major segment of the population) starts to obey it. Power, in short, should go to the strong.

According to this code, the central means of asserting dominance is through physical coercion. A sexual component of this theme, *machismo*, concerns domination of women. The more political component involves demonstration of the capacity for wielding violence. In this way violence has occupied a central place in Spanish American political culture. Its appearance does not necessarily indicate a disregard for social norms; on the contrary, it can bespeak compliance with accepted norms. Strikes, riots, coups, and assassinations do not always mean the system is breaking down; they can be part of the system itself. (Here I would offer a distinction between *governmental* stability and *systemic* stability; individual governments may tumble while the system as a whole remains intact.)

An implicit claim in the concept is that dominance, once recognized and obeyed, will bring about political order. In the well-known *Cesarismo democrático*, for instance, Laureano Vallenilla Lanz conceived of the caudillo as "the necessary policeman" to establish social control. "The authority of [José Antonio] Páez" after the wars of independence, he wrote, "like that of all the caudillos of Spanish America, was based on the *unconscious suggestion* of our majority. Our people, who can be regarded as an *unstable* social group . . . instinctively followed the strongest, the bravest and the smartest, whose personality had become a legend in the popular imagination and from whom the people expected absolute protection."

In this connection Vallenilla Lanz traced out the routinization, not of charisma, but of dominance: "leaders do not get elected," said the Venezuelan, "they impose themselves. Election and inheritance to office . . . constitute a subsequent process." Thus Vallenilla Lanz regarded dominance as a transitory (but conceptually distinct) type of legitimacy that creates the conditions for legal or traditional rule. Of course one's interpretation of the length and kind of transition would depend upon one's position. But, most importantly, Vallenilla Lanz did not condemn violence. He linked it to social order, to dominance, and by implication to charisma.

One practical consequence of legitimation through dominance is uncertainty. It is possible to proclaim dominance only so long as one is dominant (or becoming dominant). By definition, the loss of power entails a loss of legitimacy. Since people obey authority only because it is supreme, the fallen leader quickly finds his following in disarray. Partly for this reason there are very few instances of once-dominant leaders who have made successful political comebacks.

Dominance is a relatively primitive claim to political legitimacy, and the national level it has generally (but not exclusively) been associated with the rule of nineteenth-century caudillos. . . .

It is extremely important to distinguish dominance from charisma. In the first place, the dominant leader does not represent a revealed truth or moral purpose; he represents strength and, in a way, order, but not a spiritual cause. Second, the followers of a dominant person do not obey out of a sense of duty; they do so on the basis of a rational calculation, a kind of bet—that leader X will stay in power for some time—and when his time is up they commonly desert. Third, the leader pays constant attention to the size and strength of his following; without substantial recognition of his dominant qualities, he would have no credible claim to authority at all. The truly charismatic leader, by contrast, is wholly concerned with his mission; as Weber writes, in what I take to be an overstatement, "no prophet has ever regarded his quality as dependent on the attitudes of the mass toward him."

The distinction between dominance and charisma offers at least one means of classifying and analyzing the phenomenon of *personalism*. There has been a widespread tendency in literature on Spanish American politics to identify personalistic leadership with charismatic leadership. I consider this semantic equation to be theoretically untenable and empirically incorrect. It has created confusion, and, lamentably, it has also devalued the concept of charisma in the analytical marketplace. Some personalistic leaders have undoubtedly been charismatic; but others have not, and their claims to authority have really rested upon dominance. The difference is essential.

Just as legitimation through dominance prevailed in early nineteenth-century Spanish America, more recent developments have given rise to yet another assertion of political legitimacy, which I shall refer to as *achievement-expertise*. This notion rests on the claim that authority should reside in the hands of people who have the knowledge, expertise, or general ability to bring about specific achievements—usually, but not always, economic achievements. In this case authority derives essentially from the desirability of the achievement itself; the commitment is to the goal, not the means.

Political obedience is thus demanded, and presumably accorded, for nonpolitical reasons. The political structure per se loses importance. Leaders are free to adopt any method, no matter how repressive, as long as they can demonstrate progress toward the sought-after goal.

This claim first gained currency in the late nineteenth century, as the positivistic slogan of "order and progress" offered a respectable rationale for dictatorial rule. The outstanding example was the Mexican regime of Porfirio Díaz, whose *científico* advisers expressed open scorn for democratic pretensions. "Rights!" exclaimed Francisco G. Cosmes:

> People are fed up with them; what they want is bread. To constitutions teeming with sublime ideas which no one has ever seen functioning in practice . . . they prefer an opportunity to work in peace, security in their personal pursuits, and the assurance that the authorities, instead of launching forth on wild goose chases after ideals, will hang the cheats, the thieves, and the revolutionaries. . . . Fewer rights and fewer liberties in exchange for more order and more peace. . . . Enough of utopias. . . . I want order and peace, albeit for the price of all the rights which have cost me so dear. . . . I daresay the day is at hand when the nation will declare: We want order and peace even at the cost of our independence.

By this argument, political authoritarianism—Díaz's "honest tyranny," as it was called—would provide the key to socioeconomic development. Material achievement, in turn, could justify a political system. As another científico said, "The day we find that our charter has produced a million settlers, we may say that we have found the right constitution, a constitution no longer amounting to merely a phrase on our lips, but to ploughs in our hands, locomotives on our rails, and money everywhere." When Porfiristas spoke of "freedom," as they often did, they meant economic freedom—not political freedom. And, not surprisingly, when Francisco Madero started attacking Díaz, he did so on the exclusively political questions of reelection and the presidential succession. . . .

More recent military governments have made extensive use of the achievement-expertise claim. During the 1950s Marcos Pérez Jiménez proudly proclaimed *la reforma del medio físico* in Venezuela. . . . The "Argentine Revolution" of 1966 took place in the name of order and economic development. Examples abound, echoing the well-known refrain from Mussolini's Italy: The trains now run on time.

In summary, I perceive five distinct, nondemocratic types of political legitimacy in Spanish American history: tradition (mainly in the colonial period), legality, charisma, dominance, and achievement-expertise. Naturally, this does not exhaust the entire range of possibilities. It would be going too far to assert that there is *no* democratic tradition in Spanish American legalism; my point is that legality qua legality can be *either* democratic or authoritarian. Cuba's current efforts to create a "new socialist" man may offer yet another alternative. In any case, the prevalence of non-democratic, authoritarian ideals in Spanish America strongly suggests that dictatorship is not an aberration. It would seem to be a logical expression of the political culture.

Part Two
Caudillismo in the Nineteenth Century

6
Hugh M. Hamill
Hidalgo and Calleja: The Colonial Bases of Caudillismo

The chaotic years from 1810 to 1825 were, as we have seen, years in which factions struggled as much for dominance of one over another as for separation from Spain. Students find in this violent period of transition a seedbed for caudillismo, and there is much interest in the ways in which local leadership responded to the failure at the monarchic core. Caudillos sprang up in ways which would set the pattern for much of the rest of the century. It is commonly held that the wars themselves marked the point of departure for this new phenomenon: the caudillo. The essay which follows, however, argues that the very earliest leaders drew upon their natural social and kinship linkages, long common in the peacetime societies of colonial Spanish America, to create the nuclei of supporters they would rely upon in the bloody struggles ahead. The ingredients a successful caudillo would need were thoroughly extant at the beginning of the nineteenth century.

On September 16, 1810, a priest from northwest central Mexico named Miguel Hidalgo y Costilla plunged the Viceroyalty of New Spain into a struggle that marked the beginning of the wars for independence. He and his fellow conspirators exploited a complex pattern of regional unrest centered in population growth, wage reductions, commodity price rises, and antagonism toward inept and confusing government tax policies, all of which was exacerbated by Napoleon's invasion of Spain in 1808 and by drought in 1809. The result was an insurrection that drew mass support first in the Bajío region around the mining center of Guanajuato and then from what are now the states of Michoacán and Jalisco. Hidalgo's force may have numbered as high as 80,000 crudely armed and

From Hugh M. Hamill. For a somewhat different version of this essay, see "Caudillismo and Independence: A Symbiosis?" in *The Independence of Mexico and the Creation of the New Nation,* edited by Jaime E. Rodriguez O. (Los Angeles: UCLA Latin American Center, 1989), 163–74. Used with permission.

untrained followers. The charismatic fifty-seven-year-old curate made Mexico City his prime target. He withdrew, however, with the ancient capital at his mercy in early November.
Just why he made this momentous decision is due in part to
Hidalgo's awareness that a small but disciplined royalist army
had formed in San Luis Potosí and was marching south to
intercept him. This army, which later in January would inflict
a crushing defeat on Hidalgo's insurgents, was led by a Mexicanized Spanish brigadier named Félix Calleja. This essay, by
the author of *The Hidalgo Revolt,* concerns the way both men
emerged from their societies as proto-caudillos and set the
stage for a subsequent host of leaders from the military, the
clergy, and many other backgrounds.

ONE way to test the degree to which caudillaje may have been
engrained in colonial society is to examine the nature of the very
earliest responses to leadership in the crisis brought on by the
Mexican insurgency of September 1810. Who became the immediate caudillos? What pasts did they reflect? What values did they
exhibit? And whom were they able to attract? Coming as they did
at the very outset of the disruption of independence, the individual
exponents of caudillaje were not the results of Independence or of
the Early Republic. At the same time, however, their prominence
and fame made them the prototypes of many future caudillos.

The two paramount caudillos, who were products of their
societies and who made their marks indelibly on Mexico's future,
were Félix María Calleja del Rey, a Spanish brigadier, and Miguel
Hidalgo y Costilla, the curate of Dolores. These famous adversaries deserve to be compared to other pairs in Mexican history like
Cortés and Montezuma, Juárez and Maximilian, and Díaz and
Madero. At first glance Calleja and Hidalgo were completely different men. Calleja was a Spaniard, Hidalgo a creole; Calleja was
supremely self-disciplined, Hidalgo impetuous and erratic; Calleja
was a methodical military strategist, Hidalgo a mercurial and
tempermental leader without military training. To look behind
these obvious differences, however, is to find that both men fit
into a colonial ambience of well-established social networks in
preindependence New Spain.

Calleja and Hidalgo complemented each other and shared the

attributes of caudillo leadership that would become so visible later in the century. Let us accept that the power and authority which undergird caudillismo are composed of an intricate combination of personal forcefulness of character, perhaps although not necessarily charismatic; something of that peculiarly Hispanic masculinity we call machismo; a shrewd capacity to aggregate followers through kinship, godparenthood *(compadrazgo)*, professional and social ties; appeals to tradition, if possible, to solidify legitimacy; prior status through class, wealth, property, or profession; and technical and administrative expertise.

Both Hidalgo and Calleja had already intuitively built into their respective clerical and military careers solid bases upon which to operate as caudillos when they were suddenly catapulted to positions of power. Their caudillaje qualities were, of course, uneven. Hidalgo's charisma was greater than that of Calleja. For his part Calleja could far more readily claim legitimacy as a defender of the status quo than could the renegade priest, even in a system shorn of its traditional monarch.

Nevertheless, the society and its mores provided those conditions that could nurture a caudillo when circumstances favored their appearance. Just because the evidence of caudillaje is much less abundant before 1810 than afterwards, there is no reason to assume that it did not exist. To demonstrate this fully requires examination of the subtle patterns of leadership in business affairs; hacienda and mining management; government; extended families; corporate, especially Church, hierarchies; provincial village structures; and social banditry, as all these developed over much of the colonial past. Such an agenda is beyond this essay. So too is a thorough exploration of the effects that the more immediate years prior to the Grito de Dolores had on caudillaje culture. The mystique of Napoleon, for example, filtered into New Spain and stirred subliminal admiration for the French emperor on the one hand, and, then, after 1808 drew outraged but highly revealing patriotic attacks on the other. When Agustín Pomposo Fernández de San Salvador, the rector of the University of Mexico, struck out at Napoleon in a pamphlet, he warned the Scourge of Europe that "Now the Caudillo of Israel [Jesus], is the Caudillo of the Spanish people" (which is a significant contemporary use of *caudillo*). The spectacle of Spanish military heroes suddenly appearing to defend the Iberian homeland against the French invaders in 1808 and afterwards is another source of inspiration for a coming generation of Mexican warriors who would soon have their own chances for glory on either side of the military equation: insurgent and royalist.

On balance, Calleja was more important as a model for future caudillos than Hidalgo. Hidalgo may have opened the path to insurgency for other priests, such as Morelos and Matamoros, but he was clearly unique as a charismatic curate generalissimo. Hidalgo was also ephemeral because he was quickly destroyed in early 1811. Only the process of urgent republican nation-building resurrected him in mythic proportions. Calleja, by contrast, was far closer to the stereotype of the military caudillo, and dozens of leaders great and small were cast in his mold. Calleja was also victorious, a peculiarly desirable attribute for any practitioner of caudillismo.

Ephemeral as he may have been, Miguel Hidalgo is among the most studied of Mexican heroes. For all the biographical detail, however, there is much more that we would like to know about the itinerant priest. He surely had a vast network of friends and relatives throughout the Bajío (the Guanajuato region), Michoacán, Querétaro, and into San Luis Potosí and Nueva Galicia, and he naturally exploited these linkages as the conspiracy of Querétaro matured. For example, ten years earlier, in 1800, Hidalgo was invited to celebrate the mass of dedication of the new temple of Nuestra Señora de Guadalupe in San Luis Potosí, where he also chanced to attend a bullfight with Félix Calleja. Was it at that time or another that he made the ties with local clergy who would promote his cause in that city a decade later?

Hidalgo exploited his priesthood in multiple ways and yet did not let it interfere with his machismo. He was Padre de la Patria not only in symbolic ways. Even the mystery of the transvestite girl, "La Fernandita," in his entourage during the insurrection may have added sexual spice to his appeal among his supporters.

His insurgency had many of the trappings of a religious crusade, which helped Hidalgo to justify his leadership and served as a necessary legitimizing force for the *curadillo*. Hidalgo perhaps emphasized his appeals to the True Faith and sought the protection of the Virgin of Guadalupe precisely because he knew he would be attacked for usurping authority. Indeed, a royalist pamphleteer reproached him thus: "This caudillo of the insurgents has no authority to war against us; . . . such authority is an inseparable right, an inherent right of Sovereignty, and that resides in . . . King Ferdinand." (Note that Hidalgo was dubbed a caudillo, which is evidence—along with the rector's use of the term in 1808—that *caudillo* was in common parlance by the earliest stages of the crisis of empire.) Of course, Hidalgo was well aware of the traditional power of the Spanish monarch, who was excused for being a gachupin or Peninsular Spaniard by his admiring Mexican subjects. The curate skillfully employed the exhortation "¡Viva el Rey!," or "Long Live the King!," as yet another source of his charismatic legitimacy. Hidalgo also called upon his knowledge of the dynamics of his region's villages and rural estates and his awareness of economic tensions to evoke the exiled king and the Virgin and to tap a strain of intense xenophobia that focused upon the gachupins but also included those exotic monsters the French *and* the English. Hidalgo's brand of caudillismo had its limits, however. As Brian Hamnett has suggested, Hidalgo only briefly bound together the region's disparate social groups: "Since the ultimate objective was the furtherance of the political ambitions of the frustrated 'provincial bourgeoisie' this revolutionary coalition of rural workers, villagers, dispossessed tenants, unemployed urban or mine workers, *rancho*-owners, muleteers, estate administrators, local caciques, men on the make, bandits and criminals suffered internal contradictions from the start." They would eventually break apart, but only after Hidalgo's meteoric trajectory across central Mexico.

Félix Calleja came to New Spain in 1789 in the entourage of Viceroy Revillagigedo. That that wisest of Bourbon administrators should have favored the young officer from Medina del Campo in Old Castile is itself significant. Through a series of military assignments, chiefly in the north of the viceroyalty, Calleja became an expert in the geography of the realm. He was also an avid reader of history and could see himself in perspective. In 1797 Lieutenant Colonel Calleja was posted to the city of San Luis

Potosí, where he became the commander of the Tenth Brigade headquartered there. Almost at once he began the process of rooting himself in the Potosino earth and society. Within two years he had acquired land, an orchard, and a house and had the base for a future patrimony.

It was Calleja's capacity to draw about himself a powerful coterie of local members of the elite that showed his emergent caudillaje. In one lawsuit against the local intendente, which Calleja brought in 1800, he managed to gather twenty-two supporters, including a count, a knight of the Order of Charles III, the royal herald, five city councilors, two magistrates, the local tobacco monopoly administrator, seventeen hacendados, and ten merchants. Calleja spun Potosino society more tightly into his web when he married María Francisca, the niece of Don Manuel de la Gándara, the city's standard bearer and proprietor of the great hacienda complex of Bledos. The wedding in 1807 of the forty-eight-year-old Castilian and his twenty-year-old bride was a spectacular social event. In spite of his late marriage, Calleja's machismo had never been in doubt. It was said that he had a son by a Spanish ballerina. Later, when he was viceroy (1813–16), his wife bore him two children, and three more after his term expired.

His marriage to a member of the elite de la Gándara family was the capstone of Calleja's Mexicanization. It brought him closer contact with the creole aristocracy, including the Marquis of Jaral de Berrios, who later offered his sumptuous town house in Mexico City to Calleja in 1812. More to the point, Calleja soon became a frequent visitor to the Bledos hacienda and seems to have played a significant role in the management of the estate. It was at Bledos, tradition has it, that Calleja heard the bad news about the Hidalgo revolt. Well before 1810, however, Calleja had enlarged his network in other ways. Austere as he may have been, the gachupín brigadier had a common touch, and was known among the campesinos as well as among his soldiers of the rank and file as "el amo Don Félix." Whether this note of respectful affection was enhanced by his apparent taste for pulque it is impossible to say.

The military was the obvious other network that Calleja's native instincts led him to cultivate. Not only did the chain of command and his own prominence in it establish formal ties of value, but he also assiduously cultivated particular soldiers of talent who were destined to aid him in the future. It is apparent that a surprising number of early republican caudillos served their military apprenticeships not as insurgents but as royalists after the fashion of Santa Anna. To a certain degree this may have been due to Calleja's capacity to recruit able creoles and to give them opportunities that they effectively transformed into postindependence patriot careers. Thus Calleja, the proto-caudillo, nurtured as he was in the late viceregal time frame, helped create a legacy of caudillismo for the Mexican Republic. Among those to whom Calleja was able to turn when the crisis came in September 1810 were two young landed aristocrats, Miguel Barragán and Manuel Gómez Pedraza, and a young military physician named Anastasio Bustamante, who came to San Luis Potosí in 1808 and helped cure Doña Francisca's infected eye. All three would eventually pass through the revolving door of the Mexican presidency. Another key officer was Bernardo Fernández de Villamil, a peninsular whom Calleja brought into his intimate circle by marriage in January 1810 to his wife's cousin, María Josefa de la Gándara. Fernández de Villamil later became Calleja's trusted adjutant and secretary during the Hidalgo insurgency. Further linkages combined Calleja's family, the noble elite, and the military. For example, Manuel José Rincón Gallardo was the first Marquis of Guadalupe Gallardo and related to the de la Gándara clan in several ways. The marquis was also commander of the Regiment of Dragoons of San Luis and thus Calleja's subordinate. In 1815 he became godfather to Calleja's son.

When the news of the Hidalgo Revolt reached him on September 19, 1810, Calleja moved at once to prepare a defense of his region. He did so, however, with a deliberation that would be characteristic of all his future military planning. One of his attributes as a caudillo was his technical proficiency and attention to detail. His first act was instructive. He chose that very day not to raise troops but to round up funds and to interdict convoys with money and supplies he feared might fall into insurgent hands. He saw funding as an essential step to mobilization of what would eventually be called the Army of the Center.

It was only then that Calleja cashed in on his elaborate networks. "El amo Don Félix" took full advantage of his extended family, his elite coterie, and his military command. Within ten days he was able to report to the new Viceroy Venegas that the Marquis of Jaral de Berrios had agreed to make 500 armed men available from his haciendas and that he had already put a hundred mounted men armed with machetes at Calleja's disposal. This was indicative of the instant support Calleja enjoyed, and is especially significant as the marquis might have contented himself with his role as commander of the Regiment of San Carlos, which he commanded in Calleja's brigade. (Jaral de Berrios was then the second creole marquis to serve under the Spanish brigadier.) By the time he left San Luis Potosí on October 24, the Mexicanization of Calleja had paid off. The army that marched out that day to join a troop from Puebla had some 3,000 cavalry, 600 infantry, and 4 cannon, which had been founded during the weeks after the Grito. The caudillo's primary task of basic mobilization was accomplished.

The two caudillos, one a priest and the other a soldier, were both authentic products of their societies and of the value systems that rewarded public men. Both fully expected their respective righteous causes to triumph in the collision that ensued. Yet it was Calleja and not Hidalgo who brought home to Mexico City the first triumphant military parade, on February 5, 1812—just after Calleja had left the insurgent headquarters at Zitácuaro, in his words, "razed, burned and destroyed." The dramatic spectacle of a victorious army on parade with a caudillo at its head inaugurated a new era in Mexican history. The Age of Caudillismo had arrived. Firmly rooted in colonial New Spain, caudillismo would mature rapidly during the balance of the independence wars as personalist leaders increased their roles in politics at all levels.

7

Domingo F. Sarmiento

Facundo Quiroga: The Caudillo as Barbarian

Domingo Sarmiento (1811–88) wrote *Civilization and Barbarism* from exile in Chile in 1845, more than two decades before he became one of Argentina's best-known presidents (1868–74). His famous polarization of the city of Buenos Aires and the provinces of the Rio de la Plata, of *porteño* sophistication and gaucho crudity, was part of Sarmiento's polemical attack on the dictatorship of Juan Manuel de Rosas (1829–52). In this work he assaulted Rosas not directly but by a skillful comparison. In Sarmiento's hands "Bloody Rosas," the supreme gaucho, is inextricably linked to the writer's model: Juan Facundo Quiroga, the provincial caudillo of La Rioja. Sarmiento's perception of the savage nature and brutal conduct of this most notorious of gaucho chieftains during the generation after independence is revealed in the following selection. So, too, is the passion of all opponents of tyranny, not only in the 1840s but also before and after.

It is possible, however, to have another view of the type of antiliberal caudillo represented by Facundo Quiroga. E. Bradford Burns explores this possibility in the chapter that follows this one.

. . . HERE ends the history of . . . La Rioja. What follows is the history of Quiroga. That day of evil omen when [Facundo Quiroga seized power in La Rioja] corresponds to April of 1835 in the history of Buenos Aires—when its country commandant, its desert hero [Juan Manuel de Rosas], made himself master of the city.

I ought not to omit, since it is to Quiroga's honor, a curious fact which occurred at this time (1823). The feeblest gleam of light is not to be disregarded in the blackness of that night.

From Domingo F. Sarmiento, *Life in the Argentine Republic in the Days of the Tyrants; or Civilization and Barbarism,* translated by Mrs. Horace Mann (New York: Hurd and Houghton, 1868), 101–11.

Facundo, upon his triumphant entry into La Rioja, stopped the ringing of the bells, and after sending a message of condolence to the widow of the slain general, directed his ashes to be honored with a stately funeral. He appointed for governor one Blanco, a Spaniard of low rank, and with him began the new order of affairs which was to realize the best ideal of government, as conceived by Facundo Quiroga; for, in his long career among the various cities which he conquered, he never took upon himself the charge of organizing governments; he always left that task to others.

The moment of the grasp of power over the destinies of a commonwealth by a vigorous hand is ever an important one and deserves attention. Old institutions are strengthened, or give place to others, newer and more productive of good results, or better adapted to prevailing ideas. From such a focus often diverge the threads which, as time weaves them together, change the web of history.

It is otherwise when the prevailing force is one foreign to civilization—when an Attila obtains possession of Rome, or a Tamerlane traverses the plains of Asia, old forms remain, but the hand of philosophy would afterwards vainly remove them with the view of finding beneath them plants which had gained vigor from the human blood given them for nourishment. Facundo, a man imbued with the genius of barbarism, gets control of his country; the traditions of government disappear, established forms deteriorate, the law is a plaything in vile hands; and nothing is maintained, nothing established, amid the destruction thus accomplished by the trampling feet of horses. Freedom from restraint, occupation; and care is the supreme good of the gaucho.
. . .

Facundo wanted to have means at his command, and, as he was incapable of creating a revenue system, he resorted to the ordinary proceeding of dull or weak governments; but in this case the monopoly bears the stamp of South American pastoral life, spoliation, and violence. The tithes of La Rioja were, at this time, farmed out at ten thousand piastres a year; this was the average rate. Facundo made his appearance at the board, and his presence overawed the shepherds. "I offer two thousand piastres a year," said he, "and one more than the best bid." The committee repeated the proposal three times; no one made a bid; all present left, one by one, reading in Quiroga's sinister glance that it was the last one he would allow. The next year he contented himself with sending to the board the following note: " 'I give two thousand dollars and one more than the best bid.' FACUNDO QUIROGA." The third year the ceremony of adjudication was omitted, and in 1831, Quiroga again sent to La Rioja the sum of two thousand dollars, his estimate for the tithes.

But to make his tithes bring in a hundred for one, another step was required, and, after the second year, Facundo refused to receive the tribute of animals otherwise than by giving his mark among the proprietors, so that they might brand with it the animals set apart for the tithe and keep them on the place until he called for them. The creatures multiplied, their number was constantly augmented by new tithes, and, after ten years, it might be reckoned that half the stock of a whole pastoral province belonged to the commanding general of the forces, and bore his mark.

It was the immemorial custom in La Rioja that the *estrays*, or the animals that were not marked at a certain age, should become the lawful property of the treasury, which sent its agents to collect these gleanings, and derived no contemptible revenue from them, but the annoyance to the proprietors was intolerable. Facundo demanded the adjudication to himself of these animals, to meet the expenses he had incurred for the invasion of the city; expenses which were reducible to the summons of irregular forces, who assembled, mounted on horses of their own, and lived constantly on what came in their way. Already the proprietor of herds which brought him six thousand bullocks a year, he sent his agents to supply the city markets, and woe to any competitor who should appear! This business of supplying meat for the markets was one which he carried on wherever he ruled, in San Juan, Mendoza, or Tucumán; and he was always careful to secure the monopoly of it by proclamation or simple notification. It is with shame and disgust that I mention these disgraceful transactions, but the truth must be told.

The general's first order, after a bloody battle which had laid a city open to him, was that no one should supply the markets with meat! In Tucumán he learned that a resident of the place was killing cattle in his house, in spite of this order. The general of the army of the Andes, the conqueror of the Citadel, thought the investigation of so dreadful a crime should be entrusted only to himself. He went in person, and knocked lustily at the door of the house, which refused to yield, and which the inmates, taken by surprise, did not open. A kick from the illustrious general broke it in, and exposed to his view a dead ox, whose hide was in process of removal by the master of the house, who also fell dead in his turn at the terrible sight of the offended general.

I do not intentionally dwell upon these things. How many I omit! How many misdeeds I pass over in silence which are fully proved and known to all! But I am writing the history of government by barbarians, and I am forced to state its methods.

Mehemet Ali, who became master of Egypt by means identical with those of Facundo, delivers himself up to a rapacity unexampled even in Turkey; he establishes monopolies in every occupation and turns them to his own profit; but Mehemet Ali, though he springs from a barbarous nation, rises above his condition so far as to wish to acquire European civilization for himself and for the people he oppresses. Facundo, on the contrary, not only rejects all recognized civilization, but destroys and disorganizes. Facundo, who does not govern, because any government implies labor for others' good, gives himself up to the instincts of an immoderate and unscrupulous avarice. Selfishness is the foundation of almost all the great characters of history; selfishness is the chief spring of all great deeds. Quiroga had this political gift in an eminent degree and made everything around him contribute to his advantage; wealth, power, authority, all centered in him; whatever he could not acquire—polish, learning, true respectability— he hated and persecuted in all those who possessed them.

His hostility to the respectable classes and to the refinement of the cities was every day more perceptible, and the governor of La Rioja, whom he had himself appointed, finally was forced, by daily annoyances, to resign his place. One day, Quiroga, feeling inclined to pleasantry, was amusing himself with a young man as a cat sports with a frightened mouse; he liked to play at killing; the terror of the victim was so ludicrous, that the executioner was highly diverted, and laughed immoderately, contrary to his habit. He must have sympathy in his mirth, and he at once ordered the *general* (a certain call to arms) to be beat throughout the city of Rioja, which called out the citizens under arms. Facundo, who had given the summons for diversion's sake, drew up the inhabitants in the principal square at eleven oclock at night, dismissed the populace and retained only the well-to-do householders and the young men who still had some appearance of culture. All night he kept them marching and countermarching, halting, forming line, marching by front or by flank. It was like a drill sergeant teaching recruits, and the sergeant's stick travelled over the heads of the stupid, and the chests of those who were out of line; "What would you have? This is the way to teach!" Morning came, and the pallor, weariness, and exhaustion of the recruits showed what a night they had passed. Their instructor finally sent them to rest, and extended his generosity to the purchase and distribution of pastry; each recipient made in haste to eat his share, for that was part of the sport.

Lessons of such a kind are not lost upon cities, and the skillful politician who has raised similar proceedings to a system in Buenos Aires has refined upon them and made them wonderfully effective. For example, during the periods between 1835 and 1840 almost the whole population of Buenos Aires has passed through the prisons. Sometimes a hundred and fifty citizens would be imprisoned for two or three months, to be then replaced by two hundred who would be kept, perhaps half the year. Wherefore? What had they done? What had they said? Idiots! Do you not see that this is good discipline for the city? Do you not remember the saying of Rosas to Quiroga, that no republic could be established because the people were not prepared for it? This is his way of teaching the city how to obey; he will finish his work, and in 1844, he will be able to show the world a people with but one thought, one opinion, one voice, and that a boundless enthusiasm for the person and will of Rosas! Then, indeed, they will be ready for a republic!

But we will return to La Rioja. A feverish excitement on the subject of investments in the mines of the new States of Spanish America had arisen in England; powerful companies were proposing to draw profit from those of Mexico and Peru; and Rivadavia, who was then residing in London, urged speculators to invest their capital in the Argentine Republic. The mines of Famatina offered an opening for a great enterprise. At the same time, speculators from Buenos Aires obtained the exclusive right to work those mines, meaning to sell it for an enormous sum to the English companies. These two speculations, one started in England and the other in Buenos Aires, conflicted with each other, and were irreconcilable. Finally, a bargain was made with another English house, which was to supply funds, and [which] in fact, sent out English superintendents and miners. Later, a speculation was got up to establish a bank at La Rioja, which was to be sold at a high price to the national government when it should be organized. On being solicited, Facundo took a large number of shares, making payment with the Jesuits' College, which had been assigned to him, on his demand, in payment of his salary as general. A party of Buenos Aires stockholders came to La Rioja to carry out the project, and soon asked to be presented to Quiroga, whose name had begun to exercise everywhere a mysterious and terrific power. Facundo received them in his lodgings, in very fine silk stockings, ill-made pantaloons, and a common linen poncho.

The grotesque appearance of this figure was not provocative of any smiles from the elegant citizens of Buenos Aires. They were too sagacious not to read the riddle. The man before them meant to humiliate his polished guests, and show them what account he made of their European dresses.

The administrative system established in his province was finally completed by exorbitant duties on the exportation of cattle which did not belong to him. But in addition to these direct methods of acquiring wealth, he had one which embraced his whole public career—gambling! He had a rage for play as some men have for strong drink and others for tobacco. His mind, though a powerful one, had not the capacity of embracing a large sphere of ideas, and stood in need of this factitious occupation, in which a passion of the soul is in constant exercise, as it is crossed, appeased, provoked, excited, and kept upon the rack. I have always thought that the passion for gambling was some useful faculty that organized society has perverted or left in inaction. The will, self-control, and steadfastness which it requires are the same which advance the fortunes of the enterprising merchant, the banker, and the conqueror who plays for empires with battles. Facundo had habitually gambled since his childhood; play had been the only pleasure, the only relaxation of his life. But what an agreeable partner he must be who controls the terrors and the lives of the whole party! No one can conceive such a state of things without having had it before his eyes for twenty years. Facundo played unfairly, say his enemies. I do not believe the charge, for cheating at play was unnecessary in his case, and he had been known to pursue to the death others who were guilty of it. But he played with unlimited means; he never let anyone carry from the table the money he used for stakes; the game could not be stopped till he chose; he would play forty hours or more at a time; he feared no one, and if his fellow gamblers annoyed him, he could have them whipped or shot at pleasure. This was the secret of his good luck. Few men ever won much money from him, although, at some periods of the game, heaps of coin lost by him lay upon the table; the game would go on, for the winner did not dare to rise, and in the end he would have nothing but the glory of reckoning that his winnings, afterwards lost, had once been so large.

Gambling, then, was to Quiroga a system of plunder as well as a favorite amusement. No one in La Rioja received money from him, no one possessed any, without being at once invited to a game, or, in other words, to leave his funds in the chieftain's hands. Most of the tradesmen of La Rioja failed and vanished, their money having taken up its quarters in the general's purse; and it was not for want of lessons in prudence from him. A young man had won four thousand dollars from Facundo, and Facundo declined to play longer. His opponent thought that a snare was in readiness for him, and that his life was in danger. Facundo repeated that he had finished playing; the stupid fellow insisted on another game, and Facundo, complying with the demand, won the four thousand dollars from the other, who then received two hundred lashes for his uncivil pertinacity.

What consequences to La Rioja were occasioned by the destruction of all civil order? Reasonings and discussions are here out of place.

A visit to the scene of these occurrences will be sufficient to answer the query. The Llanos of La Rioja are now deserted; their population has emigrated to San Juan; the cisterns are dry which once gave drink to thousands of flocks. Those Llanos which fed those flocks twenty years ago, are now the home of the tiger, who has reconquered his former empire, and of a few families of beggars who live upon the fruit of the carob tree. This is the retribution the Llanos have suffered for the evils which they let loose upon the republic. "Woe to ye, Bethsaida and Chorazin! Verily I say unto you, that the lot of Sodom and Gomorrah was more tolerable than that which was reserved for you!"

8

E. Bradford Burns
Folk Caudillos

Sarmiento's caustic view of Facundo Quiroga and, by extension, of Juan Manuel de Rosas has been the standard appraisal
of most postindependence caudillos. Perhaps this is so because the literate Europeanized publicists and the factions and
leaders whom they represented came to dominate politically
many of the Spanish American republics in the middle and
late nineteenth century. Liberal proponents of modernization,
like Sarmiento, emerged the victors, and it was they who
wrote the histories. Neglected both politically and historio-
graphically in the process of the generalized triumph of urban
elites was what E. Bradford Burns calls *folk culture*. Indigenous societies traditionally rooted in the country and the
ancient barrios of the cities came under assault as a consequence of the independence movements. The forces of modernization were pitted against communal land tenure, Indian
languages and customs, and colonial legislation that had provided some modest protection against labor exploitation. To
defend their way of life, these threatened *folk* supported their
own caudillos. In this selection from his provocative revisionist book, *The Poverty of Progress* (1980), Burns examines both
the concept of *folk culture* and some of the folk caudillos
who, like Facundo, abhorred the liberal elites of the modern
urban centers. The most creative and successful of these defenders of traditional societies was the Guatemalan conservative caudillo Rafael Carrera, who dominated his country from
1839 to his death in 1865. Through Burns's account of his
career we get yet another perspective on caudillismo. Readers
may want to estimate where the various caudillos they meet

From E. Bradford Burns, *Poverty of Progress: Latin America in the Nineteenth
Century* (Berkeley: University of California Press, 1980), 86–94, 96–103, 105–6.
Copyright © 1980 The Regents of the University of California. Reprinted with
permission.

in this book fit along the political spectrum from elite dictator to folk caudillo.

Bradford Burns, one of the most able and influential of Latin American historians, has published extensively throughout his career at the University of California at Los Angeles. He is best known for *A History of Brazil* (1970, 1980), and for the many editions of *Latin America: A Concise Interpretive History.*

MODERNIZATION entailed dire consequences for the rural masses, who both opposed it and [saw that it] offered alternatives more suitable to their own needs. Few studies have considered those popular alternatives to the modernization pursued by the elites. Historians' customary fascination with the privileged as well as a lack of conventional documentation for the alternatives explain the silence. Because the overwhelming majority of the nineteenth-century Latin Americans were illiterate, they left few written accounts of their complaints [and] alternatives to Europeanization. . . .

José Luis Romero ranks as one distinguished scholar who has attempted to come to grips with the popular alternatives to the politics of the dominant elite in nineteenth-century Argentina. While more sympathetic to the process of Europeanization in his study, *History of Argentine Political Thought,* he nonetheless devoted much more time than the usual token discussion to the countercurrent. He termed the popular alternative "inorganic democracy," which he defined thus:

> But for many reasons the provincials opposed the doctrinaire positions and the institutional principles of the enlightened group. To these ideas the people of the interior opposed a profoundly colonial mentality and local sentiments, by which they demonstrated their new-born patriotism. . . . The people chose to obey the call of the caudillos of their class and of their own kind who sprang up on all sides, which gave support to a new authoritarianism that had some vaguely democratic characteristics since, in fact, the caudillo exalted the ideals of his people and carried to power with him a mandate to impose and defend their wishes. . . . The creoles were accustomed to

the enjoyment of immense personal liberty. The desert assured them that freedom, although at the cost of their total
exclusion from public life, which was run by the cities. When
the revolutionary movement triumphed, the creoles wanted
to transfer their feeling of indomitable liberty to political
life, since mere obedience to laws appeared to them to be
oppression. . . . From [their] . . . unlimited sense of freedom
was born a democratic desire to have their own chief rule.

The rustic rurals described by Romero had evolved a life-style
that provided them with greater equality, security, and well-being
within their own informal institutions than did the European
pattern being imposed by Buenos Aires. . . . The mutual identification of people and caudillo exemplified the "inorganic democracy" that Romero found characteristic of the Argentina interior
during much of the last century.

What Romero termed "inorganic democracy" can be related
to "folk culture," a common way of life shared by the ordinary
people; a general concept useful for the study of nineteenth-century Latin America was their adherence to ideas and values for-
mulated by the American experience over centuries. Because the
folk drew cautiously and slowly from European sources, carefully
mediating those outside influences, they did not embrace the
values and ideology emanating from Europe—and later from
North America—with the same enthusiasm and rapidity that
generally characterized the welcome extended by the elites,
wealthy, and aspiring middle class. The heavy infusion of modernization injected into national society by the urban elites in the
nineteenth century, particularly during the last half—causing
what was probably the greatest cultural confrontation in the New
World since the early sixteenth century—shattered the relationship of the folk with their environment, a relationship already
tenuous in some regions. That intrusion of broad change based on
alien values constituted the major challenge of modernization to
folk culture. . . .

[On the other hand,] from the vantage point of the Europeanized elites of the capital cities, those folk cultures and specifically
the folk societies, organized groups of individuals characterized

by a folk culture, stood as barriers to the creation of the desired "modern" state, an argument well summarized by Sarmiento.

Folk culture was based on a common language, heritage, beliefs, and means of facing daily life. It instilled a feeling of unity, loyalty, and tradition within the folk, more intuitive than codified, although folk wisdom, folk poetry, and folktales gave verbal insight into them.

In the nineteenth century, particularly during the first half, the folk culture thrived within folk societies in the countryside and in the rural villages. Those folk societies comprised small, isolated communities, which manifested a strong sense of group solidarity. The common folk culture bound people together into an intradependent, intimate, and largely self-sufficient society. A well-defined moral order in which each person knew his role and the interrelationships of individuals characterized the folk society. The folk held more to fixed laws of behavior and human existence, a contrast with the teleological bent of the Western mind. A unity of feeling and action accompanied a sense of harmony with the environment to satisfy inner needs. The combination of unity, harmony, and satisfaction comprised the soul of the people.

Education within those societies emphasized the individual's relationship to the group and inculcated in children a moral behavior honored by the community. In short, the result was to recreate in the child the patterns of the adult. Education provided continuity by passing on and maintaining tradition.

The incentives to work and to trade originated in tradition, moral dictates, community obligations, and kinship relations. In those essentially nonmaterialistic cultures, economic decisions took second place to social considerations. The system worked sufficiently well to provide the folk with employment, food, housing, community spirit, and reasonable satisfaction. Life-styles were simple; hardships were common; the disadvantages were obvious, at least to the outsider. Such life-styles repulsed the Europeanized elites of the cities. Indeed, the behavior of the folk could be neither understood nor explained within the framework of Western thought. It did not evolve exclusively from the Iberian experience, nor did it acknowledge the influence of the liberal ideology of the Enlightenment or the French Revolution. Within their own experience, however, the societies seem to have provided adequately for their members. Modest as their standards of living might have been, they deteriorated under . . . accelerating modernization, which first modified and then partially eradicated the folk societies of the nineteenth-century. . . .

Some of the leaders selected by the folk played significant roles in regional and national life. Nineteenth-century history, particularly the half-century following independence, offers a number of fascinating examples of such popular leaders, often referred to as caudillos—although, of course, not all caudillos were folk leaders. As far as we can tell, the folk expected their leader to represent and strengthen their unity, express their soul, personify their values, and increase their harmony; in short, to be as one with the people he led. Their caudillo recognized and understood the distinctive way of life of the folk and acted in harmony with it. In the eyes of the people, he inculcated the local, regional or national values—traditional values—with which most of the people felt comfortable. He exuded a natural, a charismatic, leadership of the majority, who found in him an adviser, a guide, a leader, a protector, a patriarch in whom they entrusted their interests. They surrendered power to him; he exercised it for their benefit. He embodied collective will; he incarnated authority. The fusion of leader and people had to be nearly perfect (that is, perceived by those involved as nearly perfect), and when the interplay existed both people and leader sensed, valued, and honored their interdependency. In his discussion of leadership and folk society, José Carlos Mariátegui ascribed to the leader the roles of "interpreter and trustee." Mariátegui concluded, "His policy is no longer determined by his personal judgment but by a group of collective interests and requirements." The leader seemingly arose from and blended with his physical and human environment. Thus identified with America, he contrasted sharply with the Europeanized leaders imposed by the elites.

The popularity of such caudillos is undeniable. Their governments rested on a base of folk culture, drew support and inspiration from the folk, and expressed, however vaguely, their style. Under the leadership of such caudillos, the masses apparently felt far more identification with government than they ever did under the imported political solutions advocated by the intellectuals and the elite. On many occasions the folk displayed support of their caudillos by fighting tenaciously to protect them from the Europeanized elites and/or foreign invaders.

Juan Bautista Alberdi, probably more than anyone else in the nineteenth century, studied the psychology of the relationship of popular caudillos with the masses, and he concluded that the people regarded a popular caudillo as "guardian of their traditions," the defender of their way of life. He insisted that such leaders constituted "the will of the popular masses . . . the immediate organ and arm of the people . . . the caudillos are democracy." He reiterated frequently in his writing the equation of the popular caudillo with democracy:

> Thus, the system of caudillos appears in America in the form of democracy and together they develop and progress. Artigas, López, Güemes, Quiroga, Rosas, Peñaloza, as chiefs, heads, and authorities are the product of their people, their most spontaneous and genuine personification. Without any other authorization than that, without finances, without resources, they have guided the people with more power than the governments possess.

If the folk obeyed unreservedly those popular leaders, the caudillos in turn bore the obligation to protect and to provide for the welfare of the people. The ruled and ruler were responsible to and for each other, a personal relationship challenged in the nineteenth century by the more impersonal capitalist concept that a growing gross national product would provide best for all.

Imbued with European political ideas, inheritors of the Enlightenment, the elites scoffed at the concepts represented by the folk caudillos; "barbarians" was the epithet they hurled. Their own political concepts, always highly theoretical, focused on the separation and balance of powers, equality, federalism, and other political ideas that seemed in vogue in the United States and/or Europe. Yet, their practice embraced a mixture of both their caudillismo and liberal democracy, with inclinations more toward the former. They, too, felt most comfortable, certainly more secure, with a caudillo, albeit one who represented their new values and protected their old institutions. Simón Bolívar, who authored more than one constitution, recognized the vitality of and need for just such an omniscient, omnipotent, and omnipresent leader. Speaking of his 1826 constitution for Bolivia, he revealed, "The President of the Republic shall come to be in our constitution like the sun, fixed in the center, giving life to the universe." But Bolívar's universe contrasted with that of the folk, and therein lay the potential for cultural conflict.

In his biography of Aparicio Saravia, Manuel Gálvez noted that his death in 1904 during his struggle against President José Batlle of Uruguay, the city, and foreign influence, marked the end of the era of the caudillo on horseback in the Americas. Gálvez tried to distill what Saravia represented and concluded he personified gaucho liberty, Iberia and Roman Catholic tradition, nationalist sentiments, distrust of foreign influence, an order based on hierarchy, and respect for moral values. In short, he incarnated what was Spanish and profoundly American in the Uruguayan people. Saravia well represented the not unusual alliance of folk and patriarchs who shared traditional rural values and were cautious of urban and foreign ways. Such alliances obviously crossed class lines, [which reemphasizes] . . . again the cultural nature of this nineteenth-century conflict. The hazy class lines complicate the application of customary political labels to those alliances, since the folk favored community arrangements that might suggest a rustic socialism, while the patriarchs represented, depending on one's viewpoint and/or emphasis, a type of neofeudalism or patrimonialism or neocapitalism.

Argentina history offers excellent examples of popular and populist caudillos: Juan Facundo Quiroga, Martín Güemes, Felice Varela, and Angel Vicente Peñaloza, to mention only a few obvious ones. Certainly the caudillo of greatest import was Juan Manuel de Rosas, who, in one way or another, dominated Argentina from 1829 until 1852. The masses demonstrated their loyalty by their willingness to fight for him for nearly a quarter of a century. Rosas suffered defeat and exile only when the elites enlisted the Brazilian army to unite with them to overthrow him. The concepts of these caudillos as the popular leaders of the masses and of the mutual devotion of leader and masses were as difficult for most of the Europeanized elite to accept as were the popular leaders. The identification of the masses with Rosas explains in part the negative role assigned that caudillo in official Argentina historiography as well as the historical obscurity to which a dozen local leaders have been banished. . . .

The sources for the study of an alternative history, that of the folk rather than the well-documented history of the elites, have survived to some degree in folklore. Argentina folklore, for example, including gaucho poetry, offers evidence of popular support for "inorganic democracy," with the local caudillos regarded as the defenders of the people's rights and preferences. While praising the rustic virtues of the countryside, the folklore denigrated the cities filled with foreigners and subject to European influences. . . .

Guatemala provides a handy and useful example of Indian resistance and temporary success as well as the subsequent silence accorded it in the history texts.

At midcentury the population of Guatemala numbered less than a million. The overwhelming majority was Indian, nominally Roman Catholic, non-Spanish-speaking, and minimally influenced by three centuries of Spanish rule. The Spaniards had respected much of the indigenous cultures. However, independence in 1821 elevated to power a segment of the elite that had imbibed the heady wines of Enlightenment thought and, judging the Indians to be backward, terminated the benign neglect of the Crown. According to the simile of the times, Indianism marked the appropriate infancy of Guatemala that would mature to adulthood nurtured on a European diet. In short, if Guatemala were to progress, then the Indians had to be Europeanized.

During the decade of the 1830s, the government of Mariano Gálvez energetically set out to remodel Guatemala in an effort to eradicate Indian institutions in favor of the latest European ones. As elsewhere in the hemisphere, the government favored European immigration as the guarantee for progress. In a moment of generosity—or desperation—in 1834, the government awarded nearly all the public lands to foreign companies that promised to people Guatemala with Europeans. The area conceded covered nearly three-quarters of Guatemala. Regarding the Indian communal lands as an unprogressive remnant of the past, the government proceeded to put them up for sale, a bargain eagerly acquired by a growing and ambitious mestizo class as well as by foreigners. New laws forced the Indians to build roads and ports and reestablished the burdensome head tax on them in order to finance the infrastructure that would integrate Guatemala more completely with Europe. At every turn the Indians faced increasingly heavy taxes and workloads, confiscation of their lands, and deprecation of their cultural values. At the same time the government intensified its attacks on the Roman Catholic clergy as retrograde and legislated to reduce its influence. To the Indian communities, on the other hand, the clergy remained as their last protector from a hostile, Europeanized government. They perceived any decrease in the Church's powers as an increase in their own vulnerability to exploitation or destruction. Clearly, by debilitating the only defender of the Indian masses, the elites enhanced their own position. The elites understood the organizational strength of the Roman Catholic Church to surpass that of the nascent political institutions they fostered and welcomed the opportunity to weaken a rival. Furthermore, the property confiscated from the Church ended up in the hands of the secular elites, increasing their wealth, prestige, and, ultimately, power. The many grievances of the Indians reached a climax in 1837 with the outbreak of a virulent cholera epidemic, the final proof to the Indians that the government sought to eliminate them in order to give their lands to immigrants. At that point a popular revolt, one of the major ones in nineteenth-century Latin America, broke out, and Rafael Carrera, a mestizo with firm roots in the Indian community, took the leadership.

Among the many things that popular rebellion signified, it voiced the refusal of the Indians to countenance any further exploitation and destruction through Europeanization. Their alternative was to be left alone by the elites of Guatemala City so that they could live unmolested according to the dicta of their own culture. They rejected education, culture, economy, and laws that would Europeanize them to the extent of integrating them into a capitalist economy centered in Europe. They chose to withdraw, to isolate themselves; and withdrawal was, and remains, a common reaction of the Indians before the Europeans. But withdrawal signified rebellion in regions where the elites depended on those Indians for labor and taxes. Carrera understood the Indian position; he sympathized with the desires of the Indians; and he rose to power on their strength.

During the generation 1838–65, in which Rafael Carrera dominated Guatemala, he respected the native cultures, protected the Indians insofar as that was possible, and sought to incorporate them into his government. His modest successes in these efforts assume greater significance when compared to the disastrous conditions suffered by the Indian majority during the decades of liberal, Europeanized governments that preceded and followed the Carrera period. That popular caudillo, totally unschooled in foreign theories, was a practical man who knew Guatemala and its peoples well. He had traveled and lived in many parts of the nation, always among the humble folk whom he understood. He drew from his Guatemalan experiences, in marked contrast to the elites seduced by European experiences and theories. Carrera appreciated the Indians' opposition to the process of Europeanization imposed by the Liberals. He regarded it as his principal duty to allow "the people to return to their customs, their habits, and their particular manner of living." The government, he affirmed, had the obligation of representing the majority of the people and of offering "a living example of virtue, equity, prudence, and justice." Those principles seem to have guided much of his long administration.

While Carrera repudiated the radical ideas of the Liberals, he never eschewed change. He believed it must come slowly and within the social context, a change acceptable to the people and not forced on them. An editorial in *El Noticioso* as late as 1861 decried the wholesale importation of innovations from Europe and the United States and went on to advocate the evolution from a colonial past to a national present through careful deliberation. Such gradualism generally characterized the Guatemala government under Carrera. Revisionist studies now credit that government with respecting Indian customs and protecting the rural Indians. The president held that the art of governing well sprang from the "formation of a government of the people and for the people." Accordingly, the government officially abandoned the Liberals' goal to incorporate the Indians into Western civilization. One even could argue that under Carrera the government was "Indianized." Indians, and particularly mestizos, all of relatively humble classes, participated directly in the government, holding such exalted offices, in addition to the presidency, of course, as the vice-presidency, ministries, governorships, and high military ranks. The army became nearly an Indian institution. The Carrera government was unique in Latin America for providing the political ascendancy of the once-conquered race. Significantly the "white" political monopoly was broken and never again could the minute white aristocracy govern Guatemala alone. Fundamental to Carrera's government was the decree of August 16, 1839, to protect the Indians. Commenting on the new decree, *El Tiempo* editorialized, "It is the object of public interest not only to protect the most numerous class in our society but also to encourage it to improve its customs and civilization, which can be done by providing it with the means to acquire and increase its small property holdings and industry by which it lives." Such were the intentions of the Carrera government.

The government generally succeeded in carrying out those intentions. Governmental decrees were translated into Indian languages and "protectors" appointed to serve the Indian communities. Carrera himself regularly received Indian delegations and seems to have traveled frequently in order to visit with the Indians. To lift some of the economic burden from the impoverished majority, he reduced taxes on foodstuffs and abolished the head tax. Further, he excused the Indians from contributing to the loans the government levied from time to time to meet fiscal emergencies. On the other hand, the government did not hesitate to reinstate the former alcoholic beverage controls, which included higher taxation, one means Carrera had of both increasing revenues and imposing a greater morality on the countryside. By removing many of the taxes on the Indians, which were paid in the official currency circulating in Europeanized Guatemala, the government lessened the need for the indigenous population to enter the monetary economy, thus reducing the pressure on them to work on the estates. The Indians, then, could devote that time and energy to their own agricultural and community needs.

The government took a pragmatic view of education. It encouraged a basic education, believing that for the majority of the inhabitants a simple education emphasizing reading, writing, and Christian doctrine would suffice. Higher education was available, primarily in the capital, for those desiring it. In the almost exclusively Indian Department of Sacatepequez, a decree of 1849 required each village to establish a school for boys to learn reading, writing, arithmetic, religion, and moral principles. "As soon as funds are available, those municipalities will establish schools for girls." Scholarships were to be available to defray expenses of poor children.

Of all the efforts made in behalf of the Indians none surpassed the protection of Indian lands, the return of land to Indian communities, and the settlement of land disputes in their favor. The government declared in 1845 that all who worked unclaimed lands should receive them. What was even more unusual, it enforced the decree. It was decided in 1848 and repeated the following year that all pueblos without *ejidos* [communal lands] were to be granted them without cost, and if population exceeded available lands, then lands elsewhere were to be made available to any persons who voluntarily decided to move to take advantage of them. In 1851, Carrera decreed that "the Indians are not to be dispossessed of their communal lands on any pretext of selling them," a decree strengthened a few months later by prohibiting the divestment of any pueblos of their ejidos for any reasons. Carrera thus spoke forcefully and effectively to the most pressing problem of Latin America: the overconcentration of land in the hands of the elite and the need for the rural masses to have land to cultivate. The Carrera decades witnessed increasing agrarian diversification, an escape from the monoculture that had characterized agriculture for so long. The intent was not so much to increase exports as to insure a plentiful supply of food in the marketplace at prices the people could afford. From the evidence at hand it would seem that the quality of life for the Indian majority improved during the Carrera years.

While some studies have concentrated recently on the government and programs of Carrera, scant attention has been given to the philosophical views of Carrera and of his government concerning the Indians and the many complex problems of a dual society. As has been stated, the government realized its strength rested upon Indian support and certainly exerted efforts to protect and help the Indians, but the impression often remains that Carrera acted more from realpolitik than conviction, that he was more paternalistic than egalitarian. Those paternal and pragmatic aspects of governmental policy seem most readily evident, and it should not be surprising since Guatemala inherited centuries of institutionalized Spanish paternalism. Furthermore, the anthropological thought emanating from Europe in the nineteenth century ranked the Indian as inferior, and accordingly even the most benevolent Latin American governments exercised paternalism over the native inhabitants but withheld any recognition of real equality. Indeed, the policy of most governments confronting the Indian populations was to insist on their absorption into the Westernizing patterns or their eradication. The Carrera government offered a refreshing contrast. Despite the intellectual climate in which Carrera governed, there exists some justification for speculating that certain policy makers, among them the president, maintained an unusually open and enlightened attitude toward the Indians, rare anywhere in the nineteenth century and a harbinger of ideas that would take another century to germinate. . . .

Carrera's *Informe* to the legislature in 1848 remains one of his major policy statements. In it he criticized the elites' abuses of the Indians, displayed a laudable understanding of Indian psychology, and expressed his concern for and sympathy with the Indian peoples, who, he emphasized, composed "two-thirds of the Republic's population." In his view, "humanity" and "common sense" required a fair treatment of that majority, which would be best served by the old laws and practices with which they were accustomed. Similar views were discussed on other occasions to reveal on the one hand that official philosophy did not change through the years, but that on the other hand it was difficult to overcome prejudices apparently ingrained in the Europeanized segment of the population. *El Noticioso* carried a significant essay entitled "El Antagonismo de Razas" in 1862, which expressed the official attitude in the later years of the Carrera period. While succumbing to the conclusion that European civilization was "superior" and thus subscribing to the racial implications of that conclusion, the essay warned that to accept the Anglo-Saxon version of European civilization would condemn the Indians to extermination, a condition unacceptable to the writer. The solution seemed to be the introduction of European civilization as it filtered through the more acceptable Spanish experience . . . within the framework of Spanish Europe and Indian America, Guatemala could forge its own civilization.

Within a month, *El Noticioso* returned to that theme in a clever essay, "Fantasia," signed by Miguel Boada y Balmes. The author called for nothing less than equal rights for the Indians, a singular voice in a hemisphere that at that time adamantly denied everything to the original inhabitants: "the ideal of the present is the moral, and to a certain point physical, emancipation of the Indian, his freedom to enjoy the right universally admitted to be human. . . ." The author based his arguments on the philosophical views favoring the equality of all men, on Christianity, on social justice, and on the brute economic reality that the Indians produced the wealth others enjoyed.

A further testimony to Carrera's concern for the Indians' well-being and to the interdependency of the Indian communities and the president came from the United States minister to Guatemala (1861–64), Elisha Oscar Crosby. An enthusiastic admirer of Carrera, the minister observed:

> He was always mindful of the rights of the common people, especially of the Indians. They would come sometimes in delegations of hundreds from distant provinces to lay their grievances before him, and he would sit patiently and hear all their complaints and have them inquired into, and direct redress and remedies. He had the most perfect control and confidence of all that aboriginal population. I suppose in forty-eight hours he could have assembled a hundred thousand of those Indians to his assistance if he had needed them. . . .

The characteristics marking the Carrera experience as unique in Indo-America are the respect the government extended to Indian cultures and the reluctance to push the Indian population into Europeanizing.

A willingness to respect Indian customs did not eliminate the government's attention to progress. In the relative calm of the last decade and a half of the Carrera government, the dual society both preserved the past and flirted with the future. During the closing years of the period, the newspapers commented frequently on the satisfactory pace of "progress" and "advancement," not hesitating to applaud the maturing "civilization" of Guatemala. President Carrera himself once had reminded the legislature that when he entered office his enemies expected "barbarism" to envelop the country but that he consistently had fostered "culture and civilization." . . .

The Indian victory under Carrera proved to be as transitory as the gauchos' under Rosas. The death of Carrera in 1865 reinvigorated the elites' effort to wield power, and they succeeded under the leadership of another and different type of caudillo, Justo Rufino Barrios, 1873–85. Positivist in orientation, President Barrios duly emphasized order and material progress. Under the Liberal reforms of the post-1871 period, capitalism made its definitive entry into Guatemala, which meant large-scale exportation of coffee, with all the attendant consequences for that agrarian economy. The government rushed to import foreign technicians, ideas, and manufactured goods. It did not hesitate to contract foreign loans to pay for the Europeanization. The improvement of roads from the highland plantations to the ports and then the construction of the much-desired railroads first to the Pacific and later to the Atlantic accelerated coffee production and integrated Guatemala into the world market system more closely than ever. As elsewhere, the new railroads were owned and operated by foreigners and paid handsome profits to overseas investors. The burden of financing the railroads as well as the other accoutrements of progress inevitably fell on the local poor. . . .

The judgments of the Barrios period and the Liberal reforms inevitably point to the material changes, the prosperity of the elites, and the transformation of Guatemala City into a pseudo-European capital. To balance those accomplishments [there] were a return to monoculture, declining food production for local consumption, rising foreign debt, forced labor, debt peonage, the growth of the latifundia, and the greater impoverishment of the majority. Reflecting once again the common historiographical bias, library shelves display ample biographical studies of the two nineteenth-century "modernizers," Gálvez and Barrios, while historians continue to ignore Rafael Carrera.

9

Jane M. Rausch
The Taming of a Colombian Caudillo

Plainsmen like Juan Manuel de Rosas from the Pampas of Argentina and José Antonio Páez from the Llanos of Venezuela emerged as powerful national caudillos in the immediate post-independence years. Why these *folk caudillos,* to use Burns's phrase, were able to dominate the urban elites of Buenos Aires and Caracas is a question that has long intrigued historians. The fact that other would-be military dictators from the great grasslands of South America were frustrated in their desires to control the emergent republics provides insights into the success of Rosas and Páez. In the following essay Jane Rausch, a distinguished historian of Colombia and of that country's vast eastern Llanos in particular, provides a narrative history of a Llanero chieftain, Juan Nepomuceno Moreno. Moreno served under Simón Bolívar in the Liberator's dramatic trans-Andean invasion of the Spanish stronghold of Bogotá in 1819, with its climactic battle of Boyocá. Twelve years later Moreno followed the same route in his own effort to become arbiter of Colombian politics. Moreno subsequently failed to sustain his control after he had occupied Bogotá, due in part to his limitations as a politician. He was also outmaneuvered by his own liberal allies, however, because they reflected the Andean elite's disdain for the Llaneros. Readers should consider the relative isolation and unimportance of Colombia's eastern Llanos frontier as factors in determining Moreno's fate, in comparison with very different circumstances in Argentina and Venezuela. Sidney Hook's categories of *eventful* and *event-making* leaders, which Rausch applies in her analysis, are also useful. The limits on personal power even in the heyday of caudillismo are evident here, as they are in the following essay on Martín Güemes by Roger Haigh.

From Jane M. Rausch, "The Taming of a Colombian Caudillo: Juan Nepomuceno Moreno of Casanare," *The Americas* 42 (January 1986): 275–88. Reprinted with permission.

Readers should also note the multitudes of caudillos and caciques who act in this fragmented world during and after the wars of independence. This essay should be compared with the selection by the reluctant Colombian caudillo, Rafael Núñez, later in this book.

NO statue of Juan Nepomuceno Moreno stands today in Bogotá. Most Colombians have never heard of him, and probably only a few scholars could identify him as a Llanero patriot who fought in the battles of Boyacá and Carabobo. Yet it is not too much to say that in May 1831, the action of this obscure caudillo from Casanare might have changed the course of Colombian history. Already in Venezuela and Argentina, José Antonio Páez and Juan Manuel de Rosas had used the plains as a springboard to unseat the urban elite and take command of their nations. Now Moreno, fresh from a stunning defeat of the forces of Rafael Urdaneta at Cerinza and poised in Zipaquirá with an army of fierce Llaneros, threatened to invade Bogotá, overthrow Bolívar's successor, and impose his own dictatorship. While historians agree that the events of 1831 mark a turning point in the evolution of Colombian politics, they have yet to analyze the role played by Moreno. An examination of his career suggests that his failure to seize control not only stemmed from his own personal limitations as a leader, but also was conditioned by two important trends of nineteenth century Colombian history—the subordination of the Llanos frontier to the highlands, and the emergence of a political system dominated by civilian caudillos.

Moreno's destiny was shaped by the tropical plains where he was born sometime in the late eighteenth century. Stretching eastward from the Andes for hundreds of miles, these seemingly endless grasslands merge imperceptibly with the Llanos of Apure in Venezuela. Cut by fast-flowing tributaries of the Orinoco, they experience annual cycles of flood and drought. The Llanos have little value for agriculture, but they form a natural if precarious home for herds of wild cattle and horses first introduced by the Spanish in the sixteenth century.

In colonial times, the Provincia de los Llanos, also known as Casanare, was bordered on the south and north by the Meta and

Arauca rivers and included the modern Intendency of Arauca. Spanish interest in the region quickly dissolved when conquistadors failed to discover amid its grassy tracts the fabled kingdom of El Dorado. The lack of natural resources and the barrier posed by the Andean Cordillera limited white settlers on this frontier to a handful of encomenderos, administrators, slave hunters, and missionaries. According to the census of 1778, over 73 percent of the population of 20,892 were Indians, the majority of which lived in missions administered by Franciscans, Recoletos, and Dominicans. The census also revealed that miscegenation had produced a mestizo cowboy subculture. Vaqueros, later to be called Llaneros, drove cattle from the plains up the rough trails to Sogamoso [in the Andes]. Hides and meat along with the cotton textiles fashioned by the Indians formed the backbone of the provincial economy. The War of Independence shattered the geographic isolation of the plains. During the First Republic (1810–16), Casanare became an extension of the battlefields of highland New Granada and the Venezuelan Llanos. During the Spanish Reconquest (1816–19), creole patriots fled General Pablo Morillo's wrath to take shelter in the tropical grasslands. As the republican cause lay dying elsewhere in the viceroyalty, the refugees generated a new offensive. Led by Simón Bolívar and Francisco Paula de Santander, creoles, British volunteers, and Llaneros embarked on the Liberation Campaign which broke Spanish control of New Granada at the battle of Boyacá on August 7, 1819. Bolstered by José Antonio Páez and his Army of Apure, they went on to free Venezuela at the battle of Carabobo, June 24, 1821. Reviewing this extraordinary record, a Colombian historian observed that in Casanare "the flag of Independence was never lowered, not a day, not an hour, not a minute." Throughout the war, the province remained "a sure sanctuary for the emancipatory idea, a true seedbed for the Armies of the Republic."

With Santander installed in Bogotá as vice-president of Gran Colombia, the extent of Casanare's sacrifice for the patriot victory became painfully evident. Prolonged warfare had decimated the population and livestock. The fighting had broken down the fragile textile industry, triggered the collapse of the missions, and left lawlessness in its wake, as unpaid, unemployed soldiers turned to banditry and rustling. From a modestly self-sufficient region, Casanare had become a tropical desert. In 1827 Governor Salvador Camacho resigned in frustration, predicting that the province was moving inexorably toward ruin.

While Camacho served off and on during the 1820s as political head of Casanare, military power was in the hands of Juan Nepomuceno Moreno, . . . *comandante de armas.* Like Camacho, Moreno was a native Casanareño. . . . Unlike the governor, military prowess was the key to his success. Rough and illiterate, he fought against the royalists in Arauca in 1814 and participated in the battle of Guasdualito on January 31, 1815. He was self-appointed governor of Casanare in June 1816 when Santander arrived with the remnant of the patriot army and news that the First Republic had fallen. He accepted the decision of the Arauca Junta on July 16, 1816, which confirmed Santander as commander in chief of the army. Moreno joined the patriot exodus across the Arauca River to Apure, as Morillo's troops captured the key towns in Casanare. After Páez seized control of the army from Santander on September 16 in Trinidad, Moreno fought under the command of the Venezuelan in the battles of . . . October 1816.

By February 1817 Páez felt secure enough in Apure to send Captain Juan Galea back to Casanare to revive the flickering sparks of resistance. Within a month Galea retook Chire and Pore, driving the Spanish west to the Andean foothills. Páez then appointed Ramón Nonato Pérez and Moreno to rule Casanare as military *jefe* and governor respectively. For the next year, Pérez, Moreno, and Galea fought with each other and with Páez for control of the patriot movement. Thus, when Bolívar sent Santander to Casanare in August 1818 to prepare a new offensive against the Spanish in New Granada, his first assignment was to make an end to these petty rivalries.

Within five months . . . Santander won the loyalty of the quarreling officers and molded a new army. . . . Recognizing that Moreno enjoyed great prestige among the Llaneros, Santander confirmed him as governor but permitted him to remain at the head of his cavalry squadron. In May 1819 he promoted him to colonel and commander of the First Regiment of Lancers and on June 15 to commander general of the cavalry. In this capacity,

Moreno joined in the Liberation Campaign, which, led by Bolívar and Santander, . . . crossed the Andes . . . and won a great victory at Boyacá.

After Boyacá, Santander sent Moreno back to Casanare as commander general with orders to work in harmony with the civil governor and to unify the troops in Arauca. In February 1821, the Llanero resigned this post to join Páez in Venezuela. He fought at Carabobo and in the siege against Puerto Cabello in November 1823. Having amassed a distinguished military record, he returned to Casanare, where he stayed, except for brief intervals, until his death in 1839.

During Santander's rule of Gran Colombia between 1819 and 1828, Comandante Moreno seconded Governor Camacho's pleas for programs to help the province recuperate from the ravages of war. He pressed for a tobacco subsidy, for missionaries to convert the Indians, and for doctors to attend the sick—all to no avail. Moreno protested the misguided policy of confiscating cattle for the army on the one hand and prohibiting ranchers to sell their animals in Venezuela on the other. Nevertheless, when Páez revolted in 1826, he remained loyal to [Santander].

After Bolívar exiled Santander for complicity in the conspiracy of September 25, 1828, and established a dictatorship, Moreno grew restless. He bitterly resented the Liberator's award of the haciendas attached to the Meta Missions to his Minister of War, Rafael Urdaneta, a long-standing personal enemy. Rankled by Bogotá's continuing neglect of Casanare, Moreno believed that Casanare would receive better treatment as part of Venezuela, where Páez was already passing laws which favored cattlemen. In December 1829, a congress meeting in Caracas called for Venezuela's secession from Gran Colombia. While delegates to the Admirable Congress in Bogotá tried frantically to come up with a new federal framework, Venezuela declared itself independent. Sick at heart, Bolívar resigned on March 1, 1831, and prepared to go into exile. On May 4, the Admirable Congress elected Joaquín Mosquera and Domingo Caicedo to take over as president and vice-president respectively.

Moreno was ready to make his move. On April 2, 1830, he ordered the assassinations of two [men] employed by Rafael Urdaneta to administer the haciendas of the Meta Missions, and over-threw the incumbent governor. . . . Two days later, the citizens of the provincial capital, Pore, "pronounced" for union with Venezuela. In their proclamation, they charged that the central authorities in Bogotá had reduced Casanare to colonial status by appointing officials who did not know the needs of the Llaneros, or who, because of their fear of the tropical climate, had never left the highlands. These same authorities had awarded the Meta haciendas to . . . unscrupulous men who took cattle that did not belong to them and treated the rightful owners as criminals when they protested. The citizens of Pore recalled the provincial representative to the congress in Bogotá and proposed to elect a delegate to attend the Venezuelan congress in Valencia. They agreed that General Moreno should remain in charge until the Venezuelan congress might dictate a more appropriate arrangement. Within days, . . . Arauca [and other cantons] endorsed the Pore proclamation, expressing the hope that since Casanare shared with Venezuela a common climate, topography, and public opinion, it might become part of the "representative and popular form" of government which that nation would develop.

Páez carefully monitored these events from Caracas. He denied allegations from Bogotá that he had instigated Moreno's insurrection and affirmed that, while he had submitted Casanare's request to join Venezuela to the congress, he had not endorsed the petition. On July 31 this body rejected annexation, explaining that Casanare had never formed part of Venezuela in the past and that New Granada would rightly view its incorporation as an act of war.

Casanare's status was still in limbo when General Urdaneta overthrew the government of Mosquera and Caicedo and announced a dictatorship in the name of Bolívar. Now in Bogotá, the lines were clearly drawn between the militarists, who supported the Liberator, and the civilian Liberals, who sought the return of the exiled Santander. Throughout New Granada resistance grew against Urdaneta. José María Obando and José Hilario López raised troops in Cauca. Salvador Córdoba began a revolution in Antioquia, while Juan José Neira led the opposition in Cundinamarca. In March, Joaquín Posada Gutiérrez declared in favor of the ousted

Mosquera. . . . Cauca, Panama, Magdalena, and Casanare were in open revolt. Unable to quell the anarchy, Urdaneta met with representatives of the opposition at . . . Apulo . . . on April 28, 1831. Retaining command of the army, he agreed to recognize Caicedo as head of an interim government until a convention could assemble to draft a new constitution.

In the meantime, Moreno, claiming loyalty to Venezuela, rallied support for a march against Urdaneta. On February 15 . . . an assembly in Pore [of] Llaneros [was urged] to join the fight. After some discussion, the *vecinos* resolved to send "our worthy caudillo in whom the people of Casanare have placed all their confidence," General Juan Nepomuceno Moreno, to liberate in the name of justice and humanity the people of New Granada from their oppressor.

In April Moreno set off from Pore with three hundred cavalry and four hundred infantry armed with guns supplied by Páez. Following the route taken by the Liberation Campaign twelve years before, they marched along the Morcote and Paya roads. They climbed the Andes and passed through the Páramo of Pisba, where many died of the cold. As soon as Moreno reached Socha on April 23, he wrote to General Justo Briceño and Colonel Reyes Patria, commanders of Urdaneta's army in Sogamoso, demanding their surrender in the name of liberty. The following day he occupied the town of Cerinza.

Briceño and Reyes Patria attacked on April 26. They took the plaza, but a charge by the Llaneros wielding their deadly lances forced them to withdraw. When the smoke had cleared, Moreno was the victor. He seized five hundred guns and four hundred prisoners, including Colonel Reyes, while Briceño retreated with his surviving troops to Tunja. The general proceeded to execute four captured officers, one of whom was Francisco Miranda, the son of the Venezuelan Precursor of Independence.

The battle of Cerinza imperiled the truce recently signed at Apulo. As Moreno marched toward Bogotá, enemies of Urdaneta swelled his ranks. Some of them urged him to put himself in power. The irony of this situation was not lost on historian José María Groot, who observed in 1869 that the very men who had denounced the Liberator as a tyrant were now proposing that "a

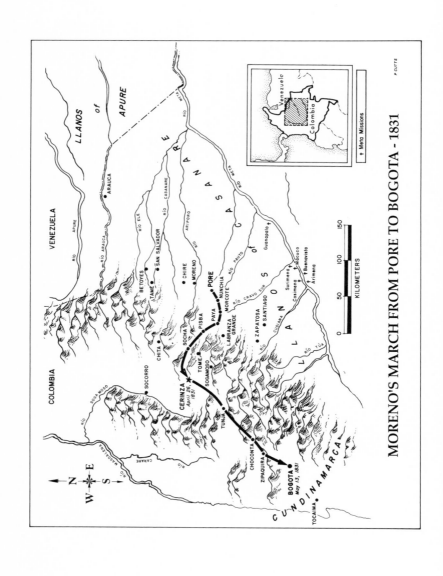

MORENO'S MARCH FROM PORE TO BOGOTA - 1831

P. CUTTS

crude Llanero" become a dictator in order to destroy the Bolivarian Party. General José Hilario López acted quickly to save the Liberal cause from such a setback. He intercepted Moreno in Zipaquirá, where he found him lying ill in bed. López persuaded the Llanero to recognize the Apulo agreement and to be guided by his orders. At best, it was an uneasy alliance. López wrote in his *Memorias*, "General Moreno was a good patriot of excellent intentions, but it would be necessary to watch him closely in order that some of his advisers might not force him to take imprudent and destructive steps."

On May 13 Moreno and López together led an army of four thousand men into Bogotá. According to Groot, the Llanero was worthy of a photograph— fat and dark-skinned *(corpulento y renegrido)*, dressed in a long blue frock coat and wearing a white handkerchief like a cap tied under his jaws, topped with a three-cornered hat trimmed with braid. The ensuing negotiations dragged on for two months, with Moreno bargaining as the leader of an "independent" Casanare, and López using the threat of unleashing the Llanero soldiers on the city as a tactic to bludgeon the opposition into accepting his demands. On several occasions, he restrained his uncouth colleague from seizing power. In the end, moderation prevailed, and President Caicedo issued two decrees, one calling for a constitutional convention, and the other permitting Santander and all others exiled for conspiring against Bolívar to return home. While the generals talked, the Llanero troops roamed the streets of the capital, harassing the residents and taking whatever struck their fancy from the stores. Groot recalled that the Bogotanos feared the "barbarians" since it was known "that their chiefs could not subject them to military discipline where there was no enemy in front of them," and that they would "kill a man in cold blood with as little emotion as killing a bull." His Liberal contemporary, José Manuel Restrepo, wrote in his diary that there were many criminals in the division of Casanare and prayed that Colombia would not be delivered "to such tigers thirsty for blood and wealth."

The highlanders breathed a sigh of relief when, with the crisis resolved, Moreno withdrew to Tunja with seven hundred men, who committed many robberies on their march. They were unwelcome guests in that city, too. The Llaneros created such disturbance that General López was obliged to march after them to restore order. On September 26, Moreno issued a proclamation bidding farewell to the highlands and returned with his troops to the Llanos.

Still to be arranged was the reintegration of Casanare with New Granada. On August 16, 1831, Caicedo invited the province to send delegates to the constitutional convention slated to begin in October. A faction led by Colonel Molina held out for union with Venezuela, but Moreno managed to bring this group into line. An election in November saw the selection of Molina and Moreno as principal and alternate delegates to the convention. On December 21 an assembly in Pore officially recognized the Caicedo government.

The events of 1830–31 which gave birth to an independent New Granada were a watershed in Colombian history. In his thought-provoking book, *The Hero in History* (New York, 1955), Sidney Hook suggests that it is just such historical turning points in which eventful figures of heroes may have a preponderant influence in determining the course of events. Hook argues that the leader who appears at the critical moment may be an "eventful man" or an "event-making man." The "eventful man" is one whose actions influence developments along a different course than they would have followed if these actions had not been taken. The "event-making man" is an eventful man whose actions are the consequence of outstanding capacities of intelligence, will and character rather than accidents of position. Both types appear at forking points in history, but the "eventful man" finds the antecedent events in a very advanced state and needs to make only a commonsense decision to make the decisive choice. The "event-making man," on the other hand, helps to create the fork in the historical road by increasing the odds of success for the alternative he chooses by virtue of the extraordinary qualities he brings to bear to realize it. In Hook's typology, it is the "event-making man" who leaves the positive imprint of his personality upon history—an imprint still observable after he has disappeared from the scene.

Considered within this context, Moreno's actions were those

of an eventful rather than an event-making man. A prototype of the caudillos who emerged in the Llanos during the Independence era, he began as a war leader who could commandeer troops and resources, holding his men together by personal ties of dominance and a common desire to obtain wealth by force of arms. The war gave him the opportunity to increase his personal fortune and to expand his base of power, but after Carabobo, he was content to remain a regional leader.

Moreno was an energetic spokesman for Llanero interests in the 1820s, but he seems to have had little genuine aspiration to control the nation. Throughout his career, he showed a willingness to subordinate himself to a higher command, first to Páez, then to Santander, and then to López. His distrust of Bolívar and hatred of Urdaneta prompted him to repudiate the latter's coup of September 5, 1830. After proclaiming Casanare's separation from New Granada, he attempted to influence affairs in Bogotá by recruiting an army and invading the highlands, fearlessly repeating the Liberator's famous trek of 1819. Yet on winning the battle of Cerinza, he was content to follow the orders of General López. Moreno's decision to join in the talks which led to the creation of a civilian-dominated republic and his docile withdrawal from the cordillera suggest that he was more a "creature of events"—to use Hook's terminology—than a master of them. Loyalty to Santander was undoubtedly a prime factor in his behavior. Moreno's return to Casanare paved the way for Santander, the "Man of Laws," to accede to the presidency and reintegrate New Granada under capable if inflexible leadership.

Yet it is curious that the rough Llanero did not make a greater effort to impose his will on a relatively vulnerable Bogotá. . . . After the Wars of Independence, plainsmen seemed fated to dominate the new nations of South America. Juan Manuel de Rosas and José Antonio Páez mobilized their cowboy supporters to take control of Argentina and Venezuela, a usurpation which Domingo Sarmiento equated with the triumph of barbarism over civilization.

While both Rosas and Páez demonstrated qualities of event-making men to a greater degree than did Moreno, their success may also be attributed to the close interrelationship between the frontier that each personified and the corresponding creole metropolis. No natural barrier sets off the Pampas from Buenos Aires, and the Andes which lie between the Llanos and the Venezuelan highlands are not insurmountable. In both colonies during the eighteenth century, exports of hides and cattle products formed a substantial portion of legal trade and contraband. Creoles living in Caracas and Buenos Aires acquired ranches. By 1810, 1.5 percent of the population of the former city controlled all the valuable grazing land in Caracas Province. Rosas was representative of a similar group in Buenos Aires. As a young man, he owned a *saladero* [meat salting plant] located several miles south of the port. By the time he became governor in 1829, he had accumulated some half-million acres of land in the Pampas. Páez began as a humble Llanero, but after the war he acquired several estates as a reward for his military service and became one of the largest landowners in Venezuela. The plains were vital to the economy of both Argentina and Venezuela in the early national period, and Rosas and Páez propped up their governments by incorporating a key segment of the urban elite whose well-being was linked to the continued prosperity of ranching.

In New Granada, accidents of geography and the subordination of the plains frontier to the highlands prevented such a union. Although the Llanos accounted for more than one-fifth of the republic's territory, they were isolated from the core population settlements by the 18,000-foot-high eastern Andean cordillera. The ranches that sprang up in Casanare during the colonial era were important locally but entirely peripheral to the viceregal economy based on the gold mines of Antioquia. Moreover, cattle could be raised more easily in many other parts of the country, where the climate was less extreme and transportation to major cities not so difficult. The Bourbon reforms did not spark an economic boom in the Llanos of New Granada as they did in Venezuela. There is no evidence to suggest that the highland elites invested much capital in Casanare before 1810, and the long war devastated the industry that had managed to develop. In 1831, as the caudillo of a remote, nonessential, frontier province, Moreno found no economic allies in the cordillera.

In addition, he faced a creole elite that was remarkably united in its hatred of the military in general and plainsmen in particular. . . . The most noteworthy outcome of the events of 1830–31 was the consolidation of civilian rule and the subsequent reduction of military participation in national politics. With their Liberal republican world view and strong dislike for any form of militarism, Obando and López, the leaders who tamed Moreno, embodied the values of the elite. Once they defeated Urdaneta, they purged all Venezuelan officers from the high command. They forced the army to accept congressional jurisdiction over promotions. In part due to their efforts, the Constitution of 1832 stated that all army and navy officers had to be New Granadans and limited the standing armed forces to a size "no larger than is indispensably necessary." Subsequent civilian governments, through drastic cutbacks in budget and personnel, terminated all military pretensions of playing a political role. Within two decades, the physical and social subjugation of the military was complete. In 1856 the army numbered only 109 men, and the highest rank was that of sergeant major.

Moreno was one of five generals after 1831 who constituted the high command, but the only one who was a plainsman. . . . A principal factor in the elite aversion to the military was its association of soldiers with uncultured, racially mixed Llaneros. Twentieth century Colombian writers . . . extol Casanare as the "cradle of Liberty." The freedom-loving cowboy, who rides the plains, lance in hand to defend liberty, has become a sacred tenet of folklore and nationalism, but . . . the generation that achieved independence took a different view. Appalled by the wretched living conditions in the Llanos, they were shocked by the cruel habits of the plainsmen. They could not forget the ferocious fighting which characterized the early years of the war. They feared that the ignorant Llanero caudillos could not control their men. Even Santander, who enjoyed the respect of the plainsmen, described their leaders in 1818 as "ignorant and without resources." "What will happen," he continued in a letter to Bolívar, "when they liberate other people less simple and natural?" *(simples y sencillos)* . . .

Moreno himself was sensitive to this prejudice. After attending the Constitutional Convention of 1832, he wrote to Santander that in contrast to Venezuela, where there was much esteem for the Llanos, in New Granada "it is rare to find a man who does not speak ill and hate Casanare . . . which was made clear to me, so that even in the Convention there were a great many deputies, who, when they heard mention of the Province of Casanare, acted as if someone had insulted them."

The highland elites harbored no fantasies of gallant, freedom-loving cowboys as long as they had to deal with a genuine Llanero, who by summoning his "barbarians," could threaten the existence of the republic. Obando and López cleverly used Moreno to achieve their own ends, but they were adamant that he should not direct the government. With diplomacy and cajolery, they convinced him to return to Casanare, and after 1831 they made sure that the Llanos frontier would never again be a threat by reducing it to abject political and economic dependency.

In summary, Juan Nepomuceno Moreno did not change the course of Colombian history in May 1831. . . . He lacked the prerequisite extraordinary intelligence, will, and character that might have ranked him with Rosas and Páez, and his actions were further tamed by the subordination of the frontier to the highlands in New Granada and the determination of the creole elite to avoid military rule under a Llanero caudillo.

10
Roger M. Haigh
The Creation and Control of a Caudillo

The standard image of a caudillo is that of an all-powerful chieftain who makes and breaks the lives of others. That caudillos might themselves have been made and broken by those who surrounded them is rarely considered. Recent scholarly attention to family history, however, has revealed a significant way in which clans and extended families or related elites became the arbiters of power and often saw their leaders not as tyrants but as tools. The late Roger Haigh was one of those historians who discovered that an apparent tyrant in the Argentine province of Salta during the independence wars was in fact the instrument of a kinship elite whose web of relations dominated the economic, political, and military facets of the region's society. Haigh began his career with this examination of the power of family structures. He then went on to the University of Utah to teach and to cultivate the enormous archive of microfilms culled from birth, baptismal, and notarial records in Latin America (and many other parts of the world) owned by the Genealogical Society of Utah. These priceless materials must be consulted by anyone bent upon the study of other ostensible caudillos who, like Martín Güemes of Salta, were figureheads created, used, and discarded by kinship elites.

ONE of the earliest caudillos was Martín Güemes. He was active in the war for independence in Argentina and ruled the northwestern province of Salta from 1815 to 1821. During his tenure in office the province repulsed several Spanish attempts at penetration. As a result of his seemingly arbitrary actions, the terms *caudillo*, *despot*, and *tyrant* are frequently used in historical treatments of his career.

From Roger M. Haigh, "The Creation and Control of a Caudillo," *The Hispanic American Historical Review* 44 (November 1964): 481–90. Copyright 1964 Duke University Press, Durham, N.C. Reprinted with permission of the publisher.

Martín Güemes was born in Salta in 1785. His father was the royal treasurer of the province, and his mother was a member of the prominent Goyechea family in neighboring Jujuy. He was one of nine children, and the subsequent marriages of his brothers and sisters were to aid him in his career. His father died in 1807, and his mother remarried into the Tineo family, thus establishing more connections of importance.

Güemes was educated in Salta; at fourteen he enlisted in the cadets and began a lifelong military career. He served in Salta until 1805, when his unit was transferred to Buenos Aires. While there he participated in the resistance to the English invasions as an aide to Santiago Liniers. In 1807 Güemes returned to Salta because of the death of his father. He remained in Salta until the break with Spain in 1810, when he was incorporated into the garrison in Salta with the rank of lieutenant.

His first command was an observation expedition into royalist Upper Peru. As a result of the expedition's success he was promoted to capitán. His subsequent military career included service with Balcarce in Upper Peru in 1811, attachment to the General Staff in Buenos Aires, and participation in the siege of Montevideo. In 1814 Güemes returned to the area of Salta with a military expedition to reinforce Belgrano at Tucumán. José de San Martín replaced Belgrano in 1814, and he commissioned Güemes to take charge of the defenses of Salta. Upon arrival in Salta he found a defensive campaign under way under the leadership of local estancieros. Commander of these groups was Pedro José Saravia, Güemes's uncle. Güemes assumed control and soon expelled the Spaniards from the province.

After securing the province of Salta, Güemes accompanied Rondeau on the invasion of Upper Peru in 1814. He fought in the battle of Puesto del Marqués, and returned to Salta in 1815. In May he was elected governor. Until this occasion his career had been completely devoted to military affairs. From 1815 to 1821 his career acquired characteristics commonly associated with caudillos, and he took actions that resulted in his being branded as a tyrant. The purpose of this paper is to indicate that Güemes was not a tyrant at all, but was created and controlled by a much older, more stable structure of power which held political, economic, and military control of the province.

Salta was situated on a trade break in the route from Buenos Aires to Lima, until 1776 the capital of the viceroyalty. At Salta all goods had to be transferred from carts to mules in order to cross the Andes. The salteños prospered from the trade passing through the city and enjoyed a virtual monopoly on the sale of mules to the caravans moving toward Peru. As a result of the profits in mules the land around the city was used as grazing land for these animals. This land was owned by several creole families who controlled most of the wealth of the province. During the colonial period these families demonstrated their power by domination of the cabildo, their mention in the records of the viceroy, and the frequent marriages with ranking Spanish officials.

The break with Spain in 1810, by eliminating Spanish officials, greatly augmented the power of the families. From 1810 to 1821 this family structure provided the basic source of strength that enabled Salta to repulse seven invasions and to earn the title "Bulwark of the North."

In an effort to determine the composition of the family structure, a search of the documents of the independence era and the colonial period revealed frequent references to several powerful families, specifically the Figueroas, Cornejos, Saravias, and Toledos. Further research into the nature of these families revealed that they controlled most of the wealth of the province and were directly related to those who controlled the remainder. These relationships were the result of a multiplicity of kinship connections, a network of families that made up the socio-economic elite of the province. The connections in kinship were strengthened by similar ethnic backgrounds, mutual economic interests, and a common, isolated locale. The family structure of Salta thus represented the combination of several types of informal group solidarities, connected intimately by repeated ties of kinship. The core of this kinship elite was composed of the families of Cornejo, Figueroa, Saravia, and Toledo.

In dealing with kinship, the uniqueness of the institution of the family is immediately apparent. The Spanish family was unusually strong due to its position, not only in custom but in both secular and religious codes. The family was formalized in law by a very detailed body of regulations governing various manifestations of family life. Among these were codes governing the dowry, entailed estates, primogeniture, and the care of adopted and orphaned children. These regulations gave the Spanish family a basic foundation in legal responsibility. The Church also gave the family additional strength. Marriage was sanctified and protected through the sacraments of the Church, and the family itself was recognized through the administration of sacraments concerning the children. This legal and religious background of the Spanish family gave it an uncommon solidarity.

The position of the family in Salta was further strengthened by local conditions. Among the most apparent of these were the relative inaccessibility of the province, the concentration of families in the isolated valleys of the province, and the difficulty of transportation and communication in the early years of the nineteenth century. These factors tended to limit the scope and contacts of the salteños with areas outside the province, produced a multiplicity of internal connections in socio-economic affairs, and restricted external relationships.

Finally and most importantly was the size of the province. The city was inhabited by nearly 7,000 people. The province held about five times that number. This relatively small population, coupled with a rather stable growth rate, could, in a few generations of intermarriages, produce a province of relatives. This extended family would have its leaders, who generally came from the elite and its affiliated families.

Economically, the four main families were estancieros, and among them they controlled most of the land in the vicinity of Salta. The first evidence of the economic strength of this group came in 1778, when the Figueroas, the Cornejos, and the Toledos were three of five donors who provided basic funds for the establishment of a royal treasury in Salta. From 1810 to 1815 the economic power of this group was demonstrated by its support of the armies of Buenos Aires in the various invasions of Upper Peru. In 1810, for example, the Figueroas donated 22,000 silver pesos to Balcarce's army; in 1812, the Saravias gave 5,000 cattle; the Cornejos also gave livestock and equipped a unit of 1,000 men to serve in the porteño force; and the Toledos supplied over 1,300 horses to the armies preparing to invade Upper Peru. For support of this kind, Feliciano Antonio Chiclana, the first representative of the junta of Buenos Aires to Salta, consistently lauded these families for rendering invaluable service to the cause of independence.

Militarily the strength of the families can best be explained by a consideration of the corporate nature of the estancia. Within the bounds of this institution the landowner was the patrón of all who lived on his land. In Salta the gaucho had acquired a sedentary position on the large ranches, working as did the cowboy in the American West. When the estancia was threatened, members of the patrón's family led the gauchos in its defense. In this manner the Cornejos managed to put in the field about 1,000 men, the Figueroas about 500, and the Saravias about 600. Together with similar units under the leadership of affiliated families, the forces of the kinship elite were consistently the bulk of the troops that defended Salta.

The union of the economic and military strength of these families was formed by a vast web of kinship connections. The Toledos and the Figueroas were related by the marriage of María de Toledo to Antonio de Figueroa. This connection between the Figueroas and the Toledos is indicative of the interconnections among the kinship elite and the other wealthy families of the region. The Figueroas and the Cornejos intermarried six times in two generations, and the Saravias and the Cornejos twice. The frequency of unions produced a superfamily which in two generations established marriages with thirty-six other leading families of the area. If the average size of a family is assumed to be about fifty members, the kinship elite and affiliated families would total about two thousand people or about 5 per cent of the population of the province of Salta. This network was the structure that controlled not only the socio-economic life of the province but the caudillo Martín Güemes as well.

The political power of the structure can best be measured by the representation of the family group in the bodies of government, in the cabildo and the provincial assemblies. The cabildo, or town council, was the principal organ of politics; the provincial assemblies were called only for special problems.

Prior to the accession of Güemes to the governorship, the power of the cabildo in provincial affairs was checked only by a representative of the junta of Buenos Aires. This representative held the position of governor of the province and presided at the meetings of the cabildo. During the period 1810 to 1815, thirty-seven different individuals held seats on the cabildo. Of this number thirty were either members of the four leading families or directly related to them. Such heavy representation gave the kinship elite an effective majority of the members of every cabildo in this period.

In May of 1815 Martín Güemes returned to Salta from Rondeau's forces in Upper Peru, and on his arrival the cabildo elected him governor. Historians have usually concerned themselves with the legality of the election and the rupture of control by Buenos Aires. The question as to why Güemes was elected has been dismissed by referring to his military reputation and his popularity with the masses. While these factors no doubt had some part in his selection, they fail to give a complete answer. He was not the only salteño with an admirable military reputation, for the province had been a battlefield since 1812; his popularity with the masses was limited to the gauchos living in the less-civilized regions of the province, and they had no political influence at all. More important than his military abilities and his mass appeal was his position in the kinship elite.

Eight men made up the cabildo of Salta in May of 1815. Seven of these were relatives of Martín Güemes, the most apparent being his brother, Juan Manuel Güemes. The connection of Güemes to the kinship elite was direct; his sister Francisca was married to Fructuosa Figueroa y Toledo; his maternal uncle, Lorenzo, was married to María Ignacia Cornejo; his paternal aunt, Bárbara Tineo, was married to Pedro José Saravia. These ties of kinship relate Martín to the four leading families of the area. His accession to the position formerly held by the representative of Buenos Aires was not usurpation of power but elimination of the only check to the power of the kinship elite of Salta by replacing a stranger with a member of the ruling coterie of families.

Güemes governed the province of Salta during a period of chaos in Argentine history. What semblance of national unity that had existed prior to 1815 collapsed with the rupture between José de San Martín and the central government under Carlos Alvear. From 1816 to 1818 the country was tied together by the Congress of Tucumán. Between 1818 and 1820 all unity disappeared, and authority was limited to the confines of individual provinces or even individual towns.

Salta had very little contact with the problems of nationhood during the Güemes administration, as the basic preoccupation continued to be survival from the Spanish power in Upper Peru. During the six-year period the province faced and repulsed four Spanish invasions, in 1817, 1819, 1820, and 1821. As governor of the province Güemes's basic concern was the defense of the area, and here he proved himself an able military commander.

The authority and power wielded by Güemes was relative to the amount of support given him by the family structure. In most matters that confronted the province, the families gave Güemes unqualified support. On such occasions he had the appearance of a leader possessing tremendous power. As long as his interest coincided with that of the group, he shared its power and it benefited from his exercise of authority. Examples of this were the Spanish invasions, the attempt of Rondeau to requisition 1,000 rifles from Salta that Güemes considered vital to Salta's defense, and his attempts to purge salteño society of Spanish sympathizers. On these issues the family structure backed him and the projects were carried out.

Politically, the kinship elite continued to dominate the province. With the exception of 1820 the cabildo of Salta was controlled by an effective majority of members of the family structure. That year a provincial assembly was established to handle provincial affairs, and the family group dominated it. Nine of the assembly's fifteen members were affiliated with the kinship elite. Its political power thus remained essentially the same during the Güemes administration as it had been prior to his taking office. The only difference was that the governor was also a member of the structure rather than a representative of Buenos Aires.

The relative military power of the families decreased somewhat between 1815 and 1821. While the ranchers still maintained command of their units, Güemes regularized the urban militia, reorganized the defenses, and created new units under professional commanders. In 1817, nevertheless, at the height of Güemes's power, after the successful expulsion of La Serna's invasion, the kinship elite held field command of four of the six divisions of gauchos, and its members occupied such key positions as Chief of Staff and Commander of the Frontier.

To measure the relative power of Güemes and the group of which he was a member, it is necessary to consider areas of disagreement between him and the kinship elite. Between 1815 and his death in 1821 there were only three serious issues of conflict between them. These were a primitive land reform program in 1817, a tax reform program in 1820, and war with the neighboring province of Tucumán in 1821. Güemes supported all three, but the kinship elite was either adamantly opposed to them or unenthusiastic.

All three were the result of a basic difference in the ambitions of Güemes and those of the kinship elite. Güemes was primarily interested in the defeat of the Spaniards, secondarily in the welfare of the province. The kinship elite was interested in its own welfare and that of the province first, and defeat of the Spanish ranked a poor second.

In 1817 Güemes attempted to reward the gauchos of Salta by absolving those who had fought against La Serna's army from paying rent to the ranchers who owned the land. The ranchers, including most of the kinship elite, opposed this assault on their property, and the gauchos' devotion to their *patrones* [masters] was seemingly stronger than their desire for rent-free land, for they refused to take advantage of the law. Güemes dropped the idea.

In 1820 San Martín urged Güemes to mount an offensive against Upper Peru. To support this military objective Güemes proposed to the provincial assembly that a system of regular taxation be adopted to guarantee him a dependable source of revenue. His proposal included taxes that would be levied on the kinship elite. The proposal was voted down and the burden of taxation was placed on interests essentially alien to the kinship elite. These were the Church, small businesses, and the urban citizenry.

In 1821 Güemes's preoccupation with the invasion of Upper Peru provoked the war with Tucumán. Civil war had broken out between Tucumán and Santiago del Estero to the south of Salta. This struggle prevented Güemes from obtaining from the other provinces military supplies which had been promised. Without this support his projected invasion of Upper Peru was hopeless. Rather than give up this project, Güemes asked the provincial assembly for permission to invade Tucumán and reopen his supply route. The kinshsip elite, by a vote of eleven to nine, gave its approval. The situation was changed rather suddenly when the salteño force was defeated by Tucumán, and the royalists began a new invasion of the province from the north. The province now faced hostilities from the Spanish to the north and from Tucumán to the south. Güemes left Salta to take command of the units facing the Spanish, and left the kinship elite in control of the cabildo. On May 21, 1821, the cabildo voted to depose Güemes and to make peace with Tucumán. This action initiated a short struggle between Güemes and the family structure that ended in his death.

The cabildo appointed Saturnino Saravia governor and José Antonio Cornejo military commander of the province. Güemes heard of this action and on May 31 he returned to the city with a force of 600 men to assume control. Seven days later a royalist force of several hundred men entered Salta in the evening and fatally wounded Martín Güemes.

After the death of Güemes a reunion of interests was accomplished. The war with Tucumán came to an end, and the forces of the kinship elite, under José Antonio Cornejo, Apolinar Saravia, and Luís Burla joined the forces of Güemes; by mid-July they had forced the royalists out of the province. Saturnino Saravia and José Antonio Cornejo, both members of the kinship elite, controlled political and military affairs respectively.

Some rather curious circumstances surrounding the death of Güemes suggest that the royalists were aided by local forces. The first incongruity was that an enemy force of such size could enter Salta without being observed. This contrasts sharply with previous salteño surveillance of royalist movements. The second curious feature was the reaction of Güemes to the trap, for he immediately assumed that it was an internal movement. There is, finally, some evidence that the royalists were assisted in their entrance into Salta by gaucho leaders such as Pedro Zavala and Angel M. Zerda. Güemes was certainly killed by royalist troops, but it is doubtful that his death was necessarily the result of a chance encounter. The abrupt end of the power struggle between Güemes and the kinship elite may have been no accident.

In summing up the relationship of Güemes to the kinship elite, the continued domination of the family structure is apparent. He was selected by it and was successful only when he enjoyed its support. On points of discord between Güemes and his supporting group he was either defeated or forced to compromise his position. Güemes was dead within a week after the final break ensued, and the family structure immediately reassumed complete control of the province. It appears that Güemes was more an instrument of the kinship elite than the tyrant of Salta.

It is not suggested that what has been learned of the kinship elite and the structure of power of nineteenth-century Salta is wholly applicable to Latin American caudillos in other areas and other eras. It does seem, however, that a similar approach to the question of caudillo power might, at least in certain cases, be more fruitful than the approaches thus far employed. It is in this regard that the present study may prove to have wider validity.

11
Francisco Bilbao
America in Danger

The description "fiery liberal" fits no one better than it does Francisco Bilbao (1823–65). Influenced by the ideas and educational theories of the great Venezuelan grammarian Andrés Bello (1791–1865), Bilbao became one of a new generation of outspoken Chilean liberals who dated their movement from the founding of the University of Chile by Bello in 1842. Banished for his iconoclastic views, Bilbao traveled in Europe (1844–50), where he absorbed the Utopian Socialist theories in vogue and witnessed some of the revolutions of 1848. On his return to Chile his radical associations soon forced him again into exile, this time in Peru. He never was able to come home again, yet his influence was felt inside Chile during and after his short life.

America in Danger, from which the following selection is taken, was published in 1863 as Bilbao's angry lament at the weakness of America before the French invasion of Mexico. In it he notes the failure of Spanish American countries to establish viable free institutions, and the corresponding growth of caudillismo in the years since independence. As he sought to explain these sorry conditions, Bilbao blamed Spain's colonial rule and, most especially, Spanish Catholicism. (It was his first vigorous attack on what he considered "thought chained to the text, intelligence bound to dogma," which led to his exile in 1844.) Here Bilbao was influenced by the writings of the French cleric Lamennais (1782–1854). Lamennais had attacked Gallicanism, was later rebuffed by Pope Gregory XVI for his democratic leanings, and then abandoned the Church to support the Second French Republic as a deputy.

Although it is abstract, Bilbao's attack on dictatorship is as forceful as the more descriptive and anecdotal *Civilization*

From Francisco Bilbao, *La América en peligro* (Santiago de Chile: Ed. Ercilla, 1941), 32–37.

and Barbarism by his contemporary Sarmiento. Especially noteworthy is Bilbao's scathing denunciation of the means by which clever caudillos circumvent fundamental laws while appearing to observe them scrupulously. The essay is also characteristic of the anticlericalism so widespread among Spanish American liberals in the mid-nineteenth century.

CATHOLICS profess the dogma of "blind obedience" and they obey an authority which they hold to be infallible. Such an affirmation produces, as we shall see, the monstrous consequences which destroy American society.

The Catholic who holds power or whose authority is fundamentally based in God . . . is naturally inclined to believe himself infallible, and since the Church will support him . . . he is strengthened in his assumption and cloaks himself in pontifical majesty. Such infallibility produces a leader who is irreproachable.

Imagine, if you will, the fury of such an authority upon seeing himself criticized, contradicted, and refuted! Political opposition is almost equated to heresy and must be exterminated at all cost *(ad majorem Dei gloriam).* . . .

Law disappears. What are constitutions, individual guarantees, and free institutions when they depend upon masses educated to blind obedience? What are they before the strong man whose knife is the law and whose supreme authority is anointed? They are nothing. So it is that there are no principles, no justice, no institutions which can resist the pressure or the threat of pressure from the authority. And politics, which ought to free the republic, provides the legal forms which only confirm the farce of elections, delegation of powers, and representation, and disguises the contaminating despotism.

The triumph of deception and of lies is all consuming; the pretense of truth and legitimacy consecrates the prostitution of the republic.

Happily these tactics are known; yet indifference spreads and political life dies out, suffocated by disillusionment. Then the first consequence of the dualism, or the opposition of politics and dogma, is the logical tendency of authority to invest itself with infallibility. The Catholic republic produces the requisite dictatorship. Machiavellianism reigns.

The tendency toward infallibility, so contrary to our legitimate ideas, emotions, and actions as selfish and partisan men, produces an unrestrained appetite for power. The achievement of power is, then, the primary goal. From this principle is born the immoral rationale that "the ends justify the means."

The contest for power in America is for some a fight for wealth; for others moral superiority, vengeance and despotism over their rivals who suffer the humiliation of defeat; others, perhaps the minority, want power to enact reforms. What is more, one must find absolution and justification to condone one's injustices.

But since there are constitional provisions which are designed to guarantee everyone his rights, and which I may not violate, I resort to obeying the "letter of the law."

The constitution says: "Thought is Free," to which I add, "within the limits established by law"—and since the "law" to which reference is made is statute rather than constitutional, I write into it these exceptions: "Thought is free," but dogmas may not be disputed, nor may systems be expounded which attack morality. And who is to judge? A commission or jury which is named in the final analysis by my authority. And so we have censorship reestablished under the name of that freest of institutions: the jury. A sublime victory of duplicity. "But the letter of the law has been observed."

The electoral power is the only power which the "sovereign people" exercise, and, indeed, the people do vote, not, however, in order to legislate directly, but rather to select their delegates who will legislate. Well enough. The majority of voters, then, express the will of the people (according to the system of delegation). This is the basis for republican authority, and it is to this end that the liberty and legality of elections consecrate the legitimacy of power.

Elections, therefore, are free. But suppose I control the election returns? Since I am the established power and have appointed the inspector of elections, what does it matter if the law is ambiguous enough to permit the same person to vote twenty times for a single candidate . . .? What does it matter if I intimidate the opposition at the polls and control the election? What is the result? My party is perpetuated in power in spite of the swindled popular will. But "the forms have been preserved"; long live the freedom to vote!

"The home is inviolable," but I violate it, adding "saving in those cases determined by law." In the final analysis it is my power which determines the "cases."

"The death penalty is abolished for political cases," but I shoot prisoners because I decide that these are not "political cases," and since I am the infallible authority I declare that these political prisoners are bandits; thus the "letter of the law is preserved."

The "Executive" may be indicted in the Chamber of Deputies and obliged to submit to a *residencia* [i.e., be subject to impeachment] for one year after retiring from office. But the Chamber was appointed by me, and it remains in office for the year after my retirement. These men who must judge me are my employees, my favorites, my creatures, my accomplices. Are they going to condemn me? No. They do not even dare accuse me. I am, therefore, vindicated, and the "letter of the law" has protected me. . . .

"The press is free." But since I select the jury, I can, with the authority of the freest of institutions, accuse, harass, persecute, and throttle freedom of the press within the very structure of liberty. The voice and opinion of a single party then reigns supreme. Infamy enshrouds the corpse of the vanquished, and I shout, "the press is free!"

It is commonly held . . . that the doctrine of the "separation of powers" is indispensable for the liberty of the Republic. But suppose that the Executive has the power to name the judges; that the Executive takes part in the legislative process; and that the Executive can employ the electoral laws to name the members of Congress; then what, in the final analysis, has become of the celebrated separation of powers?

"The guarantees which this Constitution established may not be suspended." But if I have the power to declare a state of siege in a given province or in the Republic with the authorization, as in Chile, of the "Council of State," whose members are nominated by the president himself, then what security is there for the citizen?

This miserable Machiavellianism, employing the crutch of the "letter of the law," has resulted in retrogression and bloodshed in Chile over the past thirty years. There is debate, the press is free; citizens gather freely, for freedom of assembly is a right; an almost unanimous enlightened public opinion clamors for reform; preparations are made for the elections which will carry the representatives of reform to power; and, just then, the Executive Power declares the province or the Republic in a state of siege, and the suspended constitutional guarantees blossom over the abyss of "legal" dictatorship and constitutional despotism!

And then? Either resignation or despair or civil war, etc., etc. The frightful banners of revolution are raised and blood flows on the battlefield and the scaffold. All respect for law and authority evaporates, and only force remains to proclaim its triumph in the name of liberty and justice. This is Jesuitical dictatorship.

12

Rafael Núñez

Scientific Peace: The Ideology of a Reluctant Dictator

The Church-state relationship was a central problem confronted by many nineteenth-century leaders. Some of them took a strong partisan stand in favor of close association with the Church as a means to achieve order. Most noteworthy was the quasi-theocratic dictator of Ecuador, Gabriel García Moreno. At the opposite pole were avowed enemies of clericalism such as Francisco Bilbao of Chile and the better-known Benito Juárez of Mexico.

Between these extremes other leaders took intermediate positions regarding the problem of centralism versus federalism as well as the Church-state question. Some of these leaders shifted their ground in both areas according to the politicial demands made upon them. Among these was Rafael Núñez (1825–94) of Colombia. Núñez is, moreover, a prime example of those well-educated sophisticated statesmen whom Spanish America produced in the late nineteenth century whose political vision and high principles were not always sufficient to prevent their becoming dictatorial.

Núñez entered Colombian politics in the wake of the European revolutions of 1848. Largely due to his Caribbean coastal origins, he was first associated with the liberal anticlerical faction. In 1853, as the twenty-eight-year-old vice-president of the House of Representatives, he signed the federalist constitution of that year which provided for separation of Church and state. After ten years, Núñez grew disillusioned with the radical liberal elements because of their failure to bring unity and order to the country. He did not, however, openly oppose the extreme liberal Constitution of 1863, though he managed to be absent for the signing of the document. For the next eleven years Núñez was abroad in New

From Rafael Núñez, "La paz científica," in *La reforma política en Colombia* (Bogotá, 1885), 97–104.

York, Le Havre, and Liverpool holding minor diplomatic posts and living in part by his pen. In Europe he was influenced by Spencer and the Social Darwinists and became a frank admirer of the stable English political system. On his return to Colombia in 1874 he associated himself with the moderate or independent wing of the Liberal Party, ran for the presidency in 1875, and was defeated by the Radical candidate. In 1879, however, he won the presidency (1880–82) and began to work for a constitutional reform, called by him "La Regeneración," which would counter the decentralized federalism of the 1863 Constitution. His campaign was conducted largely through an impressive series of over a hundred newspaper articles published between 1881 and 1884 and published together under the title, *Political Reform in Colombia*, in 1885.

Núñez believed that peace and internal security were requisite conditions for the nation's social, cultural, economic, and political progress. He attributed the relative backwardness of Colombia to the fact that political order within the country had been the exception and not the rule. He underscored this opinion with vigor in his article entitled, "Scientific Peace," published in 1882 and reprinted below, which made clear his belief that unbridled and divisive federalism was chiefly to blame. The rest of his essays ranged over the whole economic, social, political, and cultural life of the nation. Together they reveal Rafael Núñez as a moderate and as a statesman with perceptive abilities of a high order. How then did he become a caudillo?

In 1883, after waiting out the two-year term from which he was constitutionally barred, Núñez took his Independent Liberals into a coalition with the Conservatives and was nominated again for the presidency. Successful in the election for the 1884–1886 term, he was determined to achieve for Colombia the program he had sketched over the past three years. Núñez's shift to the right and the threat of centralization through constitutional revision provoked the Radical Liberals to revolt late in 1884. It was this brief and abortive rebellion that put in motion the events that turned President Núñez from constitutional statesman into arbitrary dictator. Impatient to enact his program, and with the revolt as a pretext, he hurried to cut the Gordian knot of slow but legal constitutional reform by supervising the abrogation of the

1863 Constitution. This act did, indeed, make possible the rapid substitution of the centralist Constitution of 1886, but it also destroyed the legitimate authority on which Núñez's office was based. In addition to this, when the constitutent assembly was called to draft the new constitution, the Radical Liberals were excluded. As will be noted in the essay that follows, the elimination of an opposition party had been one of the major complaints that Núñez had had with the Radicals during the 1860s and 1870s. "To reduce a political adversary to impotence is . . . to eliminate a cohesive element. . . ."

These twin decisions cost Núñez the achievement of the moderate regeneration he had hoped to obtain. Without an effective opposition, the Conservatives won firm control of the nation and worked a sharp reaction. The Constitution of 1886 demonstrates this fully: the formerly sovereign states were shorn completely of their power, even to the point of being redesignated "departments;" the four-year term Núñez had suggested earlier to replace the two year presidency was stretched to six, and the incumbent was provided with extraordinary powers including the right of appointment and removal of department governors; Núñez's early interest in the separation of Church and state was ignored, for the new charter proclaimed that "the Apostolic Roman Catholic Church is that of the Nation" and provided for the negotiation of a concordat with the Papacy.

A sensitive and articulate man, a fair poet, an effective prose stylist, and a capable politician, Rafael Núñez became a dictator in spite of himself. He acquiesced in a reaction which ran well beyond the politically moderate program he had proposed. Although nominal head of the state for most of the time until his death in 1894 and cloaked with enormous political authority, Núñez found the mantle of dictatorship uncomfortable. He retired frequently from the exercise of his office to leave the high altitude of Bogotá for his native coastal Cartagena. Age and ill health were clearly factors, but his ambition to retain power was also undercut by a nagging awareness that he had compromised his ideals to become a caudillo.

SINCE 1860, when the struggle between the old national parties began, a struggle which by 1863 . . . resulted in the complete triumph of liberalism, the Republic has not until now enjoyed a full presidential term of peace.

Between 1864 and 1866 there were three revolutions: one in Cundinamarca, another in Cauca, and one in Panama.

Between 1866 and 1868 there were the *coup d'etat* of General Mosquera, the counterrevolution led by General Acosta, and various local uprisings related to these two events.

Between 1868 and 1870 there were a revolution in Cundinamarca and another in Panama.

Between 1870 and 1872 there were one or two revolts in Boyacá and another in Cundinamarca.

Between 1872 and 1874 there was a series of insurrections in Panama and much unrest in Boyacá.

Between 1874 and 1876 there were disturbances and tumults throughout the Republic.

Between 1876 and 1878 there was a general civil war.

And from 1878 to 1880 there were upheavals in Panama, Antioquia, Cauca, Magdalena, and Tolima and widespread unrest.

It is only since 1880 that the country has experienced an atmosphere of perfect calm.

During the epoch between the dissolution of the old Colombia and 1860 there were six constitutional terms of four years each. Of those six terms peace prevailed only from 1845 to 1849 and . . . from 1855 to 1857.

In the course of our forty odd years of political life since 1832, the maintenance of domestic order has been the exception and civil war, the rule. In the meantime, various Constitutions have prevailed, to wit:

The moderately centralized Constitution of 1832;

The rigidly authoritarian Constitution of 1843;

The nearly federal Constitution of 1853;

The completely federal Constitution of 1858; and

The Constitution of 1863 that went so far along the path of decentralization as to embrace the fundamental principle of state sovereignty.

In undertaking the reform of each existing system, all parties doubtless believed that they were working effectively to secure, [civil] order; however, to judge from the obvious results this happy *desideratum* has not been realized since the days of the rigorously centralized Constitution of 1843.

But this Constitution was too alien to the country's dominant political feeling and to its topographic conditions for it to deserve credit as the only pacifying ingredient during the relatively long period that it was in effect. In fact it is my opinion that the intensity of the liberal reaction of . . . 1849 was due in part to the nature of the document.

If we set aside written institutions, however, in order to focus upon the effects of administrative policy assayed by the rulers, we discover that those men established policies in keeping with the national character so well that peace was maintained as a result.

The conservative administration of General Mosquera from 1845 to 1849 committed errors; but it was distinguished by the liberality with which it treated the vanquished and prostrate liberal party and by the practical guarantees which it accorded to popular suffrage.

The conservative administration of [Manuel María] Mallarino [1855–57] went further yet and with better faith along this road of generosity and foresight. In both periods, as I have said, utter peace reigned from one end of the country to the other. The administrations following those two were not characterized as tolerant and disorders occurred which were more or less general, deep-seated, and destructive.

The present administration was met by the animosities resulting from the continuous conflicts of the years 1878 to 1880; but the guarantees openly made to the conservative party, defeated in 1877 and powerless as Poland, have surely produced, for the third time, that yet rare phenomenon of a peaceful presidential term; and this without sacrificing any principles or political power.

Politics is an experimental science, like all the sciences of its kind; and if the same methods of governing, tried three times under different circumstances, have produced identical results in the preservation of order, we ought rightly to deduce that these methods of governing precisely suit the Republic and ought to be the norm for all governmental agents who wish not to release the maleficent spirit of armed discord.

But it is not only experience which counsels the adoption of a policy of conciliation to which we refer. There are, in short ample reasons which explain the fruitfulness of such a course.

Our principal parties are roughly balanced when it comes to numbers of supporters. The liberal party might be less in number but, on the other hand, it is more resolute and active. The proportion of our population which boasts some culture is slight, and the numbers of bureaucrats which that portion can supply is severely limited. The total exclusion of one party is, therefore, a major administrative error which borders upon immorality.

What is the result of such exclusion? In the first place, public service suffers from a deficiency of aptitudes. Second, many of the benefits of the competition of ideas and of healthy emulation in the conduct of public business are lost. Third, it is a fact that the domination of an oligarch [has] results which gradually undermine the fundamental principles of the established constitutional political system. Fourth, the political atmosphere becomes perverted by the spectacle of such illegitimate domination and individual consciences suffer the effects of this moral poisoning. The injustices practiced on high necessarily have their repercussions and reflections at the base of the pyramid. And finally, the leaders fall to quarrelling among themselves for lack of a counterpoise and behave ultimately like the soldiers of Cadmus who cut each other to pieces. Under such adverse circumstances . . . only a spark is necessary to produce an explosion in a society so disposed to experimentation.

It is especially important to note that since 1863 the greater part of our battles have been between members of the liberal party itself. Conflicts between liberals and conservatives have occurred only occasionally during the last eighteen years. It would seem, then, that the neutralization of our old adversaries is, in many ways, far from being a safety valve for us.

The desirable and necessary reorganization of the liberal party cannot be realized through speeches and ostentatious displays; and even less yet when everyone knows the artificial quality of the movement which is really quite opposed to the attainment of the stated objectives. . . . Some of our politicians fall frequently into the grave error of supposing that the national audience lacks the discernment to tell false notes from true ones; but the fact is that such discernment exists and the concord which so many legitimate interests demand, will not come unless a course of rectitude is sincerely adopted. Bile may be useful for something, but surely it is inadequate for the conciliation of our divergent wills.

The reorganization of a political party must begin with the unification of beliefs and with the frank pursuit in practice of the principles which compose the party creed; otherwise the simple pursuit of physical domination of the country is certain to corrupt and lead, sooner or later, to dissolution and anarchy. The reason for this is clear. Raw domination is, in essence, a business enterprise like any other, and since it does not offer tangible advantages for all partisans, those excluded from the fruits of exploitation will raise the banner of dissidence. By the nature of things men fall out as the magnetism of material benefits wanes unless, and only if, ideas unite them.

The fear of a common danger is another, though less durable, agent of party harmony. To reduce a political adversary to impotence is, then, to eliminate a cohesive element which might replace absent or diminishing moral bonds.

These are not paradoxes, but realities which have been encountered frequently throughout our agitated contemporary political history.

Whenever we or our closest friends express ourselves in these terms, others immediately try to suggest that we are bent upon turning down the road to conservatism. With like reasoning, the French revolutionaries . . . guillotined each other until the Empire came and concluded everything in a horrible Olympian carnival of blood. The conservatives know perfectly well that profound philosophical convictions separate them from us, yet for that very reason we must show only the most careful respect for their religious creed. What does unite us to their political community today is our sterling liberalism. This brand of liberalism leads us frequently to shield the conservatives against the intransigence [of the radical liberals] which threatens and persecutes us as well because of the plain fact . . . that we replaced them in running the government in response to the persistent will of a people long fatigued by years of violence. Such intransigence born of the lamentable wedding of overweening vanity and ambition would seem, to put it bluntly, the legacy of the Zipas [who ruled the Chibchas] and of the Kings of Spain.

The administrative policy of the present [Núñez] administration has been the result of serious reflection and of experience. Far from wishing to destroy the community to which men of good faith adhere, that policy would save it following the counsel of a rigorous and abundant logic. The evidence of our progress along the path of salvation is already manifest everywhere. If shortsighted men would only compare 1873, 1875, and 1879 with 1881 they must realize that the harsh mountain of hatred has been reduced to a negotiable hill. Still the drums of revolt beat again and from time to time new alarums run the spectrum of absurdity; but the battalions do not respond, only a few professional rebels and small squads of caudillos heed the call to arms. The mass of the people remain confident and tranquil.

13

Carlos Octavio Bunge
Caciquismo in Our America

A product of the late nineteenth century, the Argentine sociologist, novelist, and educator, Carlos Octavio Bunge (1875–
1918), first published *Our America* in 1903. The book went
through many editions; the following selections are from the
sixth edition, to which Bunge's brilliant contemporary, José
Ingenieros, contributed a long introduction. Influential and
popular because of its virulent attack on Spanish character
and because it evoked the Social Darwinist and Positivist
thought then in vogue, *Our America* provides for us an important insight into the fin-de-siècle pattern by which the phenomenon of caudillismo was explained and justified to contemporaries. Bunge found the Spaniards chiefly to blame for
the "cacicability" of the Latin Americans, but, from his bla-
tantly racist perspective, he also charged that Indian and black
admixtures had produced resignation, sadness, laziness, and
decadence to go with Spanish arrogance. Bunge, however, was
confident that Argentina could expect a bright future based
on energy and progress because so many white European immigrants were flooding into the country. On the other hand,
he hurled no moral anathemas at such a contemporary dictatorship as that of Porfirio Díaz (1876–1911), which he held to
be a "blessed despotism" and a relatively successful attempt
to bring order and progress to what he considered an innately
slothful mestizo society.

THE politico-philosophical conception of the republic, understood as a democratic society whose citizens possess not only the
right but also the duty of governing the *res publica* by means of
representatives elected for that purpose, is essentially European.
It was born in Greece from whence it passed to Rome. It was the

From Carlos Octavio Bunge, *Nuestra América: ensayo de psicología social*, 6th
ed. (Buenos Aires: Casa Vacarro, 1918), 224–48.

great innovation which Europe contributed to ancient history, reacting to the autocracies of the Orient; it was some sort of *prechristian Christianity* since it advanced the principle of equality, if not for all men at least for those citizens who composed the nation. The republic is, therefore, neither Asiatic nor African but rather a severely European institution belonging only to the purest of European races. . . . Even though in the Middle Ages monarchic forms were adopted, these monarchies were more republican than they were autocratic; the republican principle remained latent in the people, and was revealed in communal liberties, parliaments, guilds, and so forth. England was always a monarchic republic; she forced her kings to agree to the Magna Carta and she executed Charles I. . . . Switzerland is a typical republic. In the Germanic states and the countries of the North, the most absolute princes respect certain popular liberties. In France, the Revolution demonstrates that beneath monarchic despotism there throbbed profound republican sentiments. Even in Italy certain aristocratic republics, which were *sui generis*, persisted through the medieval centuries.

It is only just to note that neither in Spain nor in Portugal was absolutism confused with tyranny. The caesarist principle of the *princeps legisbus solutus* [the prince is unrestrained by law] had few defenders, and was generally fought by theologians and canonists who sustained the opposite doctrine, accepted by canon law: *princeps tenentur et ipsi vivere legisbus suis* [the princes themselves are also bound to live according to their own laws]. The decline of the admirably democratic organization of the twelfth- and thirteenth-century councils was the result of multiple causation. Among these causes ought to be weighed the influence of Moorish blood which *Africanized* the population of the Peninsula to a certain point. Alexander Dumas, a mulatto who well understood the character of the Africans because of his own psychological affinity, once coined a graphic phrase when he said, with that insolence and exageration common to his ethnic bastardy, "Europe ends at the foot of the Pyrenees." In spite of this, Charles I and Philip II contrived to reduce communal freedoms and privileges only after extensive bloody fighting. . . .

On the other hand, we know that the [precolumbian] indigenous Americans were quite as absolute as the most powerful oriental autocracies; and we know that the African Negroes bore their servility to their fierce petty kings to such a degree as to speak to them only when prostrate, to kiss their footsteps, and to eat their excrement!

Adding together the Afro-Hispanic antecedents (although these were not of decisive importance) and the Indian experience, it is difficult if not impossible to suppose that democracies might have been improvised with success in Latin America after independence. The cabildos were the only bastions of the ancient Spanish communal liberties, and they were most certainly shabby bastions! On the other hand, the North American people at the time of independence possessed a certain republican individualism in their ideas, in their customs, in their institutions, and in their blood dating back to Caesar and Hamilcar, even to prehistoric times! For them, the republic is natural, original, and pertinent; among the Spanish Americans it must be perforce imitative, conventional, and hybrid . . . and so it is that "no people can be great unless it cultivates its own character"; I almost prefer for "Our America" the satrapies of caciques which are open, honest, and unmasked. Were it possible, I would even use ancient Indian names! . . . Let us be true to ourselves! . . .

The *cacicability* of each Spanish American nation is in inverse proportion to its degree of European blood. For this reason the tyranny of Rosas over Buenos Aires, which was the most European of the Spanish American states, was also the bloodiest in Hispanic American history. . . . Mexico, in contrast to Buenos Aires, is perhaps the most Indian country in America and there the despotism of Porfirio Díaz has been the most pacific and most prolonged.

One would suppose that the cacique, in order to possess the requisite psychology, ought always to be either mestizo or mulatto. A pessimist might think that the position would be repugnant to a pure European, that political success in the Spanish American countries is dependent upon being more or less swarthy. Such is not the case. The strong race is always the white race. And, given the human vanity of the European, the white man is tempted to play the cacique quite as much as any Mandingo, which explains well enough why some thoroughly pure Goths have disguised themselves and, crowned with brilliant plumes, have grasped a lance bloody to the hilt in order to rule. . . .

I find [a related] key to the curious Hispanic American phenomenon of caudillismo or caciquismo in collective sloth. Among indolent people it is easy for the most active to be outstanding. Then the rabble, composed of those citizens who are too apathetic to think and to act for themselves and take responsibilities, gladly abrogate their sovereignty. . . . To whom? To him whose qualties best inspire confidence and who knows best how to capture the sympathy of everyone. . . . Is he the most able? One presumes so; but he need not be as long as he is the most feared and beloved.

Although it is in the best interest of everyone to entrust the plumed spear of symbolic authority to the most competent, it is in the best interest of the individual, who wishes to thrive in the shadow of power, to have a close personal friend for governor. It is for this reason that caciquismo sometimes produces regimes of the most shameful compliance. A cacique must have friendships before personal merits and he must maintain them in order to maintain himself in power. But what about such things as laws, the national wealth, progress? They matter little if there is no social pressure to combat degeneration and injustice! . . .

In the career of a cacique there is always an initial stage in which he deceives the mob with feigned and superficial virtues. . . . Once securely in power, it is customary to strip himself of such appearances as one might remove an uncomfortable suit of clothes which restrains one's movements. Once the first praiseworthy and virtuous impression is made, the verdict is in and it is irreversible because the public will no longer take the trouble to revise the first impression. . . . Why bother to investigate, to revise judgement, perhaps to condemn? It would be a great deal of work; it is much easier for one to be quiet; and, far better yet, to serve and to flatter the cacique . . . because the reward, at once received, would recompense his whole clan, man for man. . . . There is no concern for independence or individual strife. Such implies individual effort which is so often arduous and really the province of commerce, industry, the arts and sciences; the object of life is, after all, rest and relaxation. . . . The gods have created men that they might watch them repose in elegance. If the sheep rest more than the shepherd, let us be sheep not shepherds! . . .

It would be a great error to suppose that caciquismo must always be a retrograde and tumultuous system. Caciquismo is not anarchy, nor tyranny, nor reaction; it is simply laziness, nothing more than laziness. Only in abnormal times has the cacique appeared, as in the eyes of Sarmiento, like a spectre enveloped in a tattered red poncho brandishing his lance as if it were a scythe.

It may be that the genesis of caciquismo was in anarchy; but, in the course of the evolution of American history, it has acquired a pacific form, perhaps the most pacific of demagogic and even democratic governments. . . . By "pacific" I mean that the conflict of ideas and of parties is avoided; whatever agitation there is, is reduced to personal feuds between one cacique and another. The people, restrained by their incurable native indolence, will leave them to fight it out, unperturbed, as simple spectators who do not commit themselves in advance to the triumph of one or the other. Such is the nature of the *civilized caciquismo* of our modern age, so thoroughly in contrast to that of our medieval period. It is a long distance from Facundo Quiroga to Porfirio Díaz!

14
Luis González
The Dictatorship of Porfirio Díaz

The Mexican caudillo, Porfirio Díaz, was effective master of his country from 1876, when he first assumed the presidency, until he was ousted by the Revolution in 1911. Few caudillos in Spanish American history wielded their power more pervasively—to a point—or provoked a more profound reaction in their societies when they fell than did Díaz. In spite of the fact that his thirty-five-year dictatorship has been meticulously studied, scholars disagree about how best to assess Don Porfirio. Among the most trenchant analyses of the Porfiriato, as the era is known, is that by Luis González, one of the deans of Mexican historiography. González is best known for his prize-winning microhistory of a rural community, *San José de Gracia: Mexican Village in Transition* (1974). As readers will discover, he writes with grace and wit. The essay, of which this excerpt is the conclusion, is not only a penetrating critique of the Díaz epoch, but it also explores with sensitivity the nature of dictatorship. Thus it adds to our store of perspectives and definitions.

Included in González's remarkable insights is his insistence that Díaz was such an ardent patriot that "the mass of the population . . . developed a vigorous nationalism" in his time that is the base for "the patriotic liturgy prevalent today." He further argues that while much is made of the censorship which prevailed in Mexico and which is attributed to the "omnipotent dictator," "the greatest censorship . . . was due to the dominant orthodoxy among the people." At least until the aging dictator began to lose his deft control during the last decade of his rule, the González analysis suggests the patterns Eric Fromm explored in his *Escape from Freedom*. In his effort to find a place in the spectrum of authoritarian rule for the

From Luis González, "La dictadura de Díaz," in *Dictaduras y dictadores*, edited by Julio Labastida Martín del Campo (México: Siglo Vientiuno, 1986), 161–78. Reprinted with permission.

Porfirato, González concludes that the Díaz regime was neither a tyranny nor a paternalistic state. It was, however, a dictatorship because, by his definition, it was "structurally evil [and hence] destructive of liberty."

[DÍAZ'S death in 1915] closed out his chance to shape any further the historical judgment of *la dictadura porfírica,* or the Porfirian tyranny, as his greatest enemies call it, or the patriarchy of Don Profirio, according to the accounts of his sympathizers. If by tyranny we mean a form of corrupt, cruel government without laws, ruled by the tyrant's caprices which work only for his advantage and that of his lackeys, then certainly the Porfirian regime was not tyrannical. If we call a government patriarchal or paternal where a "Papá" reigns with profound love for the people whom he considers his children, an indulgent, sentimental, and benevolent progenitor who, when he punishes someone, says, "it hurts me more than it does you," the Díaz government did not know how to nor did it wish to achieve the tenderness of paternalism. Perhaps this was because military fathers are by nature more rigorous than run-of-the-mill fathers. We are dealing with a regime which never contradicted the ideals of liberalism, but which never conceded the label of liberal democracy.

The Díaz regime was a dictatorship, which is to say a style of government concentrated in one person or group, less inhuman than a tyranny and more rigid than a paternalistic rule, which is apt to emerge in order to rectify a chaotic or warlike situation. According to Eduardo Haro, a dictatorial government "is centered essentially in the person of the dictator, to whom one must attribute every merit . . . and which is above [the laws and the spirit of the laws] . . . and is capable of repudiating and modifying them." Dictatorship is something which is opposed to the ideal that no one should govern or direct anyone else, and there are many styles which correspond to this. In this light there are dictatorial regimes which only impose the dictates of the proletariat; others, bourgeois doctrines; still others, the imperatives of the aristocracy, and, above all, the ideals of a church or an army. There are gold-braided [oropelescas], vulgar, and romantic dictatorships like that of Don Antonio López [de Santa Anna] and classical types like the Porfírica. Corrupt ones abound and stoic ones are scarce; the former take advantage of the people in order to enrich themselves and the latter to construct pedestals. Dictatorships which come through like lightning are less frequent than those of long duration. According to the times either they comport themselves with generosity or they are spy ridden and oppressive. None are morally good.

The Porfírica dictatorship refrained from being revolutionary and in the service of the proletariat on the one hand, and of being conservative and submissive to the interests of the feudal class on the other. Some friendly gestures for the workers and for the great landholders were insufficent to grant the dictatorship either the title of a labor government or that of the landed elite. In balance it was neither at odds with clerical powers nor was it a religious dictatorship. Only during the first decade was it somewhat praetorian. If it served any group at all, this was the bourgeoisie or capitalists and, for that reason, the epithet which fits best is bourgeois or liberal dictatorship. Some adjectives which also apply include durable, nationalist with cosmopolitan trimmings, honest or nearly so, persecutorial, and authoritarian.

The Díaz dictatorship "had lasted longer than nature would seem to permit," as Alfonso Reyes put it, but that was during a historical cycle when it was fashionable for governments to grow very old, as in the cases of the reigns of Queen Victoria in the United Kingdom, Franz Joseph in Austria, Mutsu Hito [in Japan], Christian IX in Denmark, Alfonso XII in Spain, Abdul Hamid II in Turkey, and Leo XIII in the Vatican. . . .

The extraordinarily long rule of Díaz sought not to be autarkical; it never thought to isolate itself from the world, to close its doors and shutters to investors, ideologues, artistic currents, and external fashions. It is said, with reason, that it loosened up in order to attract money and immigrants, Positivism in its French and British forms, and French fashions in dress, food, homes, mirrors, sofas, and decorations. Not only the dictator but those who made up the elite of the dictatorship during its zenith and its sunset considered themselves scrutinized by the outside world, and they desired that the powerful and famous nations would look upon them without contempt, that the blond people of Europe and the North would feel themselves at ease in their homes, that the influx of opera companies and modistes de Paris would be constant, that our architects would find inspiration in the art nouveau and that our authors would follow the footsteps of Zola, Hugo, and Baudelaire. The Porfirian elite was unquestionably anxious to be worldly. However, side by side with the vice of *extranjerismo* [fondness for foreign culture], the virtue of nationalism grew vigorously, especially among the lower classes. Porfirio Díaz was profoundly patriotic and he eagerly sought to give shape to his country. Díaz, unlike any president before him, fulminated against regionalism in the name of national unity. Thanks to the nationalist propaganda of the Porfiriato, the mass of the population, which had not known nor felt themselves to be Mexican in previous epochs, developed a vigorous nationalism during la Porfírica. The patriotic liturgy prevalent today is the work of the Porfiriato. Between then and now there have only been the addition of some names to the patriotic hagiography, a few dates to the calendar of patriotic holidays, and technological advances to the complex liturgy of speeches, campaigns, cheers, fireworks, parades, floral offerings, [and] allegorical floats . . . with which we are accustomed to venerate and corrupt our flag.

Don Porfirio was nationalist and honest in spite of the fact that the chorus of científicos and more than a few of their comrades in arms were neither one nor the other. The social crème de la crème adored the golden calf. The governing class devoted their working hours to lucrative business affairs and their leisure ones to the life of the parvenu. The liberal elite was well disposed to make itself rich. The chief sins of the new social cream were concupiscence, avarice, greed, as well as the unbridled search for comfort, but Porfirio Díaz was the exception in his own way. He was also a porphyry obstacle against a picaresque administration, a dike against those desirous of enriching themselves from the public treasury. Dishonesty among public servants is not the most notable characteristic of the Porfiriato. There were shameless sorts, principally among the científicos, but they were not the thieves who set the tone of the Porfírica dictatorship. We should remember, with Fuentes Mares, that the Porfiriato, before its decadence, was very "honest."

There is heavy emphasis on the rigid censorship practiced in the days of Don Porfirio, and it is customary to attribute the gag to the omnipotent dictator. The greatest censorship, however, was due to the dominant orthodoxy among the people. These preferred order when it was demonstrated that it did not comport well with liberty. The majority agreed to do without many liberties in exchange for pacification. In economics, however, the principle of laissez faire was scrupulously respected to the point of injustice. From the point of view of the workers each day brought less opportunity for organization, strikes, and protest. In the field of labor the dictatorship was increasingly persecutorial. In the field of religion, the opposite was true; public worship in the streets and plazas was reestablished [after the ban on such activity during the Reform]. As with the Church, reconciliation with conservative political enemies was public and notorious. There were restrictions on things having to do with gambling and the prohibition of bullfights and cockfights. The opposition press never circulated in the light of day. The championship for the absence of liberties, however, was won without question by women. Domestic morality was highly puritan and restrictive.

The Porfírica autocracy is a mixture of the concentration of power in a single superior will, of noncompliance and respect for the law, of voluntary abandonment of criticism on the part of intellectuals, of official censorship, of generalized indifference toward elections, and of arbitrary nomination *[por dedazo]* of those responsible for legislation and for compliance with the laws in the states and municipalities. Don Porfirio gathered more personal power than any other ruler of independent Mexico. According to the words of Alfonso Reyes, "the great caudillo animated by unreproachable love for his country has charge of the conscience of everyone. Even the morality of individuals depends upon his decisions. . . ." Presidential cabinet ministers, Supreme Court justices, deputies and senators of the Congress of the Union, governors of the federal entities, army generals, bishops, legislatures, city councils, and every mother's son endeavors to conform his tastes to those of the caudillo and can do no other than to grow pale and even tremble before his august presence, majestically erect, with arrogant glances to the right and left, with a threatening voice and few words. For never having been given to tears or sentimental, Don Porfirio would have given the impression of being made of porphyry.

If there could have been good dictatorships, that of Díaz would deserve the judgement of kind *[bondadoso]*. However, as dictatorships are structurally evil because they are destructive of liberty, they put in doubt the intelligence of the people; foment cruelty, idiocy, discipline, and servility, and promote the robotizing of human beings. The dictatorship of Díaz can only aspire to the title of relatively less evil, less spectacular than that of Napoleon Bonaparte; less harsh than oriental despotisms; not as cruel as those of Hitler and Stalin nor as idiotic as that of some Hispanoamerican dictators today.

marina   marques
                                         thlaca

Above, Fernando Cortés (1485–1547), one of the earliest caudillos in Spanish America, manipulates Moctezuma through his emissary *(right)* with the vital aid of his interpreter and lover, Doña Marina or Malinche, in 1519. The print is from Diego Durán, *Historia de las Indias. (Courtesy Carol Maturo) Left*, The Mexican priest Miguel Hidalgo (1753–1811), with Ignacio Allende and others in his network beside him, exhorts his followers in September 1810 with his Grito de Dolores. The print is by José Guadalupe Posada. *(Collection of Hugh M. Hamill)*

Felix Calleja (1753–1828), a Mexicanized Spaniard married into the creole elite, rallied his local network in San Luis Potosí to create an army that thwarted Hidalgo's insurgents in January 1811. He was viceroy 1813–1816. *(Collection of Hugh M. Hamill)*

Simón Bolívar (1783–1830) achieved his successes as Liberator of Gran Colombia through his supercaudillo qualities and suffered his defeats at the hands of the regional caudillos whom he could not control. *(Organization of American States)*

José Antonio Páez (1790–1873), the Venezuelan Llanero, helped Bolívar defeat the Spanish, but asserted his own caudillaje to make Venezuela independent in 1830. He dominated the politics of the early republic. *(Organization of American States)*

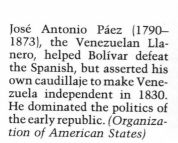

Juan Nepomuceno Moreno (?–1839), a caudillo who served under Bolívar, came out of the Llanos of Colombia in 1831 in an aborted attempt to impose himself and his region's interests on the politicians of Bogotá. *(Courtesy Jane Rausch)*

Juan José Flores (1801–64), a Venezuelan follower of Bolívar who became first president of Ecuador in 1830, was a caudillo committed to the belief that monarchy was most appropriate for Spanish America. *(Organization of American States)*

José Gaspar Rodríguez de Francia (1766–1840), better known as Dr. Francia, "El Supremo," masterminded not only Paraguay's independence from Spain but also from Buenos Aires (in 1811 to 1813). Among the shrewdest of caudillos, Francia ruled Paraguay until 1840. *(Organization of American States)*

Juan Manuel de Rosas (1793–1877), most famous of Argentine gaucho caudillos, dominated the La Plata region from 1829 to 1832 and from 1835 to 1852. The obligatory wearing of red, and other psychological warfare tactics, fostered nationalism under Rosas. *(Organization of American States)*

José Rafael Carrera (1814–65) was the dominant force in Guatemala from 1839 until his death. A folk caudillo, he promoted the traditional interests of Indians against the Liberal pressures to modernize. *(Bettmann/Hulton)*

Antonio López de Santa Anna (1794–1876) as an old man, about the time he made his final—and fruitless—effort to return to power in Mexico in 1867. His role as a military caudillo was greatest between 1833 and 1855. *(Organization of American States)*

Francisco Solano López (1826–70), an ambitious Paraguayan caudillo with a fanatical following, led his country into a heroic but suicidal war against Argentina, Brazil, and Uruguay (1864–70). *(Organization of American States)*

Rafael Núñez (1825–94), a Liberal Colombian politician and essayist from coastal Cartagena, served as president from 1880 to 1882 and from 1884 to 1894. Disillusioned by federalism, he shifted toward conservative centralism and became a reluctant caudillo in the process. *(Organization of American States)*

Porfirio Díaz (1830–1915), about the time he first became president of Mexico in 1876. This portrait of Díaz in his prime suggests the character of the most successful of Mexican caudillos in a different way from the next, more familiar picture. *(Organization of American States)*

Porfirio Díaz as an octogenarian, just before his overthrow in May 1911 during the first stages of the Mexican Revolution. Compare his appearance in uniform with his unadorned civilian appearance thirty-five years earlier. *(Library of Congress)*

Victoriano Huerta (1854–1916), the Mexican caudillo who ousted Madero from the presidency in February 1913, is here surrounded by his staff at the time of the U.S. invasion of Veracruz in April 1914. *(UPI/Bettmann)*

Alvaro Obregón (1880–1928) and Pancho Villa (1877–1923), two of Mexico's most formidable caudillos, meet with U.S. General John Pershing at El Paso in August 1914, soon after Huerta's defeat. *(UPI/Bettmann Newsphotos)*

Juan Vicente Gómez (1857–1935) used his political finesse, managerial ability, oil profits, and ruthless repression of dissidents to master Venezuela from 1908 until his death. *(Library of Congress)*

GENERALISIMO RAFAEL L. TRUJILLO M.
Benefactor de la Patria

Rafael Leonidas Trujillo Molina (1891–1961), the nearly totalitarian caudillo who dominated the Dominican Republic for thirty years, appears here in a 1938 portrait as the "Benefactor," a title that baffled Jesús de Galíndez. *(Library of Congress)*

Left, The Monumento a la Paz de Trujillo, finished in 1954, commemorates the achievements of the "Benefactor" during his first quarter-century in power. It towers two hundred feet above the city of Santiago. *(Library of Congress) Below,* Trujillo was skillful in the cultivation of foreign relations, especially with the United States. Here he welcomes Vice-President Richard Nixon with an *abrazo* during Nixon's visit to the Dominican Republic on March 1, 1955. *(UPI/Bettmann)*

Above, Anastasio "Tacho" Somoza García (1896–1956) of Nicaragua, quite as skillful as Trujillo in foreign relations, here receives a medal of honor from Mayor Vincent Impellitteri *(left)* in New York City in June 1952. His astute wife Salvadora ("Yoya") watches Mrs. Impellitteri. *(Library of Congress) Right*, Juan Domingo Perón (1895–1974) and Eva Duarte de Perón (1919–52), the year before she died of cancer. He is holding two toy-pistol cigarette lighters presented to him by a visiting U.S. publisher. *(UPI/Bettmann)*

Marcos Pérez Jiménez (1914–) was nurtured in the military system of Venezuela's Juan Vicente Gómez. Although quite as oppressive as Gómez, he lacked the master's skills during his dictatorship from 1952 to 1958. *(Organization of American States)*

Francisco Franco (1892–1975), who proudly claimed the title of "El Caudillo," poses on April 1, 1954, for an official portrait to mark the fifteenth anniversary of the end of the Spanish Civil War (1936–39) that brought him to power. *(Library of Congress)*

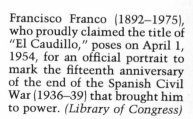

Anastasio "Tachito" Somoza Debayle (1925–80), a cardiac patient, exercises in his fortified bunker in January 1979, six months before he was ousted from Nicaragua by the Sandinista Revolution. *(UPI/Bettmann)*

Fidel Castro (1926–), uses his oratorical gifts to exercise his leadership authority in a speech on July 26, 1984, to 100,000 people, marking the thirty-first anniversary of the beginning of the Cuban Revolution. *(UPI/Bettmann)*

Augusto Pinochet (1915–), who used the role as chief of staff of the Chilean army to exert power after the overthrow of Salvador Allende in 1973, here shows how fit he is to govern on his seventieth birthday. *(UPI/Bettmann)*

Alfredo Stroessner (1912–) of Paraguay, seated on the right in this picture, enjoys the company of Generalísimo Franco *(middle)*, and Prince Juan Carlos *(left)* after a state dinner in Madrid in 1973. Franco died two years later; Stroessner endured in power until 1989. *(UPI/Bettmann)*

Manuel Noriega (1938–) celebrates his survival after an aborted coup by rebel officers in Panama in October 1989. Two months later Noriega was ousted from power in the U.S. invasion. *(Reuters/ Bettmann Newsphotos)*

15
John J. Johnson
Foreign Factors

Thus far the nature of caudillismo has been explored primarily as an internal or domestic problem in Spanish America. In this essay John Johnson examines factors which are external, or "foreign," by which the author means "nondomestic or nonnational as opposed to nonregional." Stressing the roles that immediate neighbor states as well as more distant powers, especially European and North American, have played in the continuum of dictatorial absolutism, the author suggests that subtle external influences, such as bank loans and philosophical systems, may have been as important as more direct pressures. Although this essay focuses primarily on the nineteenth century and was written from the immediate post-World War II perspective, readers will find much of enduring relevance. Johnson's discussion of political exile, for example, with the attendant "menace of political malcontents operating from neighboring states" and the consequent need to meet the emergency by increasing "the already multiple powers of the chief executive," has obvious relevance to recent Central American history.

John Johnson's distinguished career has included the managing editorship of *The Hispanic American Historical Review* and the authorship of several influential books, among which *Political Change in Latin America* (1958), with its focus on the "middle sectors" in the society, and *Latin America in Caricature* (1980) are best known.

[A]MONG an important segment of Latin Americans who concern themselves with the problem of dictatorship, foreign factors, when considered, are most often those originating outside Latin

From John J. Johnston, "Foreign Factors in Dictatorship in Latin America," © 1951 by Pacific Coast Branch, American Historical Assn. Reprinted from *Pacific Historical Review* 20, No. 2 (May 1951): 127–41, by permission.

America, rather than those foreign to any one given nation. In this study the term *foreign* will be considered as nondomestic or nonnational, as opposed simply to nonregional. . . . Two types of factors will be considered—those emanating from the outside and . . . which the peoples of the individual nations were more or less helpless in controlling, and those coming from the outside but which were or are due to the practices and thinking of the peoples who go to make up the separate states.

Much has been made of the failure of certain European countries and the United States to give adequate material and moral support to the cause of Latin American independence between the years 1810 and 1825. . . . On the other hand, the British loans of the mid-1820s have received relatively little attention. Actually, it would appear that those loans did as much to promote the cause of dictatorship in Latin America as any single factor originating outside the area up to that time. And in retrospect it is perhaps not too harsh to say that England did several of the new republics a gross injustice by making funds available to them—an injustice on at least three counts. The loans were made because there was a vast surplus of investment capital resulting in lower interest rates in England and not because the investors were misinformed as to conditions in South America; in fact a number of volumes and articles in English had appeared which objectively presented the situation and pointed out the inherent dangers. A greater injustice stemmed from the fact that at the very time when the chief executives in the various nations, personalists by nature and representatives of minority groups, should have been forced to go to their own peoples for support, they were in several instances freed from that responsibility by the British loans. The first crop of strong men quickly comprehended how much easier it would be to grant concessions to foreigners in return for loans than to derive revenue by taxing those who controlled the wealth. That the leaders learned the lesson well is evidenced by the number who came to power and retained it by means of hazardous borrowing abroad.

Finally, British merchants followed British pounds—merchants who were anti-Catholic, merchants who were accustomed to English law and who soon wearied of the legal maneuvers of the people with whom they were dealing, merchants who came to disdain the very people with whom they were carrying on commerce. A flourishing trade was the desire of the businessman, and just as the dictator learned the advantage of foreign loans, so the foreign trader quickly appreciated the virtues of authoritarian government.

The British loans did not save the young republics from economic chaos. Payments were soon discontinued on interest as well as on principal. It was not long before there developed in England an unhealthy collective concept: "Latin America." Embittered by financial losses and apparently vastly ignorant regarding the area, they made little effort to distinguish between Argentine and Chilean, between Peruvian and Bolivian. To the Englishman the Latin American peoples were all the same, all anarchic, untrustworthy, and ruled by despots concerned only with their own welfare and that of their coteries. London investment brokers turned their backs on the struggling nations, not to return in most cases until midcentury. It was a generation later (ca. 1880) before British capital was joined by that from the United States. For several decades thereafter English and United States capitalists and technicians, welcomed by the various Latin American government officials who mortgaged the future of their countries in the belief that the problem of communications was to be solved, concentrated on the construction of railroads. Latin America was doomed to be disappointed. Money was raised abroad. Valuable technical knowledge was supplied which made possible some of the great engineering feats of the nineteenth century. But it would be difficult to prove that funds or technical advice were utilized in the best interests of the recipients. At the end of the fifty-year railroad-building spree, Latin America awoke to the fact that proffered assistance from Europe and the United States had contributed little to the developmental pattern. Each nation had railroad lines, with varying gauges, in most cases leading from the interior to the nearest port, so that raw materials could be shipped more easily to Europe and the United States. Not a single country in Latin America had a railroad system.

Mexico's predicament is illustrative. Under the dictator Porfirio Díaz a series of north-south lines was constructed which directed the wealth of Mexico away from the political center and served primarily as feeders for the east-west lines across the United States.

If economic dislocation is a factor conducive to dictatorship, as it surely is, then the responsibility of the foreigner concerned with railroad building is large, how large it is impossible to say. Certainly there is plenty of evidence that the foreigners who shared in the program regarded the various nations as economic colonies of Europe and the United States rather than as sovereign powers.

Of the foreign factors accounting for dictatorship and for which the several Latin American countries themselves must assume a considerable degree of responsibility, the most obvious is perhaps diplomatic asylum and its corollary, exile. Diplomatic asylum, in a sense a form of extraterritoriality, by the eighteenth century played a decreasingly important role in the relations of nations with a Western European background. However, with the rise of the Latin American republics the institution took a new lease on life. . . .

One of the earliest grounds for upholding asylum and exile stemmed from the rigid caste system, carried over from the period of Spanish domination. The jails and prisons—poorly constructed and with few provisions for sanitation and comfort—were unfit, or so it was thought, for the elite of society; and it was this group for whom diplomatic asylum was almost wholly reserved. Tied to this argument was that of the economic plight of the new states. The construction of prisons strong enough to retain a prisoner and at the same time comfortable enough for persons of the upper stratum was beyond the financial means of the embryonic republics.

Coincidental with these considerations was the more widely used defense of saving the most capable man power. . . . In the ensuing struggles for power, diplomatic asylum and exile seemed to offer the surest and most economical means of conserving the ruling class. The loser, whether morally right or wrong, was assured a place of retreat so long as asylum was respected. Protected by a foreign flag, he could await the cooling of tempers, marking time while in most cases arrangements were made for his passage into exile.

Each of the arguments presented above was openly espoused and had merits, but it would appear from the records that while they were offered to the populace as warrantable reasons for clemency, a self-survival rather than a moral, economic, or social basis ordinarily was the primary cause for tolerating asylum and exile. Each leader was aware that in the next shuffle of the cards the help of the lately defeated statesman or ousted warrior might be needed desperately. Furthermore, the victor was not oblivious to the fact that it paid to set a good example. If he displayed leniency in triumph he might more rightly expect mercy in adversity. Nor was it likely that in an area where political changes came at an amazing pace, the man temporarily on top could forget that it was probably his predecessor who had said, "I have the choice of respecting asylum and eventually letting my enemies go into exile or shooting them."

The step from asylum into exile was short and exile has contributed time and again to dictatorship in the countries to the south. With the opposition perched across the border, the individual commanding at home could see real and imaginary threats to the fatherland. One method commonly seized upon to meet emergencies in Latin America has been to increase the already multiple powers of the chief executive. In more cases than not the person in control thus has been able to meet the menace of political malcontents operating from neighboring states; moreover, in cases of failure, his successors usually found it advisable to assume dictatorial power. That is only part of the story. The chief executive, in preparing to meet the danger from the outside, frequently increased the military strength of his country. Then, if the perils did not materialize, an enlarged armed force was left without a major assignment, reluctant, nevertheless, to be demobilized. This posed a thorny problem for the president. Too often he sought to solve it by stirring up trouble with the neighboring state by accusing it of harboring or giving encouragement to elements hostile to the established order. Impending war or war itself has resulted. In either case the defense of the honor of the country made it possible for the ruler to strengthen his position, while increased tensions served to divert attention from unpleasant realities at home. Nor has it been too unusual for the army to find its own way out of the dilemma by overthrowing the incumbent and seizing power for one of its own leaders.

The extent to which the Latin Americans can be held responsible for dictatorship resulting from asylum and exile can be fairly definitely established. On a slightly different level of responsibility are some factors contributing to dictatorship which have resulted from the inclination of the official and upper-class Latin American to imitate the United States and certain countries of Europe. . . .

Throughout the nineteenth century many of the elite of the various republics received their education in Europe, and today that same class is taking advantage of opportunities in the United States. This means that the formative years of many of the leaders of Latin America—political, literary, social, and economic—have been spent away from their home countries.

A considerable number of those who went overseas for their training or simply for travel became imbued with new ideas which they later wanted to see applied in their native lands. It is a truism that much of what they absorbed was not adaptable to the social and political environment of their homelands. . . . Decade after decade [after independence] the influences of foreign education continued to be felt in various ways, until finally no less an authority than the great Argentine thinker, Juan Bautista Alberdi, rose vindictively against scholars trained abroad. Writing in the 1870s he charged a section of them and their disciples with fomenting civil discord and, because of their advocacy of local autonomy, held them largely responsible for the continuance of the federalist-centralist struggle which was plaguing much of the area. In the opinion of Alberdi the Latin American youth who went abroad to study often came almost wholly under the influences of professors who were far removed from the realities of life, who were enthralled by radical theories, and who were often rabid champions of decentralization. After making this observation, Alberdi concluded that "the youth whose mind is molded in this school, in these ideas, returns to America a demagogue in every sense of the term, a bachelor in revolutions, a seditionist by principle."

It should be noted that Alberdi's concern is, by implication, primarily with the foreign-trained intellectual as a rabble-rousing idealist eager to reform his fatherland. He does not accuse his villain of being a dictator, because after the first wave of despots, several of whom had European experiences, the foreign-trained scholar ordinarily did not assume that role. Rather he was the "disloyal opposition" who in playing the part of agitator afforded those who opposed him additional grounds for appropriating dictatorial powers. . . .

Latin America has felt the impact of many philosophies originating in Europe, but of those that have influenced the politics of the republics, the Positivism of Auguste Comte seems to have contributed most directly to dictatorship. Francisco García Calderón, Peruvian literary figure and diplomat, writing shortly before the turn of the nineteenth century, stated that Positivism was then the dominant political philosophy in Latin America. After emphasizing the appeal of Comte's "law and order" to the political factions, he added that, "Minds formed by Catholicism, even if they have lost their faith, demand secular dogmas, and verities organized in a facile system: in short, a new faith, and the positivist philosophy satisfies that craving. At the same time material progress, based upon scientific development, and the utilitarianism which exaggerates the importance of wealth, find in positivism, which disdains futile ideologies, a system adequate to industrial life."

Of the [Spanish American] nations where [Comte's] philosophy met with acceptance, Mexico experienced the most noticeable impact. Brought [there] in modified form during the presidency of Benito Juárez, Positivism's emphasis on order and progress was construed to serve the ends of the new ruling class that had emerged during the 1850s. Its provision for a type of Social Darwinism admirably served the ends of the select and arrogant members of the cult generally referred to as the científicos. The self-made materialists comprising the group after the midnineties played a prominent role in shaping the thinking of the aging Porfirio Díaz.

Order, efficiency, improvement were their slogans, and were to be achieved at any cost to the nation—and the price was high. It is certain that for a decade and a half the científicos kept Mexico on the road to material progress, but it is extremely doubtful whether they were fully aware of the social implications of the change from an agricultural to an industrial economy, whether they were at all cognizant of the significance of the shifting of peoples and the bringing of large numbers of laborers together in relatively compact units. The científicos not only helped to retain Porfirio in control, but their stranglehold on Mexican politics survived until destroyed by other dictators with their own axes to grind.
. . .

Part Three
Twentieth-Century Dynamics

16

Lyle N. McAlister

Dictators and the Military

Among the many facets of caudillismo, none has attracted
more comment than the role of the military. Since it is commonly held that he who controls the army controls the state,
a critical examination of the relationship between dictators
and armed forces is in order. The following essay provides a
remarkably durable taxonomy that helps us comprehend civil-military relations and the role that dictators have played in
their association with the army. Lyle McAlister's four types
of civil-military states (Praetorian, Gendarmist, Garrison, and
Civilist) serve well to help us understand twentieth-century
cases both in and out of this book. His purpose is not to
present paradigms as conclusions but rather "to illustrate a
point to encourage the asking of questions." The wisdom
he brings to the subject from his broad knowledge of Latin
American history is revealed in his criticism of many analysts
who think "the military is conceived of as a force external to
and interfering with 'normal' historical processes rather than
as an integral element in them."

Lyle McAlister is a noted historian of Mexican military
institutions. His book, *The "Fuero Militar" in New Spain,
1764–1800* (1957), is a classic study that helped open up the
modern examination of the late Spanish American Empire. It
is characteristic of his breadth of interest that his most recent
book, *Spain and Portugal in the New World, 1492–1700*
(1984), should survey the first two centuries of that same
empire and the Portuguese Empire as well.

IT is hardly necessary to assert that the armed forces have been
important factors in the historical development of the nations of
Latin America. By bringing into association men from all parts of

From Lyle N. McAlister, "Civil-military Relations in Latin America" *Journal of
Inter-American Studies* 3 (July 1961): 341–50. Reprinted with permission.

the national territory, by posing as the incarnation of the national spirit, and by teaching patriotism and exalting national virtues, they have been a significant influence in overcoming regionalism and localism. By providing an avenue for advancement for members of lower social strata, they have encouraged social mobility. In many countries they have contributed to the transition from traditional to modern societies through their work in constructing communications systems, their emphasis on general and technical education within their ranks, and by their demands for industrialization. In the political sphere they have repeatedly overthrown the governments that created them; generals have employed the forces entrusted to them to make themselves heads of state; military factions have intervened in the political process in support of specific economic objectives or of broader ideologies. In a less spectacular fashion, the armed forces acting through political parties, as in Mexico, or through officers occupying cabinet posts have exerted powerful influences on public policy. . . .

Much of Latin American history has been written in terms of "Progress toward Democracy" or "The Struggle for Democracy." Within this teleological system the armed forces are regarded as "Obstacles to the Achievement of Democracy." Now no rightthinking person would deny that democracy is a desirable goal and it would be mean-spirited indeed not to wish the Latin Americans success in their struggle toward it. Yet, this conceptual framework encourages simplistic interpretations and explanations. The military is conceived of as a force external to and interfering with "normal" historical processes rather than as an integral element in them. In this position it can conveniently be regarded as a constant whose importance is recognized and accepted but which need not be described or analyzed systematically.

[If] the importance of the military as a power factor in Latin America is accepted and the nature of its relations with the civil elements of the state can be regarded as a discrete historical and sociological problem, what is the scope of the problem and how may it be defined? The most commonly used term to describe the role of the armed forces in Latin America is "militarism." In the sense that it means the use of military force or threat of force to achieve nonmilitary ends, it is adequate. It has, however, two disadvantages. To many scholars it has a more specific usage; that is, a system or way of life which glorifies war, in which the military is a high-status profession, in which an entire nation is oriented toward military virtues and mores, and which has strong imperialist overtones. Such a system may have existed in Paraguay during the dictatorship of Francisco Solano López, and the G.O.U. in Argentina may have aspired to it. It has, however, been atypical of Latin America. Also, it does not cover instances in which armed forces have been nonpolitical and, if the problem is to be viewed broadly, such instances also require description and analysis. Another commonly used expression is "the army in politics," but this term also excludes situations where the military has been nonpolitical. Moreover, it seems rather too mild an expression with which to describe the praetorian excesses of some Latin American armies in the nineteenth century. "Civil-military relations" is also open to the latter criticism. It is, however, comprehensive enough to cover the range of phenomena involved in the problem and its accepted usage elsewhere is an argument for its adoption by Latin Americanists.

[What then] is the structure of the problem? As H. Stuart Hughes remarks, historians are reluctant to make distinctions and tend to view their problems as all of one piece. Thus *pronunciamientos, cuartelazos, golpes de estado, machetismo,* militarism, praetorianism, and all other instances where armed forces transcend their purely military functions tend to be viewed as phenomena of the same order and explainable with more or less the same formula. Sometimes these phenomena are even confused with military history. This is equivalent to regarding the Assumption of Mary and the exercise of the ecclesiastical patronage as belonging to the same order of things or of teaching surgery and medical sociology in the same course. In fact a diversity of patterns or systems of civil-military relations has existed in Latin America and each pattern consists of complex interactions involving the structure, status, and power of groups, both civil and military, and the motivation of individuals, as these several elements are influenced by the political, social, and economic environment. Thus the role of the Brazilian officer corps in the overthrow of the Empire, the institutionalized gangsterism prevailing in the contemporary Dominican Republic, and the pronunciamientos of Antonio López de Santa Anna are sharply different examples of civil-military relations involving different types of civil and military elements interacting in different environmental situations.

At a schematic level several types of civil-military relations in Latin America may be defined. The first might be called the "Praetorian State." It is characterized by the frequent overthrow of governments by military revolutions or coups d'etat for nonmilitary purposes. It tends to be associated with a high degree of social and political disorganization and a low degree of professionalism within the armed forces. Examples are Mexico during the first thirty years of the republic and Venezuela before and after the dictatorship of Juan Vicente Gómez. The second might be described as the "Gendarmist State." It emerges when a single individual, generally but not always a military man, uses a mercenary army to make himself master of the state, imposes social and political order, tames the army, and uses it as a gendarmery to maintain himself in power. The dictatorships of Gómez in Venezuela and Anastasio Somoza in Nicaragua are examples. The third type, after Harold Lasswell, is the "Garrison State." In it the military not only dominates or strongly influences the political system but it attempts to militarize the state and society at large. It occurs in connection with deep fears of aggression from the outside or strong aggressive tendencies within and is associated with a relatively high degree of political and social stability and a professionalized military establishment. Paraguay under Francisco Solano López might be taken as an example of this type. As noted above, it is atypical of Latin America. Fourth, is the "Civilist State." It is characterized by civil supremacy over the military and exists in relatively stable societies with professionalized armed forces. [One example is] Argentina between 1861 and 1930. . . .

It should be added that these are ideal types in the Weberian sense. They do not exist in pure form and may shade or metamorphose into one another. Thus a strong caudillo may in certain circumstances transform a praetorian state into a gendarmist state as in the case of Porfirio Díaz and Rafael Trujillo, or the weakening or death of a leader or pressures within a society may turn a gendarmist state into a praetorian state as, for example, [in] Mexico after 1910. Changes in the social or economic structure within praetorian or gendarmist states may result in the emergence of a civilist pattern as in contemporary Mexico, while conversely, political, social, or economic strains within a civilist state may result in the emergence of praetorian or gendarmist patterns as in the case of Argentina after 1930 or Colombia after 1949. These paradigms, it should be added, are not intended to present conclusions. They are devices to illustrate a point and to encourage the asking of pertinent questions.

17

Russell H. Fitzgibbon

Continuismo: The Search for Political Longevity

As the essay by Peter Smith makes clear, legitimacy was an abiding concern of most caudillos. In a society where a premium on forms exists and where documents provide justification for political behavior, many power seekers have sought to give authenticity to their uprisings by the hallowed pattern of plan and pronunciamiento. Once in control, the elaboration of new constitutional forms has been a standard practice. Though refined in the twentieth century such constitutional reliance was firmly rooted in the nineteenth century, as Francisco Bilbao has so vigorously demonstrated. Constitutions, however, commonly set limits either upon the length of the term of office or upon the reelection of the chief executive or both. A dilemma then presents itself to the new master who would build a life term for himself at the same time that he attempts to acquire legitimacy through respect for the law embodied in the constitution. (The dilemma is the same, if less acute, for the duly elected and hence legal president who wishes to go beyond his constitutionally limited term.) One solution to his dilemma is continuismo; its nature is explored in the following essay. Readers may conclude with Smith that "one might well construe . . . constitutions as efforts to legalize dictatorship rather than to implant democracy."

Russell Fitzgibbon, a prominent authority on Latin American politics, limits his attention to Caribbean and Central American cases during the 1920s and 1930s. It is clear, however, that the adroit cultivation of continuismo has been pursued avidly by caudillos like Castro, Pinochet, and Stroessner during the last half-century. That "Tacho" Somoza learned the arts of continuismo well and taught them to his

From Russell F. Fitzgibbon, " *'Continuismo'* in Central America and the Caribbean," *The Inter-American Quarterly* 2 (July 1940): 56–74.

sons is thoroughly demonstrated in the essay by Alain Rouquié in this volume.

. . . *CONTINUISMO* . . . is the practice of continuing the administration in power in a Latin American country by the process of a
constitutional amendment, or a provision in a new constitution,
exempting the president in office, and perhaps other elective officials, from the historic and frequent prohibition against two con-
secutive terms in office. The precise form of the constitutional
change may vary—the general pattern is simple and uniform.

Cuba was easily the dean of experimenters with the device.
General Gerardo Machado y Morales was elected president of
Cuba in the balloting of 1924, to take office May 20, 1925, under
a campaign pledge limiting him to one term in office. Machado,
who had resigned a cabinet position years before in protest against
the reelectionist plans of his then chief, José Miguel Gómez, declared in his election manifesto in September 1924 that "a Liberal
President cannot be reelected. This is now a noble tradition—the
most noble of this party." The General seemingly slammed the
door shut, locked it, and threw away the key when he declared in
July 1927 that "a man whose lips had never been defiled by a lie,
would lower his dignity, and dishonor himself, if after a political
labor of twenty-five years during which he opposed the principle
of re-election with the word and the sword in two revolutions, he
should now accept the principle for himself."

If Machado had locked the door upon himself he proved a
skillful locksmith, however, and soon found a way of opening
it. The Machado-dominated Cuban congress in the spring and
summer of 1927 passed a set of resolutions aimed at a comprehensive amendment of the constitution. Among other changes, the
presidential term was to be lengthened two years. All went legally
until May 9, 1928. The congress submitted the series of amendments, as was required of it, to a special convention on May 9,
1928, which, the same day, adopted a resolution asserting that
"the Constituent Assembly does not vacillate in reaffirming that
General Gerardo Machado y Morales, because of the obligation he
has contracted and because of his role as founder of the Republic,
is unavoidably bound to accept a new presidential period."

The convention concluded its simple task two days later but with the omission, inadvertent or otherwise, of the provision regarding the prolongation of Machado's term for two additional years. It specified instead that the single, six-year term provision should become operative with the first subsequent election. The changes became effective as part of the constitution on publication in the *Gaceta,* May 11, 1928.

With the way constitutionally cleared Machado became the candidate of all three political parties in the 1928 elections, held on November 2, and was chosen without opposition to succeed himself, "ignoble," "undignified," and "dishonorable" though it was! The first of the recent attempts at continuismo thus became history.

The contagion of continuismo spread first in the Caribbean. The Dominican Republic next fell victim to the malady. . . . A symptom of what was to come had manifested itself in the Dominican Republic even before the Cuban changes of 1928. Horacio Vásquez had assumed the presidency in Santo Domingo (as the capital was then named) on July 12, 1924, under a constitution of June 13, 1924, which established a four-year term for the chief executive with ineligibility for an immediately successive term. The fruits of office apparently tasted sweet, for in 1927 a constituent convention revised the basic law to provide, among other changes, a two-year extension of the terms of the president, vice-president, and members of the congress. The change, effective June 16, 1927, legally continued Vásquez in power from 1928 to 1930. Presidential provisions in the constitution again were juggled in 1929 when an additional amendment on June 20 restored the four-year term for the head of the state and at the same time removed the prohibition on reelection. A further political insurance policy for the ruling régime was the revision of the electoral law of 1924 in a manner which convinced the opposition parties that an attempt to win through election was impossible.

With these changes on the statute books, President Vásquez announced in 1929 that he would be a candidate for reelection in May 1930. Political tension increased throughout 1929 and came to a head early in 1930.

Vásquez's refusal to meet the demand for minority representation on the local election boards was the clue for revolution, which broke out in the north on February 23, 1930, and was carried through to success five days later by the ousting of the régime in power. Chief factor in the success of the insurgents was the defection of General Rafael Leonidas Trujillo Molina, commander of the government forces and an erstwhile private in the United States Marine Corps during its occupation of the island republic. A provisional president, General Estrella Ureña, set presidential elections for May 16, 1930, and himself became the candidate for vice-president on the "government ticket" headed by Trujillo. The withdrawal of the opposition nominees two days before the election permitted the choice of the favored candidates without a contest. [Trujillo's skill in the use of continuismo during the next thirty years is revealed in the next three essays in this book.]

It was not surprising that with these repeated and presumably successful demonstrations of the efficacy of continuismo in the Caribbean republics, the contagion should spread to the neighboring mainland governments of Central America. The first to undertake such experimentation was Guatemala, the efforts of which were, indeed, practically concurrent with those of Haiti. Guatemala had had a long, unenlightened political history, alternating between despotism and virtual anarchy. After kaleidoscopic changes in the control of the executive branch late in 1930, General Jorge Ubico came to the presidential palace on February 14, 1931, through elections held February 6–8. The constitution promulgated January 1, 1928, established a six-year term for the president and prohibited reelection during the twelve years following the expiration of the term. The whole emphasis of the relevant articles in the 1928 constitution was on the prevention of indefinite continuance in office, nepotism, and allied problems.

Ubico moved quickly to consolidate his position in the presidency. The Partido Liberal Progresista, the candidate of which Ubico had been in his campaign for the presidency, soon became a well-knit personal following. Taking time by the forelock, the president on May 5, 1935, won for his Liberal Progressive party, by methods which may be guessed at if not documented, a majority of the seats in an Asamblea Nacional Constituyente, created to consider revision of the basic law. The constitutional assembly, which held only seventeen sessions, worked from the basis of a draft constitution submitted to the Junta Preparatoria and by the latter to the full assembly. While Ubico's message to the first plenary session of the assembly contained no reference to the possibility of his own reelection to the presidency, it was a foregone conclusion that with the proceedings under full executive control some provision pointing in that direction would be an easy and logical way out.

The constitution retained the 1928 provision (Article 66) that twelve years must elapse from the expiration of an initial term before a president could again occupy the office. The assembly then provided for the holding of a national plebiscite on the question of continuing Ubico's term of office. This step—convenient substitute for a regular presidential election—was consummated on June 22–24, 1935, and resulted in an officially announced vote of 884,703 to 1,144 in favor of the continuance of General Ubico in the presidency until 1943. Following this overwhelming popular mandate the constituent assembly duly decreed certain transitory provisions under date of July 11, 1935, the first of which provided that "The Constitutional Presidency of General Jorge Ubico shall end on March 15, 1943, and with such an object the purpose of Article 66 of the Constitution remains in suspense until that date. . . ."

The Guatemalan nucleus of continuismo spread fan-wise in Central America, first to Honduras, successively to El Salvador and Nicaragua. . . .

The last country—to date [i.e., 1939–40]—to attempt continuismo was Nicaragua. The prelude was the political campaign by which General Anastasio Somoza, head of the Guardia Nacional, became president in 1937. He had in 1934 announced his entry in the 1936 campaign, although he was doubly barred on constitutional grounds by the fact that he was a nephew by marriage of the incumbent president, Dr. Juan Bautista Sacasa, and by his headship of the national guard. The political situation was further complicated by the alleged complicity of General Somoza in the assassination by national guard members of General Augusto Sandino, long an opponent of United States Marine occupation of Nicaragua, on February 21, 1934. Somoza more formally entered the presidential race with a statement published in September 1935 in *El Cronista* at León, traditional Liberal stronghold, promising that he would "eliminate all other candidates who bar my path" to the presidency. The political situation tightened as the 1936 elections approached, and on June 6 of that year Somoza forced his uncle out of office. A Somoza partisan became provisional president, and on June 15 the Liberal party gave the national guard chieftain its nomination. The elections on December 8, 1936, were farcical: Somoza received approximately 117,000 votes against 1,100 given his exiled coalition opponent.

Continuismo flowered in Nicaragua with less than half of Somoza's term gone. Dr. Carlos A. Morales, a Liberal justice of the Supreme Court, suggested in an article in *La Prensa* at Managua, the capital, on May 14, 1938, that steps be taken for the revision of the constitution. The congress in August passed the necessary legislation for elections to an Asamblea Constituyente to convene on December 15. The elections, held on November 6, resulted in the choice of twenty-seven Liberals, eleven Conservative Nationalists (the pro-Somoza wing of the Conservative party), and seven Conservatives. The president on December 8 issued detailed "provisional regulations" for the government of the constituent assembly, and the plenary sessions opened on December 16. The main work of the assembly got under way early in February 1939 when it began consideration of an 18,000-word draft constitution. This task was completed some seven weeks later with publication of the document in the *Gaceta*.

The 1939 constitution contained several provisions bearing on the presidency. In the first place, after specifying a six-year presidential term, it provided flatly (Article 204) that "the immediate reelection of the President is forbidden." Other seemingly rigorous restrictions upon eligibility and succession were included. A "joker" appeared in Article 350, though, in the statement that "The amendment of the provision which prohibits the re-election of the President of the Republic and those concerning the duration of the presidential term . . . cannot be decreed except for future need, in order that the amendment may not be a detriment or a help to the officials in service at the time of its promulgation."

In the first of several transitory provisions, the constituent assembly arrogated to itself the function of electing "a citizen who is to exercise the Presidency of the Republic during a term . . . from March 30 of the current year [1939] to May 1, 1947." In the article immediately following, the constituent assembly, with the model of its two northern neighbors before it, transformed itself for an eight-year period into the ordinary legislative congress. In compliance with its self-imposed mandate to choose a president for the ensuing term, the assembly voted on March 24, 1939, the prize going to Somoza with forty-six votes as against seven for Fernando Guzmán, a prominent Conservative party leader. In his inaugural address on March 30 Somoza declared that "One of my greatest ambitions was reformation of the Constitution to represent the will of the People!"

One should be extremely cautious in drawing conclusions and moral judgments about continuismo. . . . It is in order, however, to raise a few questions and, perhaps, to venture highly tentative answers.

Why has the practice under discussion been so localized? What conditions in the body politic favor the entrance of such an infection? How incompatible is it with what we define as "democracy"? It may even be proper to ask if it is a disease, i.e., an undesirable manifestation. Two explanations may be suggested as possible and partial answers to the first question. The simple fact of geographic nearness encourages an imitation of political trends and techniques which neighbors have adopted. A certain vague common denominator underlies the countries of "the American Mediterranean," variant though their ethnic composition, their economic interests, their social structures, and other factors are. In the second place, the location of the countries concerned within the sometime international political orbit of the United States induced a certain lip service to constitutional forms as such. . . . The average Latin American constitution has been more symbol than instrument, however, and it is understandable why, with any external examples of this sort seemingly stressing form, the Central American and Caribbean governments should be concerned with such an aspect. The anomaly appears in the willingness and casualness with which on more than one occasion the régimes endeavoring to preserve the appearance of legality have departed from the prescribed legal methods of effecting new constitutions or constitutional amendments. Viewing the whole picture, the question of sheer constitutionalism becomes artificial and dogmatic.

Continuismo has been favored in middle America by just those conditions which nurture dictatorship—and to just the same extent. A high degree of illiteracy, of political inarticulateness and even unconsciousness, of governmental concentration, all make for those expressions of exaggerated personalism of which this legalized perpetuation of control is a form. Dictatorship has been a normal rather than unusual type of executive development in most of the countries under consideration, and continuismo is but a natural result of a dictatorship which wishes to give the color of legality, either for domestic or foreign eyes, to its continuance. Costa Rica is a country of greater literacy, more general popular participation in political expression and consciousness of governmental problems; these factors have a very pertinent relationship to the entire absence of any suggestion of the adoption of continuismo in that country.

The practice seems to be in direct and immediate contradiction to political democracy as we know the term. It is naïve, of course, to assume that in any of the countries the constitutional perversion has been accomplished in other than the harshest and most arbitrary sort of manner. The exiled opponents of the various régimes have been loud and persistent in their charges of constitutional perversion and violated democracy. Such charges are naturally to be discounted because of the personal elements entering in, but they certainly contain a strong half-truth. . . .

Continuismo cannot be regarded as a problem in and by itself. To detach it from its environment is to consider the image in a mirror as unrelated to the object which causes it. Continuismo is simply a reflection, a symptom, and a result of the larger problem of dictatorship.

18
Rafael L. Trujillo Molina
A Dictator Extols Democracy

One of the most successful practitioners of continuismo in the Caribbean was Generalísimo Rafael Trujillo, dictator of the Dominican Republic from 1930 until his assassination in 1961. As notorious for his totalitarian methods as any caudillo in history, "The Benefactor" developed his propaganda machine to a high level of efficiency. He was particularly concerned with the image of himself and of his regime that was projected abroad. Laudatory biographies were presented as gifts to libraries, professors, and public officials all over the United States, and major metropolitan newspapers ran expensive full-page advertisements praising Trujillo. The following essay is characteristic of The Benefactor's efforts to seek legitimacy in the eyes of the world. It was first given by him as the inaugural address to the Hemisphere's delegates to the Thirteenth Pan-American Sanitary Conference at Ciudad Trujillo (now Santo Domingo) on October 2, 1950. Revised and published again five years later, "The Evolution of Democracy in Santo Domingo" stands as the remarkable rationale of a Spanish American dictator who made the trains run on time. The anti-Communist emphasis is particularly revealing, for this is what made him the prototype of the Red-baiting dictator who knew best how to ingratiate himself with the United States during the Cold War. Only about 30 percent of the speech is reprinted here. It should be closely compared with the next document by Jesús de Galíndez, which was also published in 1955, and with the analytical essay by Howard Wiarda and Michael Kryzanek which follows that by Galíndez.

. . . DEMOCRACY acts according to the needs and characteristics of each particular group, actuated and governed by the objective

From Rafael L. Trujillo Molina, *The Evolution of Democracy in Santo Domingo,* translated by Otto Vega, 2d ed. (Ciudad Trujillo, Santo Domingo: Dominican Government, 1955), 10–64.

structure of each particular society. Democracy is action: economic, religious, political, social, human action—in a word, action which evolves and operates in accordance with the traditions,
the history, the ethnology and the geography of each group, provided of course it is primarily directed towards the improvement
of the community.

All during the course of my influence in Dominican affairs,
the nation has been administered in accordance with this basic
and determining criterion. The results speak for themselves and
so far I have no reason for regrets in my executive program. . . .

In 1930, . . . after eighty-six years of bloody warfare, social
unrest, poverty, and want, we had failed to solve any of our problems: there were still no schools, no hospitals, no employment,
no boundary, no roads, no currency, no banks, no agriculture, no
industry (except the sugar latifundium), no public buildings, no
social security, no electric power, no university, no irrigation
system, no bridges, no money, no appreciable production. Not a
single step had been taken by 1930 toward regaining our financial
independence. . . .

The Republic was limited to the static maintenance of a
minimum of services wholly dependent on a meager budget essentially designed to meet the overwhelming debt. . . . The spirit of
Dominicans [was] dejected by hopeless skepticism. Wealth unde-
veloped, services paralyzed, trade inactive, the capital city destroyed, creditors demanding payment, public opinion divided
into countless individual factions of a primitive nature, local boss-
ism as active as ever, and, in the background of the whole picture,
"the monster of armed rebellion trying to raise its Hydra head."

Such a picture was enough to discourage even the most enthusiastic and optimistic. But I had confidence in the country's future,
in the good faith of my people, and in the immanent will of God.
I had the patience and the faith to undertake and carry out a
program of government which was embodied in a single word:
build!

As had happened repeatedly before, the financial crisis of 1930
brought about a political crisis. Factious ringleaders plotted revolt
and some of them started the nation on the road to civil war. . . .
I was convinced that the generalization of a new upheaval would

mean final collapse. The Republic could not stand . . . further proof of its unfitness for self-government. Dominicans were not responsible, of course, for many of the fundamental aspects of the situation, which was actually the inevitable upshot of poverty and economic subservience; but surely in the end the tragic balance of chaos would fall upon our shoulders.

The year 1931 passed amid great difficulties. Revolt began to appear everywhere and it became necessary to subdue more than one revolutionary attempt. . . . It was impossible to think of a new period of bloodshed, wastefulness, and executive irresponsibility at a time when all the energies, the thinking capacity, and the self-respect of Dominicans ought to be bound together in a single effort for national regeneration capable of leading us along the righteous path of civility to the only revolution possible: the revolution against the public-administration methods hitherto responsible for the wasteful depletion of the sources of our common welfare. That long-coveted revolution could not come from the horse-riding guerrillas, or from turmoil, or from anarchy, or from shameful poverty, or from lack of faith, or from the narrow-mindedness of local chieftains, or from foreign intervention, or from subservience. The revolution had to be brought about by the way of thoughtful reconstruction, sacrifice, peace, and order.

While the government confronted these serious difficulties in maintaining order, I also had to face the financial crisis. I was not willing to maintain peace by dint of subduing the seditious spirit of Dominicans—fundamentally a consequence of profound social inadequacy—simply in order that our creditors might enjoy a maximum guarantee of payment. My purpose was to make of peace an instrument of the revolution itself; to give peace a constructive, positive social meaning. To do that it was necessary to eradicate the basic problems and to perform, under the guidance of government, a thorough transformation of our essential values. . . .

In the course of four dark and anxious years we . . . [had] succeeded not only in surviving and avoiding final collapse but in becoming an example of honesty and efficiency. . . . Notwithstanding this accomplishment, our efforts had only given us a moment of rest. We had rid ourselves of oppressive demands, but nothing had yet been accomplished towards real liberation. Further proof on our part was needed and the people had to be educated and prepared for it.

In August 1934 [I took] the oath of office for a second presidential term. . . . Amidst the serious difficulties encountered during my first term since 1931, I undertook to organize a political force which could join me in carrying out the arduous program I had outlined. However plausible my intentions might have been, they required the support of public opinion and a sense of national responsibility profoundly conscious of our common welfare. Therefore the Dominican Party made its appearance on the nation's political arena. That staunchest supporter of my Administration stands today as a living expression of the constructive ideals of a whole Dominican generation.

The Dominican Party represents a paramount effort of organization against the self-indulgent, factious methods of policy-lacking groups. Thanks to its disciplined and purposeful existence, the Republic has attained national objectives of far-reaching import. Dominicans of all times and even the foreigners who ruled us on various occasions struggled vainly in search of those objectives. The formation of a stable, majority-carrying political body was one of our major requirements, one of the basic prerequisites for the desired change. The principle of authority could not be effective without a coherent grouping of the masses around a well-defined program. With public opinion divided into a hundred different interfighting groups unable to find the way to national unity, it was impossible to take any serious steps towards regeneration. . . . It was not a case of facing mere routine difficulties, such as are bound to exist even in organized and well-established democracies. We were struggling against veritable organic deficiencies. . . .

The experience of our barren and tormenting past had driven us into a state of unbelief and self-distrust from which it was vital to emerge. But first a series of psychological elements had to be created in contrast without past background. That was the mission I entrusted to the Dominican Party. As its name suggests, the Party's activities are carried out on a nationwide basis and the organization is not incompatible with any other serious movement aimed at our social and political rehabilitation. . . . Respect for the law, the spirit of cooperation and association, the sense of collective unrewarded responsibility, mass-subordination to the principle of authority—sum and substance of any stable social organization—were conditions that had not taken root in our national conscience before 1930. It was therefore our duty and responsibility to create this series of intangible and imponderable elements, just as much as it was—but perhaps with greater urgency—our duty and responsibility to build roads and bridges, hospitals and schools. So long as strong foundations were not laid for a new Dominican ethical code, we could not hope for a revision of our frustrated past. The change would have to begin at the very root of our national spirit, at the bottom of our attitude toward life itself.

Without a working institution, without an active organization, without a flexible, disciplined, and responsible force identified with the government's constructive aims, the fulfillment of such aims . . . would have never materialized. When I thought of creating the Dominican Party, I did not have in mind just another party. I was thinking in terms of a Dominican social substratum capable of carrying out the vital rehabilitation program upon which our life as a nation depended. As an inevitable consequence of our peculiar social conditions, the Party has been an instrument of civilization.

The change in our character is so obvious and the practice of cooperation is now so deeply rooted in our population, that the following data, which I consider of the utmost importance as they point to social events of the first magnitude, will be sufficient to dispel any doubts in this respect: on September 15, 1947, compulsory military training was established by Act of Congress. . . . By the time the registration deadline provided by the Act was reached, 448,607 citizens had already complied with the requirements of the law—in this case a law dealing with so thorny a subject as military conscription. During 1949, 33,862 citizens received training and only 240 were, for legitimate reason, exempted from the service. There was not a single case of desertion! . . .

On various occasions criticism has been directed against the Dominican Party as constituting a one-party system offering no possibility for opposition. This contention lacks any valid foundation inasmuch as the Party was originally formed with the same contingent of old factions which had eventually disintegrated and become weary owing to their inadequacy and lack of faith. I should like to stress that men from each and every one of the political groups in existence before 1930, as well as others who had nothing to do with those groups, have been active in my Administration. It is apparent that a new partisan school of thought has come into being in this country which will prevent a reversion to the outmoded system of anomalous, subservient factions whose activities were responsible for many a national calamity and to be sure for the failure of Dominican democracy in the past. Independently of the government party's influence, public opinion has evolved freely towards the formation of a well-defined labor movement and towards constitutional recognition of women's political and civil rights. Both actions are of course consistent with contemporary political trends which, while running parallel with governmental action, are wholly independent of it.

Moreover, public education and every cultural activity sponsored by the government have been conducted in a free and purely objective manner and have never been under the influence of interested foreign movements. The same can be said of religious activities and of all other activities inherent to our national or to resident aliens, *provided that such activities are not aimed at destroying or hampering the great task of national reconstruction to which we Dominicans are morally committed by command of our ruinous past.* [Trujillo's emphasis]. If a price must be paid for regeneration and revolution, then we must pay that price in order to live under God and according to the standards of present-day civilization. I am well aware that my work, being human, is not perfect. There are shortcomings and deficiencies. But thus far the good results achieved greatly outbalance the expectations and hopes of even the most optimistic of Dominicans of 1930, of the Dominicans of my own generation. . . .

I have pointed out that each and every one of our national problems awaited solution when the government was entrusted to me, and that these problems, at the same time, called for a well-intentioned hand. The question of demographic organization, which was uppermost among our problems in 1935, could not be met successfully without a scientifically conducted census, hitherto lacking, of our population. This task was undertaken immediately and good results were achieved. In 1936 a likewise thoroughly planned scientific statistical system was set up throughout the country as a fundamental prerequisite to the organization of many other essential public services. . . .

Meanwhile far-reaching reforms and innovations were being brought about by sheer dint of effort. No action involved greater urgency, insofar as our domestic affairs were concerned, than that of raising the low stagnant level of our economy and our production. As we are primarily an agricultural country and were at that time devoid of any other immediately accessible source of wealth, no problem was so pressing as the development of the agricultural and livestock industries. . . .

In order to cope with the unfathomed problem of our agriculture, the government adopted a threefold policy comprising irrigation, farm colonization, and distribution of lands, water, seeds, and implements to farmers, free of charge. The government also undertook an ambitious campaign for farm mechanization and improvement of cultivation methods designed to help farmers obtain the greatest possible profit from their work. . . .

The system of land distribution among farmers lacking financial means was begun in 1935 through the establishment of a Board of Agricultural Protection in each of the country's provinces. This action was completely independent of the farm colonization system. Thus far 3,530,057 *tareas* [approximately 588,343 acres] of land have been distributed among 104,707 people. At an average price of $3 per tarea, the value of these lands would amount to $10,590,171. The land grants are made outright, with the sole provision that recipients prove that the land is kept under cultivation. The only effective method of combating idleness is by helping everyone to work for himself. The beneficiaries, almost a hundred thousand strong, who are now small landowning farmers, were so many potential idlers whom we have rescued from the pitfalls of indolence and indulgence that they may gain sustenance for their families. Wanton loafing is strictly forbidden by law in this country. Moreover, I should like to point out that none of the large private enterprises, operating in this country, or even several of them combined, including those controlling the largest properties, maintain in production an area of land equaling that which the government has distributed among the small, needy farmers. . . .

From 1908 to 1935 only 857 kilometers of road had been built throughout the country with funds coming from various loans. This road network was insufficient to carry the volume of the nation's trade and agricultural production. So long as production is not accessible to good roads, it cannot be considered as a source of wealth. It was therefore necessary to build roads and permanent bridges. During the last twenty years more than 2,929.13 kilometers of highways and 380 bridges have been built throughout the country at a cost of $20,692,653.97.

The expansion of agricultural production and of our resources in general called for increasing industrialization of raw materials. The government took upon itself the program for industrialization. The first step towards this end was the establishment of the Industrial Slaughterhouse and Refrigeration Plant in 1944, through which development of the livestock industry was begun. Later a cement plant was installed. In 1948 the government purchased the Chocolatera Sánchez, one of the best plants for industrialization of cacao in existence in Latin America. In 1948 also a large incinerating plant was installed at the capital for proper disposal of refuse and for utilization of certain residual matter for industrial purposes. This plant is considered by experts as the best of its kind in the West Indies. . . . Likewise, other basic industries representing a total initial investment of $6,671,850 have been established under official sponsorship. . . .

In 1930 the school situation here was quite deficient. Enrollment throughout the country that year included only 50,739 students and attendance was very low. When I became President, there were only 526 educational centers in this country, the University included, and illiteracy was very high because rural schools were practically nonexistent. It was precisely the time, also, when the pressure of conditions under the economic crisis caused the closing of many schools. . . .

This situation was alarming. Anything might have been expected to happen save that so essential a service as public education should become paralyzed. Now then, even amidst the financial crisis, substantial steps were taken not only to forestall the continuation of this evil but to improve the service and insure its normal operation. From then on budget appropriations for education have increased steadily up to $3,661,932.50 in 1949, and up to $8,836,927.27 for 1955.

The change in the field of education can be appreciated from the following data: school enrollment, including the University's, was 250,684 students during 1949 and average attendance was 86 percent. At the present time there are 5,727 schools functioning in this country, with a combined enrollment of 344,560 students.

The University of Santo Domingo, the oldest in the Americas, has a current enrollment of over 3,000 students. In order to house it decorously, the government is building on the capital's outskirts a University City consisting of a number of buildings for the various departments and schools. When completed, this project will presently house the Schools of Medicine, Pharmacy, and Dentistry, the Institute of Anatomy, and several laboratories. . . .

The pith of the changes that have taken place in administrative methods and in the general way of life of our people must be found in this simple formula of government: the greater the volume of active and productive wealth, the higher the quality and the number of public services. A nation's wealth must be the measure of its inhabitants' welfare.

This sound policy is making it possible for us to invest hundreds of millions of dollars over a short working period for the purpose of raising the standard of living of a people dejected by four centuries of adversity. We do not hold that everything has been done already, but we do believe that what has been accomplished has placed us firmly on the open and definite road to recovery. . . . The budget of the Department of Health in 1930 amounted to $160,854.75. At the time there were only 30 hospital beds available for maternity cases in the entire country . . . ; there were 484 beds in general hospitals, twelve medical dispensaries, one in each Province, and a few understaffed sanitary brigades, made up of medical students, to combat endemic diseases in rural areas.

With such meager resources it was practically impossible to

make any serious attempt to improve sanitary services in the country. At the same time it was quite difficult, not to say impossible, to launch a program of sanitation such as conditions demand, so long as the Treasury situation remained unchanged. To set up efficient sanitary services and establish social security we needed money and resources which we lacked and which, moreover, I was unwilling to procure abroad under onerous and enslaving conditions.

Progress thus far in the fields of sanitation and social welfare has been attained through our own means invested in relative proportion to the growth of fiscal revenues and with the sole support of the Dominican Party. The magnitude of these programs would in itself be a source of pride to my administration. At the present time there are twenty-nine hospitals operated by the Department of Public Health with 6,000 beds available to patients, ten maternity hospitals with a total of 1,000 cribs, plus another 1,000 beds belonging to welfare establishments and social-security centers supervised by government departments, and eleven hospitals and one clinic made available by the Social Security Chest, with a total of 1,088 beds. . . .

But that is not all. Public health is not solely dependent on hospitals and medical services. There are other elements indispensable to the maintenance of good health and the general welfare. . . . To live well one must have decent quarters, eat adequately and sufficiently, drink potable water, bathe every day, drain all wastes, dress properly; in short, it is necessary to possess a series of material elements without which it is impossible to live in good health. To this end we have brought forth a general program of urbanization and a social-welfare program. . . .

This long-range program [included] the paving of streets in all cities, construction of sewer and drainage systems, opening of new streets and avenues, building of public markets, racetracks, zoological gardens, installation of electric light throughout the Republic and, last but not least, . . . the construction of a chain of modern hotels as a basis for the promotion of the tourist trade. . . .

While no binding concordat between the Dominican Republic and the Holy See, existed then, our government took it upon itself to build a goodly number of churches dedicated to the Roman

Catholic faith, which is that professed by the Dominican people. Our far-ranging rehabilitation program could not be considered complete if it failed to take into full account the religious functions and the most intimate spiritual needs of the people. Government relations with the Church have always been very cordial and this circumstance has enabled the two to execute a full-fledged building program [into] which the Administration has invested very considerable amounts of money. It includes building for seminaries, for churches throughout the country, parochial houses, Catholic colleges for men and women; it includes also the supplying of ornaments as well as direct help and subsidies to congregations. Preferential attention is given to all endeavors aimed at fostering Catholic sentiment. The vicissitudes of the past also cast the shadow of ruin over religious institutions and lessened religious fervor. Now a government truly concerned over the fate of its people could not look upon such a loss with indifference. Therefore we undertook to make up for it with fully as much enthusiasm and patriotic feeling as we put into our civic improvement.

The establishment of social-welfare services was uppermost in my mind from the very earliest days of my Administration and this objective has been consistently pursued. At the outset . . . it was clear that the government was not financially able, at the time, to attend to such services, [so] I decided to organize them under the auspices of the Dominican Party. But those early attempts were as mere trickles against the sea of destitution in which our needy classes drifted helplessly.

However, my will to improve conditions was unshakable. In 1933 I sponsored the first Dominican Medical Congress with a view to studying and properly classifying the grave health and social-welfare problems that our people had confronted from time immemorial. . . .

[The resulting] program has been completed in all its phases. The growth of social-welfare services called for the creation of permanent specialized agencies and these are now operating under the Department of Social Welfare. . . . We have built comfortable dwellings in social-betterment districts in various communities throughout the country. These districts are endowed with every requirement under modern urban development. We have built shelters for the aged, and farm reformatories for boys. We have built recreation centers for workers, maternity clubs, nurseries, sewing centers for female workers (with an attendance of over six thousand), and elementary schools for illiterate adults. Complete medical services are maintained for the care of children and free milk-distribution stations, established throughout the country, contribute effectively to preserving the health of needy children.

In closing my remarks bearing upon governmental action on social problems, I should like to refer to the work done to improve throughout the relations between capital and labor and to raise conditions among the laboring class within the framework of those relations. . . .

In 1932, . . . I submitted to Congress a bill for a Workmen's Compensation Law to bring labor-accident regulation into line with the practical demands of modern life. In 1938 two bills were enacted, one dealing with the Dominicanization of labor which provided for a 70 percent minimum participation of native workers in all commercial, industrial, or agricultural enterprises, and the other pertaining to the sabbath as a day of rest and to closing hours. In 1941 a new bill was adopted providing for the cash payment of the salaries and wages of agricultural workers. . . . In 1942 I sponsored a substantial amendment to our Constitution aimed at bringing about wider action by the Administration in favor of the laboring classes.

The time elapsed since 1935 has been industriously and profitably employed in Santo Domingo. In twenty years every value in our community, material as well as moral, has undergone a substantial change. Not a single feature of our national life has failed to go through the machinery of sound, progressive action, though the invigorating outcome of this prolific period cannot be appreciated in its true measure while the programs undertaken are still in full process of development. Nonetheless, from a population standpoint, the results have been abundant. The 1950 census shows an increase in population of 700,000 inhabitants over those in the 1935 census; and while our present population does not yet fill our potential capacity, I am certain that it will not be long before the two million Dominicans counted this year will have arrived at a shining goal of plenitude. The elements of security, health, and cleanliness now prevailing in this country will doubtless yield results even more gratifying in the days to come.

I have purposely reserved for the latter part of this account reference to our military institutions and their work during the past few years. Without a foundation of individual and collective security, without a definite agent for order and peace, setting the wheels of progress in motion would have been utterly impossible. While it is true that the Republic has had courageous and seasoned fighters to defend its independence on the field of battle, it is no less true that we never had an adequate military organization designed to uphold internal peace and to safeguard freedom for the nation's civil institutions.

To organize this was quite as necessary as establishing other services. A nation cannot fulfill its historic destiny unless it has armed forces and a military spirit. The career of arms, within the framework of its role as a safeguard, is indispensable among national institutions. To create and organize the armed forces of the Republic is as noble and essential a task as is the building of schools, hospitals, ports, or banks, provided of course that by their creation and organization the other administrative services will not be impaired. . . .

We Dominicans were in the midst of our efforts at rehabilitation when the hectic period of readjustment following World War II came about. We had fulfilled loyally the obligations imposed on us by that conflict and far was it from our minds to suspect that we, the loyal and devoted supporters of Democracy in that struggle, were to be the victims of the extremist and demagogic storm that followed the cessation of hostilities. But the tempest vented its fury upon us and, had our new national spirit not been cast in so solid a mold, we would have met with disaster.

In 1942 war conditions brought me back to office. Side by side with the United States we entered the armed conflict in view of the treacherous Pearl Harbor attack. Postwar conditions in 1947, which were even more dangerous to us than the actual period of hostilities, compelled me, against my wishes, to continue in office. The Dominican Party and the people at large would not consent to shifting the responsibility of government in the face of

the dangerous contingencies prevailing at the time. By an imperative command of circumstances, I was and still am the core of
that responsibility. Therefore I could not, either as a man or as a
leader, turn my back upon the most elementary duties of one who
was to be tested at a difficult and perilous juncture.

Since the early months of 1946 the existence of a definite
coalition of governments against the prevailing order in this country made itself apparent. The political phenomenon of that coalition developed in violation of both the spirit and the letter of the
Inter-American System, was counter to the staunchest juridical
principles governing international relations, and went against all
rules of international law. The Dominican Republic was complying strictly with all obligations incumbent upon it in the international field and undoubtedly stood as a positive element of progress and civilization in this geographical area. None of the
governments involved in the plot had cause or reason for ill will
toward us. But the plot subsisted with all its implications and by
mid-1947 it had become an outright threat of war.

The conflict involved deep ideological differences. Here was
an advancing nation eagerly seeking the gist of its own existence;
here indeed was a small country on the road to self-sufficiency,
where order and cooperation were the very essence of institutions.
And there were the others, disjointed and misguided, bent on
carrying beyond their borders the noxious spirit of the new economic and political systems. We represented the national, in
terms of democratic advancement; they represented the international—the Marxist revolution—intent on social and economic
domination. The actual promoters of the coalition could not have
been concerned over the needs of the Dominican people, whom
they neither know nor love. . . .

We met the situation with calm and composure but with
firmness as well. At the very moment when we were bringing to
an end, through a substantial cash payment, the age-old process
of the foreign debt—that hotbed of evil in our wasteful past—the
haunting specter of a new disintegration hovered over us. The
downfall of the government through social and political interfer-
ence by alien systems, would have given rise to chaos in this
country. Therefore we decided to resist, and not merely for our

own convenience but also to test the very nature and raison d'etre of the Inter-American System. This decision entailed great sacrifices. On one occasion I pointed out that national defense during that period subtracted from our public treasury over $20,000,000 which would have yielded a better harvest had they been devoted to the nonmilitary investments for which they were originally intended.

When I became fully aware of the extent of the political, economic, and military forces that were gathering to disrupt the Republic's rehabilitation program, I tried of course to build up adequate defenses. The Communist plotters knew that we lacked arms to face an event of such magnitude as they were readying. Our resources had been channeled toward promoting a production and wealth that served to meet the requirements of other countries during the war years, and were not used for excessive armament which we never considered necessary for our own democratic way of life.

At the end of 1945 we took steps to acquire in the United States certain war matériel—a very limited amount of it. The Department of State flatly refused to approve the necessary licenses, thereby closing all doors for consideration of our security. Had an attitude more akin to understanding prevailed, our subsequent sacrifice for defense would not have been so burdensome and onerous. To show the measure of that sacrifice, suffice it to say that in order to manufacture our own weapons we had to put $5,000,000 into an industrial war plant.

It was contended at the time that the munitions requested by the Dominican government were not necessary for the nation's defense. The Department of State put it bluntly and distinctly that inasmuch as no threat whatsoever existed against the Republic's security, our government could seek to arm itself only for aggressive purposes. We, the friends of law and order, the ones responsible for what stands to this day as the most genuine program of democratic rehabilitation in Latin America, had to endure the bitterness of this unwarranted rebuke while the agent of anarchy and the promoters of disorder and confusion remained free to plot against a loyal country.

Communism found us alone, but indeed not lacking in courage and strength to thwart its designs and ward off its influence in the Caribbean. We did not even receive moral succor from an unbiased press. American newspapers either held off in a frigid, baffling silence favorable to the Communist scheme, or, to go along with the plotting governments, plunged into a foul campaign to discredit our country and its leaders.

Events moved with pressing swiftness. Hardly had a year transpired since our request for war matériel when, with the knowledge and forbearance of all, we found ourselves facing the most dangerous operation for military attack in our history. Responsibility for this operation rested upon several governments. Subsequent investigations by the Organ of Consultation of the Organization of American States evinced the full scope of that responsibility. The event, unparalleled in the Americas, was undeniably a result of the change international relations have undergone. Now extremist ideas and extremist methods militate against all national limitations and seek to extend themselves beyond geographic frontiers to turn these into a mere symbol of independence that will not be a hindrance to the impulsive ways of Marxism.

This far-reaching implication of the Dominican case was not opportunely minded by those who ought to have regarded it and pondered it most carefully. Our efforts to make that state of affairs understood were unavailing, and the blunder cost us treasure and energy untold. But we have no regrets over this because in the end we derived a profitable lesson in solitude. This humble country of the Caribbean anticipated the bewildering, world-shaking events of today and initiated the great battle that will decide the fate of Western Civilization.

19
Jesús de Galíndez
Inside a Dictatorship

Jesús de Galíndez, a Loyalist in the Spanish Civil War, came to the Dominican Republic and lived there for six years. He describes his residence in the following essay. As a teacher in the Dominican School of Diplomatic Law and legal adviser to the Government's Labor Department, Galíndez ultimately became too sympathetic to the workers' cause to suit Trujillo. He may also have had ties to the anti-Trujillo underground. Feeling threatened, he left in 1946 and settled in New York, where he pursued a doctorate in political science and served on the faculty of Columbia University. Meanwhile, Galíndez devoted much of his energies to a methodical accumulation of information about Trujillo's dictatorship. The spirited and humorous account here reproduced, first published in one of the Hemisphere's best-known and widely circulated journals, is one of the reasons Galíndez was marked as a prime enemy of Trujillo's state. His doctoral dissertation, completed early in 1956, was a sober and damning analysis of "The Era of Trujillo."[1] Negotiations for its publication in English had just begun when, on the night of March 12, 1956, Jesús de Galíndez mysteriously disappeared from his apartment in Manhattan, never to be seen again by his friends. Subsequently, well-publicized investigations indicated that Dominican agents abducted, drugged, and then smuggled Galíndez out of the United States as an "invalid" aboard a light plane piloted by a young American flyer, Gerald Murphy, who later disappeared himself. Once in the Dominican Republic, Galíndez was apparently murdered.

Jesús de Galíndez, who "knew more about Trujillo than anyone else in the whole world" (according to his Columbia colleague, Frank Tannenbaum), may have done more to discredit Trujillo after his death than while he was alive. Only

From Jesús de Galíndez Suárez, "Un reportaje sobre Santo Domingo," *Cuadernos Americanos* 80 (March–April 1955): 37–56.

the Pinochet regime's car bombing of the Chilean exile Orlando Letelier and Ronni Moffit on the streets of Washington, D.C., in 1976 may have been more of an international cause célèbre than the macabre disappearance of Galíndez. Like the Ecuadorian journalist Juan Montalvo (1832–89) who exulted at the assassination of the dictator Gabriel García Moreno in 1875 by saying, "My pen killed him," the shade of Jesús de Galíndez may have taken grim satisfaction over the riddled body of Rafael Trujillo in 1961.

I arrived in the Dominican Republic at the end of 1939 as a consequence of the Spanish Civil War in which I had fought as a good Basque in the Loyalist army. The majority of our refugees went to Mexico; but I was only twenty-four, with an excess of illusions, and reluctant to be one of the nameless mass. I wanted a small country where none of my fellows were going, for there alone would there be opportunities for me to blaze a trail in the New World. I had visited the Dominican legation in Madrid during the days of the siege, and the memory of some favors extended me gave me the inspiration to present myself at the consulate in Bordeaux where I acquired the visa which narrowly rescued me from Europe in the last North American ship. I . . . stayed in the Dominican Republic . . . for more than six years; six years during which I came to identify myself with the Dominican people as a brother and had the opportunity to live under one of the most picturesque political regimes that has ever existed in the world.

The Dominican Republic divides with Haiti the central island of the Antilles. In 1492 Columbus was captivated by its natural beauty, and from its shores later on departed almost all the great discoverers and conquerors. In its capital, Santo Domingo de Guzmán, there came to flourish a small viceregal court at the beginning of the sixteenth century. . . . Later the first Spanish colony in the New World fell into decay; and the attacks of Drake and other meddlesome corsairs preceded the settlement of rude pirates on its more inaccessible coasts; these later gave origin to the French colony whose slaves proclaimed a Negro republic at the beginning of the nineteenth century which took the indigenous name, Haiti. Three dates and two bloody wars led the way to

Dominican independence snatched successively from Spain in 1821, from Haiti in 1844, and from Spain again in 1865; finally to suffer yet again in the twentieth century the occupation of North American marines from 1916 to 1924. Innumerable civil wars and more than one dictator spatter her national history over the last century; but at the same time she is able to pride herself on the oldest . . . cathedral in America, on her abundance of illustrious writers beginning with the poetess Leonor de Ovando in the sixteenth century, and on her luxuriant natural wonders. . . .

But in the last twenty-five years this exuberant and tragic land has offered the observer a curious phenomenon. . . . For the Dominicans who endure it the Trujillo regime is a daily drama which silences lips and oppresses hearts. For alert foreigners the benefactor and his megalomanias are a treasure of incredible surprises which merit divulgence.

I confess that when I applied for a visa for the Dominican Republic I did not even think about who would be the president, so engrossed was I in carving out a new life for myself. My first knowledge of "Generalísimo" Rafael L. Trujillo Molina was acquired accidentally in that same Dominican consulate in Bordeaux. We were waiting in line for our passports to be countersigned in a room dominated by the portrait of an imposing personage wearing a hat with a white plume. One of my companions asked the consul, "Is that your president?" and the consul replied somewhat strangely, "No, he is not the president; he is the benefactor." My friend and I looked at each other uncomprehendingly; but, we thought shrugging our shoulders and putting our doubts to rest, bah? American doings.

I would soon discover the mystery of that "benefactor." I believe that my first Dominican political lesson was received near the Caribbean Sea at the Christopher Columbus Institute which the first refugees to arrive in the country opened. . . . One of our daily visitors was a creole journalist named Gimbernar . . . who was accustomed to boast of being one of the most faithful "Trujillistas." With a pride incomprehensible to us he bragged of being the only deputy who had resigned "by word of mouth." A few weeks later I heard some other comments no less incomprehensible from the lips of [the rector] of the University . . . , on whose *finca* [country estate] we who were aspirants to the faculty were accustomed to gather. President Peynado was dying and it seemed natural that Vice-President Troncoso de la Concha would fill the vacancy; nevertheless, the rector assured us in language which appeared sibylline, "The chief wants me to be the new president, but I have told him that Pipí ought not to resign."

Only some time after was I able to clear up these puzzling mysteries. In benefactor Trujillo's Dominican Republic there are elections, for what they are worth. . . . According to the official election returns . . . in 1952, 100 percent of the voters cast their votes for all the candidates, from the president to alderman, including senators and deputies. But Trujillo—el "jefe" y "benefactor"—makes them sign beforehand undated resignations of their elected offices. Afterwards, from time to time, he has only to add the day's date to one of these resignations and publish it simultaneously "suggesting" the name of the new congressman in accordance with Article 16 of the Constitution—for of course the Constitution is always applied to the letter—according to which if there is a vacancy in a popularly elected post the chief of the former incumbent's party presents a slate of three names from which the party caucus selects the substitute. In such a "constitutional" way the wirepulling of deputies and senators is an everyday affair. With reason our journalist friend boasted of being the only one who "resigned" by word of mouth, for there are legislators who learn about their resignations when they arrive in Congress without previously knowing what is going to happen. Even worse was the case of the Minister of Foreign Relations who, in the presence of a European Chief of Mission, ordered his Protocol Officer to find out why the newspaper whistle was blowing, then had to suffer the shame of being told that his own resignation "had been accepted."

Don Pipí Troncoso de la Concha finally became president, but later on he also had to give it up. This was one of the funniest episodes of the political operetta which I witnessed in the Dominican Republic. . . . It happened in the general election year 1942. Trujillo had been president from 1930 to 1934 and from 1934 to 1938; in 1938 he decided to take a little trip through Europe and he therefore saw to the election of his lieutenant Peynado, the president who died shortly after our arrival. At the end of the interim government of Vice-President Troncoso, all Trujillo's favorites were in a quandary because with the date approaching there were no signs which clearly revealed the new "president." It was only rumored that in this year of 1942 there would be a "fight"; this was because some months earlier the Dominican Republic had gone to war with the Axis Powers and circumstances requiring that there be at least a democratic façade, it would seem that to set up another candidate for defeat would be a simple matter. The only difficulty was that under Trujillo there only existed one party: the Dominican Party, boss: Trujillo. Thus any fight would be difficult no matter how well contrived.

An opposition party had to be organized rapidly. And one morning we breakfasted to sensational news: the awaited opposition party had been created, but it was called . . . the Trujillista Party! What's up? We had the answer the following morning; heavy type in the morning press informed us of the incredible news that the President of the National Directive Council of the Dominican Party had applied for admission to the new Trujillista Party and had been admitted at once. That was the signal; and everyone rushed to join the two parties.

For several months we witnessed a volcanic election campaign during which the public functionaries and the would-be bureaucrats scurried from meeting to meeting of both parties. The difficulty was in distinguishing one party from the other, because all the orators had but one subject: the most enthusiastic adulation of Trujillo. And we went on not knowing who would be the triumphant candidate and who the defeated.

The first convention was that of the Dominican Party, the traditional. The emotion of the delegates was uncontainable, for it was suspected with good reason that they would be "the victors." Finally there rose to the podium the President of the National Directive Council, the same one who had applied for admission to the opposition party; at last we were going to know the name of the favorite to be elected. But, what emotion!, the name which came from his lips as the nominee was none other than that of Generalísimo Dr. Rafael L. Trujillo Molina, benefactor of the country. The ovation was overwhelming; there was no longer any doubt that "they" would be the winners. Immediately there was a debate as to who should constitute the special commission which would communicate the good news, the surprise, to Trujillo. It is said that when the commission arrived at his estate, San Cristóbal, the Chief was taking his morning horseback ride and received the congratulations of the commissioners with an eloquent gesture of modesty: they could drink in celebration but as for *himself* he would continue his horseback ride without excitement, being above such human emotions. The following day the press presented us with a full page headline which said: "I will go on riding" [*Seguiré a caballo*]. . . .

"I will go on riding" was from that point on the slogan of the election campaign; the entire country was filled with posters with the equestrian figure of the Generalísimo, and a composer improvised a merengue with the symbolic refrain, "And I go on riding, said the general." The pinnacle of adulation was reached in an immense billboard . . . in the principal street of the capital city—Ciudad Trujillo, naturally—painted by an Italian jeweler who had until recently been an enthusiastic supporter of Mussolini . . . ; the poster read without the least shame: "I will go on riding said the Chief. And we will follow you on foot." It need hardly be said that Trujillo was elected president unanimously, for the Trujillista Party hurried to endorse his candidature. Thus ended that peculiar opposition party.

But the operetta did not end here. The elections were in May and the inauguration was to be celebrated in August; there were too many months of anticipation. The President of the Chamber—"antitrujillista" just a bit earlier—hurried to point out how difficult the situation was with the country at war; the Dominicans needed Generalísimo Trujillo at the helm at once, so it was necessary to find an immediate solution. This was easy; again the Constitution was brought into the game. On Monday we read the news that the Minister of War (incidentally, Trujillo's younger brother) had resigned and that President Troncoso had named Trujillo the Great for the post; on Tuesday President Troncoso resigned in an emotional session before both Houses; and, always in accord with the Constitution, the Minister of War occupied the vacancy provisionally. The rest of the combination was simple;

a little afterwards the president of the Senate, Porfirio Herrera, "resigned" and don Pipí was elected Senate president; the president of the Chamber of Deputies, Peña Batlle, "resigned" in his turn, and Herrera was elected Deputy President; Peña Batlle was named Minister of the Interior, his predecessor going on to occupy some other post which I have forgotten, and so on successively. What I cannot be precise about is who was the functionary who resigned from everything and was left without a job in this beautiful "constitutional" arrangement. . . .

All these memories which pile up as I write I became aware of little by little. . . . Already that muddy vision of the consulate in Bordeaux, the portrait in white plumage, seemed far removed. Now I was coming to know the Trujillo of flesh and blood; and many other things besides. Since I arrived in the country, I was able to admire the beautiful, multicolored neon sign which "President" Peynado rushed to have erected on his house the day he was "elected": "God and Trujillo." Advertisements for the Lottery proclaimed: "Be rid of poverty, and Trujillo forever." The capital city had had its name changed from that which Columbus had christened it to that of Ciudad Trujillo; it was located in Trujillo Province, and that which adjoined was named Trujillo Valdés (in memory of papa); there were also provinces called Benefactor, Libertador, San Rafael . . . ; the highest mountain had been rebaptized Trujillo Peak. It was incredible the notoriety reached by that man. Above all for me the best continues to be the sign which I saw on the door of the Nigua insane asylum: "Everything we owe to Trujillo."

How did this glorious operatic "generalísimo" appear? One of his many genial traits was that he won all his ranks without having fought in any campaigns. . . . His official history began in the years of the U.S. Marines' occupation of Santo Domingo; a young man from San Cristóbal named Rafael L. Trujillo was one of the few Dominicans who prepared himself to enroll in the ranks of the National Guard created in order to maintain order by the Army of Occupation. On retirement in 1924, Trujillo boasted the rank of captain; and in the Treaty of Evacuation it was stipulated that the officers of that Guard would go over and become officers in the new National Police. Captain Trujillo made a rapid career, with his native intelligence and North American training; soon he was Chief Colonel of the Police, which he reorganized completely with officers in whom he had confidence; and by 1927 he had become General in Chief of the recently created army. Then he had his chance. Since 1924 the President had been the old caudillo of the past civil wars, General Horacio Vásquez, against whom some forces from Cibao in the north of the island revolted. . . . General Trujillo hurried to reaffirm his loyalty to President Vásquez and advanced with his forces from the capital in order to combat the rebels; but secretly he had conspired with the latter and may have been their leader from the beginning, so that the rebels peacefully occupied the capital while Trujillo's troops remained inactive, "unable to find the enemy"; President Vásquez had to flee the country. . . . Months later Trujillo was elected president after an electoral campaign in which the police, whom he had reorganized, were much more effective than political rallies; and not long afterwards all his collaborators who might have put him in the shadows were purged: Vice-President Estrella Ureña was lucky enough to end up exiled in the United States; but another member of the Provisional Cabinet . . . was simply assassinated.

Thus began in 1930 the "Glorious Era of Trujillo." . . . It is an era which is carefully acknowledged in official documents and public buildings. For instance a law issued by a ministerial official must be dated on such and such a day in 1955, 112th year of Independence, 89th of the Restoration, and 25th of the Era of Trujillo.

The human side of this political personage is most interesting and worthy of a novel. . . . He has been married three times; the first appears to have occurred before his star had risen high in the zenith, and the light mulatto characteristics of his famous daughter Flor de Oro perpetuate the memory of a wife discarded when General Trujillo judged it necessary to have a more presentable Señora Trujillo. The second did indeed belong to high society, but she did not satisfy the new President's ideal of beauty; whereupon, in order to marry a third time, he did not hesitate to change the divorce laws. . . . Later the law was modified again because Trujillo lacked a male heir. He sought to acknowledge as his the illegitimate boy born to his third wife a little while before her divorce from a Cuban who denied the child's paternity. Years later Doña María de Trujillo wrote a most curious newspaper column on Sundays which bore the title "Moral Meditations."

This son is the famous "Ramfis." . . . At nine years of age he was named Brigadier General, which for a time provoked widespread rejoicing from everyone. When he reached fourteen, the newspapers duly told us that he had renounced his general's commission in order to begin a military career from the beginning. . . . The [subsequent] letters of congratulation from any number of secretaries of states, senators, and deputies . . . sought to proclaim such an act as a model to be imitated by Dominican youth.

Well, the resultant model could not be anything else but encouraging to the youth of whatever country because new cadet Trujillo climbed rapidly, one by one, all the ranks in the army until he became general at twenty-three. . . . At the same time he took his doctorate in law and obtained the highest decorations of the Orders of Christopher Columbus, Juan Pablo Duarte [a hero of Dominican independence in 1844], and even Trujillo.

. . . Trujillo has a third legitimate child, who was baptized Radamés, who was a colonel, I believe, at seven or eight years of age. [The Benefactor's] younger brother, Hector, is a general in the army and currently President of the Republic; another brother is brigadier general honoris causa and owns a radio-television station; another brother who died—a suicide—also had the rank of general. One brother-in-law is a retired major general, another holds high rank in military aviation, and a third administered the Lottery until a short time ago.

Trujillo's enemies are accustomed to speaking of his reign of terror. The cases which they mention are perfectly true, and I have had occasion to know personally some of the most recent victims. But his most powerful weapon is hunger. Nothing can be done in the Dominican Republic without demonstrating not only that one is not an enemy of the government but also that one is its avid supporter. Any official petition, including passport applications and import declarations, contains a line for the inclusion of the number and date of one's membership in the Dominican Party. Even the closest favorites know they are at the mercy of the merest caprice; and Trujillo enjoys proving that they are dependent upon that caprice. It is as easy to ascend to the highest offices as it is to be left destitute and even end up in prison.

I recall some cases in point. . . . In 1944 the man who had been Ambassador to the United States was transferred back home with the high position of Advisory Ambassador to the Secretariat of Foreign Relations. When this happened, we were about to celebrate the First Centenary of the Republic and all the ambassador's wife's friends knew that she had brought with her all the dresses necessary for the celebration, and the many receptions and parties. Well enough, but just two weeks before the beginning of the celebrations, Ambassador Troncoso was suddenly dismissed from office so devastatingly that there was no doubt that he had suffered total political disgrace; he was not even "elected" deputy as is the custom when the disgrace is partial. It need hardly be said that he remained isolated at home during the weeks of rejoicing and not even his friends dared invite him to private receptions. Ah, but as soon as the celebrations had ended he was named a member of the Cabinet, I believe as Secretary of the Treasury. In short, the ambassador had been punished by missing the Centenary as a naughty child is punished by missing his dessert. The worst of the matter is that he accepted the new position.

Such political disgrace suggests other complications. In Trujillo's Dominican Republic there is a scale of value for disgrace: A [deposed] minister might expect election as a senator, or, further down, a deputy; still worse he might be left with just the automobile and house the Chief had given him in bonanza days or disgraced further by walking on foot through the streets. A major fall from grace meant complete retirement from public life and real difficulty in gaining any sort of living. It is well to remember that but few ended up in jail; it was usually enough to crack the whip.

After so many years, almost everyone has become accustomed to a life of uncertainty. Punishment or promotion is accepted with the same resignation.

A member of the Trujillo cabinet told me in a fleeting moment of confidence and of personal irony that the Chief had made "a flock of tame sheep" out of the Dominican people. But from time to time someone blows up and contrives to escape into exile, where he joins the ranks of the "revolutionaries." Then the whip descends on his relatives, some of whom hurry to sign all the necessary documents to disavow the traitor, often publishing a statement to that effect in the newspapers; if they do not, the vengeance which cannot reach after the exiles reaches them.

[With respect to Communism in the Dominican Republic] it is well to give our attention to the eloquent parody on democracy carried out by Trujillo in 1946. World War II had just ended and many dictatorships were toppling; it was à la mode to "democratize." In the Dominican Republic this was easy; it was enough for the President to give the order.

The process had actually begun in December 1941 when the Japanese attacked Pearl Harbor. Within a few hours the news spread through the capital that the Dominican Republic was going to declare war on the Japanese Empire. . . . Curious as to how war is declared, I went to the Chamber of Deputies, where all the lawmakers were gathered ready to vote with their accustomed unanimity. But hours passed and the ceremony was not begun. This was because Don Pipí was President rather than Trujillo and he had to wait for cabled instructions from the benefactor, who was in the United States. . . . Finally this cable arrived, the President sent his message to Parliament requesting their approval in order to declare war, the senators and deputies voted "yes" (including those who had been Germanophiles the day before), and the President signed the declaration of war on Japan. But then arose the major problem: to whom should the declaration of war be read? In Ciudad Trujillo there was no Japanese diplomat. It was finally necessary to rout out of bed a poor Dominican merchant who had the bad luck to be an importer of Japanese goods and also, as a courtesy, an honorary consul. This astonished fellow listened to the solemn declaration of war before he was hauled off by the police as a "suspicious person." Two or three days later we were also at war with Germany and Italy.

And the war was won. Trujillo was one of the victors, one of the champions of democracy. It was then that the "democratization" of the regime really began. . . . In 1946, Trujillo sent an agent to Cuba in order to interview the exiled Dominican Communists there; among them was Periclito Franco. The Dominican Government offered them guarantees that they could reorganize publically in the Republic. The Communists accepted, several of them returned to the country, and the so-called Popular Socialist Party was for a time the only opposition party whose activities and propaganda were tolerated. . . . I do not know how fully the Communists took advantage of this opportunity, for I left the Dominican Republic at the beginning of 1946; but Trujillo's moves were clear from the beginning: by the eve of the 1947 elections he could confront the country saying that her only enemies were the Communists and that he was disposed to save the Dominican Republic from the Communist danger. . . .

This time Periclito ended up in jail with all those deceived youngsters, Communists and non-Communists, who had fallen into the trap. But "democratization" went right on. The elections of 1947 were the only ones during the Trujillo era which saw a "struggle" between three presidential candidates: Trujillo the Great, Don Fello Espaillat (who was Secretary of Economy before he was ordered to join the nominal opposition), and Panchito Prats as representative of a flaming Labor Party. . . . A few days before the election all of the deputies published their support for the saviour candidate; . . . the list included none other than the "labor" candidate Panchito Prats. It need hardly be said that Trujillo won. Some time later, Panchito returned as an "elected" deputy of the official Dominican Party; Don Fello Espaillat simply died.

Today [1954–55] the Dominican Republic has returned to its normal course. No longer is it necessary to "democratize." The Dominican Party (chief: Trujillo) is the only one; its "anti-Communism" is the topic of the day; the presidency is proudly occupied by the youngest brother in the dynasty; and Trujillo is again the benefactor . . . as in the days of my arrival in the Dominican Republic.

Notes

1. An English version was eventually published: Jesús de Galíndez Suárez, *The Era of Trujillo: Dominican Dictator* (Tucson: University of Arizona Press, 1973). For the Spanish version see *La Era de Trujillo* (Santiago de Chile: Editorial del Pacífico, 1956).

20

Howard J. Wiarda and Michael J. Kryzanek

Trujillo and the Caudillo Tradition

The third essay in this collection that treats the Trujillo regime was written sixteen years after "The Benefactor" was gunned down. Unlike Trujillo's own advertisement for himself and Galíndez's witty attack on the regime that consumed him, this analytical essay provides not only historical perspective but also a political and developmental model to help arrive at a balanced view of the Dominican Republic between 1930 and 1961. The authors are well known Latin Americanists. Howard Wiarda's many works include assessments of such major topics as corporatism and the prospects for development throughout the Hemisphere as well as penetrating studies of the Dominican Republic. He is among those scholars who warn against the application of Anglo value systems in the evaluation of Latin American socites. Michael Kryzanek is the author of a text on United States–Latin American relations.

This essay was contributed by Wiarda and Kryzanek to a special issue of *Revista/Review Interamericana* devoted to "Caribbean Dictators and Strong Men." In it they establish a list of criteria to measure caudillo regimes and then test the items against the historical record. Of particular importance is the stress they put on the dynamics of change over the three decades of Trujillo's rule. The caudillo's success was due, they argue, to his skillful employ of authoritarian techniques and his remarkable empathy with Dominican aspirations, especially in the 1930s and 1940s. In their analysis of the early years of his dictatorship, Wiarda and Kryzanek employ the model of authoritarian government worked out by Juan Linz in his study of the Franco regime in Spain. They show, however, that Trujillo became increasingly oppressive and rigid,

From Howard J. Wiarda and Michael J. Kryzanek, "Dominican Dictatorship Revisited: The Caudillo Tradition and the Regimes of Trujillo and Balaguer," *Revista/Review Interamericana* 7 (Fall 1977): 417–35. Reprinted with permission.

especially in the 1950s, to the point that he became totalitarian. That transition, they argue, put him out of touch with his people and led to his assassination.

Students interested in the more recent history of caudillismo in the Dominican Republic should consult the last half of this essay, which deals with the subsequent rule by Joaquín Balaguer after 1966.

"You must remember, Howard, that there is a little of Trujillo in every Dominican."—A prominent Dominican historian and politician, as told to one of the authors

LIKE styles in bathing suits, interpretations of political phenomena are marked by fads, phases, and cyclical, almost yearly change-overs. For a time during the Kennedy era, we rushed missionary and Peace Corps–style to condemn all dictatorships and embrace the democratic Left. Then, under the influence of Juan Linz's typology and sympathetic treatment, authoritarian and even semifascist regimes were again legitimized as areas of research inquiry. Now [in 1977], under President Carter's human-rights campaign, we seem again to be indiscriminately hostile and condemnatory toward all authoritarian regimes and practices.

Many of the older generation of Latin Americanists, as well as some of the newer ones, have been both more constant and more discriminating in their treatment. [For example,] in a slim volume published [in 1960], Rosendo Gómez usefully distinguished between constitutional presidents, demagogic caudillos, military guardians, and paternalistic caudillos. . . .

The present essay draws upon the earlier literature in fashioning a model, or more accurately a set of characteristics or checklist, of modern caudillo rule. It then proceeds to examine and reinterpret the Trujillo regime in the Dominican Republic in the light of this model.

The Caudillo Model

Without at this time rehashing the old theses of whether authoritarianism in Latin America is a product of cultural, social, political, racial, economic, geographic, or historic factors, it may confidently be asserted that strong centralized rule, or the aspiration thereto, has long been a hallmark of the area. At present, centralized authority is concentrated in the executive branch, particularly the office and person of the presidency. The modern-day caudillo president, as Frank Tannenbaum used to argue, is comparable in his powers to the Aztec emperors; or, one can look at the imperial presidency in Latin America as an extension of the absolutist concepts of imperial Spain and Portugal. And, although the term "caudillo" is used frequently by historians to distinguish the ruder strong men of the nineteenth century, as R. A. Humphreys emphasizes, "the dictator of the present age . . . is the heir of the nineteenth century caudillo." But if there is perhaps more continuity than differentiation between the nineteenth- and twentieth-century caudillos, it is also the case that new social and economic pressures, new ideologies, new forms of organization, and new techniques of control have shaped the regimes of the more modern dictators. The model and discussion below seeks to address both these continuities as well as the changes that have occurred in the caudillo tradition, with special reference to the Dominican Republic.

No claim can be made that the list of descriptive characteristics given below is all-inclusive. The list was fashioned by the authors as a convenient device to describe the nature of leadership in a caudillo regime. Other observers would likely include different characteristics or give the present ones different emphases. Nevertheless the list is a useful heuristic tool which we found helpful in analyzing past and present Dominican regimes. If others find it useful in thinking about caudilloism in other contexts, that is well and good; but it must be emphasized that what we are presenting is a set of characteristics with only modest pretensions to greater generality and no claim to being a full-fledged paradigm of caudillo rule. . . . The following is offered as a general description of some major leadership patterns and characteristics in a caudillo regime:

1. Caudillo leaders come generally (although not exclu-

sively) from the military and rely principally on the military for support.

2. Caudillo leadership is characterized by a strong personalistic style and way of dealing with the citizenry.

3. Caudillo leaders govern in a paternalistic and highly centralized manner.

4. Caudillo leaders tend to remain in office for an extended period of time (continuismo).

5. Caudillo leaders generally govern in an autocratic fashion, which often implies suppression of the opposition, the creation of official, government-sanctioned parties and other agencies, the effort to eliminate other, potentially subversive power bases, and a dictatorial hold on power.

6. Caudillo leaders have generally avoided what North Americans would term democratic norms of governance; instead they tend to erect organic state systems.

7. Caudillo leaders generally develop public policies designed to enrich themselves and their clientele, to perpetuate themselves in power, and to preserve the status quo that they have established.

8. Caudillo leaders tend to see little sharp difference between the public and private domains; they operate within a patrimonialist conception and often use their office and the apparatus of government for personal gain.

9. Caudillo leaders, particularly in the circum-Caribbean area, have seen the advantages of developing close ties with the United States government; by the same token they tend to be aggressive in curbing internal communist activities.

10. Although caudillo leaders may govern in an authoritarian fashion, which is often a reflection of their own society's general norms and expectations, they may not become totalitarians. There are limits beyond which a caudillo leader may not go. Ruling in a tyrannical fashion violates the informal but widely understood social contract or "rules of the game" governing the caudillo's relations with political society and justifies rebellion against his regime.

With this set of characteristics in mind, let us look now at the [regime] of Trujillo. . . .

The Trujillo Regime: A Reinterpretation

The regime of Rafael Leonidas Trujillo Molina, 1930–61, has been widely characterized as a bloody tyranny, as indeed during certain periods it was. The early books on the regime, such as those by Bosch, Galíndez, and Ornes, cast Trujillo in the evilest and "blackest" of terms as a despot, usurper, murderer, assassin, fascist, megalomaniac, and totalitarian. Some refer to him condescendingly as "swarthy." All of these characterizations, with certain qualifications, undoubtedly have a certain validity. But they no longer offer the only perspective on the Trujillo regime.

By the late 1960s other views began to be presented. Three major influences helped shape the newer interpretations. The first was the new emphasis on developmentalism which, when applied to the Dominican Republic, emphasized not just the sordid nature of the Trujillo regime but also its centralizing, consolidating, nation-building achievements. The second was the Linzian distinction between authoritarianism and totalitarianism and the more-or-less sympathetic presentation of the authoritarian alternative which made it somewhat easier for scholars to discuss Trujillo's authoritarianism in rational and functional terms rather than from the point of view of automatic condemnation. The third was the publication of Robert Crassweller's superb biography of Trujillo which, though weak on the historical continuity of his regime within the long tradition of Dominican caudilloism, presented Trujillo's life and activities sympathetically and made them understandable (though not necessarily commendable) within the context of Dominican society and culture. This approach has been bolstered in recent years by a whole body of literature and perspective that looks at Latin American experience and institutions more sympathetically, instead of through the biased perspectives of the United States. The discussion in this part of the paper seeks to analyze, sort out, and fuse what is useful in these varied interpretations.

There can be no doubt Trujillo was, first of all, a caudillo and bloody dictator, in conformity with the list of characteristics presented earlier. He rose up through the military, and the armed forces always remained the primary support of his regime. His rule was personalistic and charismatic. He governed in a paternalistic and highly centralized manner. . . . He governed autocratically, brutally suppressed all opposition, created an official party and a raft of other official agencies, and eliminated all potential sources of challenge to his regime.

Though Trujillo was a man of action more than an ideologue, [his] advisers were attuned to the ideological currents of the 1930s and helped Trujillo fashion the organic, neo-corporatized state system that was eventually established. Trujillo's public policies were designed to help enrich the ruling family, to perpetuate it in power, and to preserve the new status quo he had established. Trujillo operated within a patrimonialist tradition and saw little or no separation between the public and the private domains. Trujillo carefully cultivated his relations with the United States, part of which involved posing as the Hemisphere's foremost anti-Communist. Finally, Trujillo took pains to operate within the parameters of the Dominican political tradition, though toward the end, as we shall see, he overstepped its boundaries and was overthrown.

While it is clear, thus, that the caudillo model above closely describes the Trujillo regime, it is a static description rather than a dynamic one. It provides little sense of the ebb and flow of events, changing developments and societal contexts, the corresponding changes in the Trujillo dictatorship, and how his regime first enjoyed widespread popularity and then fell outside the national consensus. Let us try to provide these perspectives now, by concentrating on the insights provided by the newer literature.

First, it is important to think of the Trujillo regime within a development perspective. The context of the times is important. Trujillo came to power in 1930 upon the heels of the collapse of the old oligarchic order. He stepped into and filled a power-and-legitimacy vacuum brought about by the fact that while an older system had disintegrated, no new or modern one had as yet emerged that was sufficiently strong to take its place. In this sense Trujillo's was a transitional regime. He provided the national order and stability in which a new period of growth and consolidation could ensue. After a devastating hurricane leveled the capital city in 1930, he rebuilt it—while increasing his own power in the process. He modernized and greatly expanded Dominican agriculture and presided over the first stages of industrialization. He modernized the army, the public service, the banking system. He built roads, airports, highways, public buildings, aqueducts, port facilities. He provided the national infrastructure that had heretofore been lacking. Of course these accomplishments came at considerable costs in personal and political liberty, and few projects were undertaken which did not profit the Trujillos. Still, Trujillo presided over an unprecedented era of modernization, development, and nation-building. It was not just by blood and tyranny that he stayed in power for thirty-one years but because of real accomplishments as well.

A second useful perspective for reinterpreting the Trujillo regime is provided in Linz's model of authoritarianism. Linz described an authoritarian political system (Franco's Spain), as distinct from a totalitarian one, as having limited pluralism, a "mentality" but not necessarily a guiding ideology, no intensive or extensive political mobilization, a ruler who exercises power within formally ill-defined limits but actually quite predictable ones. This description fits the early Trujillo regime nicely (though whether it fits the later, more totalitarian Trujillo system is a point we must also consider). Particularly relevant for this discussion, and serving also as a link to the previous point, is Linz's comment that authoritarian regimes are the outcomes of the breakdown of more traditional forms of legitimacy. Authoritarian regimes, he says, are therefore modernizing in that they represent a break with traditional forms, introducing criteria of efficiency and rationality, personal achievement, and even a degree of populist appeal. "Authoritarian rule," he concludes, "might be an intermediate stage in or after the breakdown of traditional authority."

By thus rationalizing authoritarian regimes such as Trujillo's, Linz's formulation helped legitimize the study of them. The model also provided a useful tool by which to distinguish authoritarianism from fascist totalitarianism and thus to analyze the Trujillo system. Although it is outside the scope of this paper, it may be suggested that a useful comparative study might be done of similar authoritarian modernizers: Salazar in Portugal, Franco in Spain, Perón in Argentina, Vargas in Brazil. Trujillo's rule was probably bloodier than these, but that should not blind us to other attributes of his regime. A strong populist-authoritarian-corporatist-organicist-developmentalist streak runs through all of them, providing fertile ground for fruitful comparative analysis.

The third major influence leading to a reinterpretation of the Trujillo regime was the Crassweller biography, coinciding with a new and more general body of literature arguing that Latin America must be looked at sympathetically and through its own eyes, rather than from the perspective of the United States and its institutions. This approach had several implications for our understanding the nature of Trujillo's rule.

First, the Trujillo regime must be looked at in its historical context. After the first "golden" fifty years, Hispaniola experienced one of the most miserable histories in all Latin America, marked by regression of its social and economic institutions, abysmal poverty, repeated foreign occupations, dependency, and lack of development. Virtually all of the island's subsequent history, first as a colony and then as an independent nation, may be looked on as an effort to overcome these historic deficiencies, resurrect the glorious sixteenth-century model, and earn a renewed, albeit modest place in the sun. This Trujillo did. He filled the organizational and institutional void. He increased the population and filled the empty space. He created modern structures and agencies. He developed the economy and paid off the foreign debt. Little known is the history of how he took over many foreign-owned properties and "Dominicanized" the economy. He achieved military parity and then superiority vis-à-vis the Dominican Republic's historic threat, Haiti, which had twice the population. His country and its vote were courted in international circles; Dominican accomplishments in various fields were recognized and skillfully manipulated by Trujillo to identify the accomplishments of his regime with rising Dominican nationalism. Of course all informed Dominicans were also aware of the abuses and sometimes the high comedy of the arrogant, pretentious Trujillo "society." But most . . . were discerning enough to take pride in the accomplishments as well. Trujillo had in various areas restored some of the traditional glory, helped give the Dominican Republic a bit of lustre and pride, and restored in part its respectability. These factors were probably more important than any instruments of despotism in explaining the longevity of Trujillo's rule. Further historical perspective is lent to the Trujillo regime if we remember that Trujillo was very much in keeping with the long tradition of Dominican caudillo rule and was not, for a long time, outside the mainstream of public opinion and support. Historically in the Dominican Republic, only strong governments—Santana, Báez, Heureaux, Trujillo, now Balaguer—have been nation-builders. Democratic rule is admired as an ideal, a goal to strive for, but democratic governments—Espaillat in the 1870s, Bosch in the 1960s— have been weak, short-lived, inefficient, and characteristically unable to hold together the wrenching centrifugal tendencies and divisive clan politics that [make up] . . . Dominican political society. Most Dominicans recognize this; hence their loyalty and support, by both cultural tradition and political experience, have often gone to strong men-on-horseback. Trujillo was such a strong forceful leader, as well as a builder of his nation; and so long as Trujillo operated within the parameters of acceptable Dominican political behavior, his regime was widely supported.

A class/racial perspective also sheds new light on the Trujillo era. Trujillo was of middle-class social origins and of a mulatto racial background. So were the fellow military officers and henchmen who came to power with him in the 1930s. Trujillo had wrenched political and eventually social and economic power away from the white, aristocratic ruling classes who had dominated the national life up till then. He took pains to embarrass these haughty *tutempotes*, whom Bosch would also later denounce so effectively. The Trujillo era was thus not just another in the long line of Dominican strong governments but symbolized a class and caste shift in the way power was organized as well. For the majority of Dominicans, themselves of modest social origins and mixed racial background, Trujillo's ambitions and accomplishments provided something they could admire and identify with. Since they were largely unaffected by the abuses of the dictatorship, these other factors took on added significance in explaining the strong popular support Trujillo long enjoyed.

Trujillo organized one of the tightest and most close-knit dictatorships the world has ever seen. This political variable is also important in explaining his popularity and longevity. He succeeded in tying society and polity together more tightly, binding up more "loose ends," than any other Dominican president. Two intriguing propositions follow: If it is in fact the case that the ideal model to which Dominicans look historically is that similarly tightly integrated, prosperous, developmentalist model of early sixteenth century imperial Spain, of both the mother country's and Hispaniola's own "golden age," then Trujillo came closest of all succeeding Dominican rulers to resurrecting and reestablishing this "ideal type." And if it is also the case, as many Latin Americanists are now arguing [in 1977], that an integrated, organicist, tightly coordinated, and corporatist (in the broad sense) regime constitutes the generally preferred developmentalist model of Latin America and toward which the aspirations of its elites and people are directed, then the Trujillo regime, along with Salazar's in Portugal (although the latter was certainly more "corporatist" in a formal-legal sense), constituted one of the closest approximations ever realized to that kind of system. That again helps explain the widespread popular acceptance of the Trujillo regime. It also gives it an importance that reaches beyond the confines of the Dominican Republic and makes it an especially exciting case on which to develop comparative perspectives.

These new interpretations from diverse perspectives on the Trujillo regime come together in a consideration of Dominican aspirations. In addition to the aspirations for development and a measure of national dignity already alluded to, the Dominicans, modern survey research seems to indicate, prefer an "organic democracy" to the inorganic sort that Bosch tried to provide. That does not imply necessarily that they prefer Rightist, conservative, stand-pat regimes. Dominicans also demand social justice. But they perceive that all these things can best be achieved through a closely integrated and caudillo regime that ties all the strings together, not one patterned after the looser, open-ended, hurly-burly, laissez-faire pattern of North American democracy. . . .

But if caudilloism, Trujillo, and "organic democracy" are so close to the mainstream of Dominican politics and widely supported and even admired— helping to explain, as the quotation with which we began this paper says, why "there is a little of Trujillo in every Dominican"—then why, one legitimately asks, did the regime so ingloriously fall and come to be so widely hated. Although the reasons are complex and multifaceted, a useful starting point is provided by applying a time perspective. Trujillo came to power as a caudillo with widespread popular support and retained that support through the 1930s and 1940s, as the regime and the country developed. But in the 1950s Trujillo began to overreach himself, went too far, overstepped the boundaries of permissible *authoritarian* behavior and employed such tyranny and oppressive controls that they verged on *totalitarianism*. In addition, time and societal change had passed the Trujillo regime by. Whereas before he had been an accommodator of new social interests, now he used brutal repression to hold back any change. As he became more and more of a tyrant, running roughshod over both individual rights and corporate group *fueros*, resistance, in the time-honored fashion, grew. In 1961 he was assassinated, not by those desiring a new inorganic form of democracy and a complete changeover of "the system," but by elements who wished only to adjust the regime to the newest realities, restructure it along modernized lines, and inherit it for themselves.

21
Alain Rouquié
Dynasty: Nicaraguan Style

Alain Rouquié, former Director of Research at the Fondation
Nationale des Sciences Politiques in Paris and French Ambassador to El Salvador, includes the following analysis of the
Somoza dynasty (1933–79) in his thoughtful treatise on militarism in Latin America. In it he seeks "to understand how
the armed forces can support personal, and even family, dictatorships and the degree to which one can describe patrimonial
tyrannies as military regimes." In doing so he questions how
a dominant family uses the armed forces and what sort of
resources assure their loyalty. Rouquié demonstrates that the
Nicaraguan National Guard had its fortunes fused with the
extended family of Anastasio "Tacho" Somoza at least from
the assassination in 1933 of Augusto César Sandino in which
both were implicated. With the Guard's help Tacho and his
two sons, Luis and "Tachito," who succeeded him, became
ever more proficient in promoting continuismo during the
forty years after Fitzgibbon wrote his article. The intimate
ties between "Tachito" and the National Guard help explain
the emergence of the antirevolutionary Contras during the
decade after the Sandinistas took power in Managua in 1979.
Readers may debate whether Rouquié's comparison of the
Somoza family with the Mafia is valid.

THE dictator-generals of the nineteenth century in Latin America
were rarely professional military men. We use the Latin American
term "caudillo" for them, but it is more accurate to call them
"political entrepreneurs" who made use of a variety of means—
most often force, but also ideology—to further their enterprise of

From Alain Rouquié, *Military and the State in Latin America,* translated and
edited by Paul E. Sigmund (Berkeley: University of California Press, 1987), 156–
65. Copyright © 1987 The Regents of the University of California. Reprinted with
permission.

enrichment and personal power. The government belongs to the one who can seize control. The state is available for the taking because there is no state. The daring hacendado transforms his peons into soldiers, and distributes Mauser rifles instead of pickaxes; "he harvests wheat in time of peace, gathers in men in time of war." A partisan chieftain calls himself "general," and if he is lucky he becomes one of the heavy-handed patriarchs whose picturesque tales loom large in the history of the continent.

In Venezuela in the twentieth century, "General" Juan Vicente Gómez waited for the right moment to seize power from his comrade Cipriano Castro after serving as his faithful second in command, and allowed the petroleum whirlwind to modernize the country and the state. This precocious native of the Andes administered his family's hacienda in Táchira on the Colombian frontier at the age of fifteen. He distrusted the army and only reluctantly accepted the foreign military missions, which he played off against each other. He seems to have believed—correctly—that educated officers and semiautonomous institutionalized armed forces were in contradiction to his rude personal style of government. Men who had a little bit of power and owed him nothing were potentially dangerous. He knew so well who his adversaries were that with the help of petroleum he died in his bed in 1935 after twenty-seven years as dictator.

However, the confusion, or at least the customary identification, of dictators with generals does not come only from the fact that civilian despots in the tropics don gold braid. It is true that repressive and narrowly personalized tyrannies have used the army as their instruments, and its officers have been their principal beneficiaries. The military pronunciamento has become a modernized form of political entrepreneurship. The professionalization and bureaucratization of the army have made personal uprisings more and more difficult, but nevertheless the coup has made a deep impression on the collective memory. In addition a military neo-caudillismo has appeared in certain national and organizational circumstances, the analysis of which is helpful in comprehending the nature of military power.

We also tend to identify dictators with generals in the apparently disorganized state of the politics of the continent because there is no fundamental difference between the governing style of the caudillos in uniform and that of their civilian counterparts. The institutional element is almost absent in a number of cases in the nineteenth century in which the general-presidents seem to have deliberately ignored the impersonal objective norms that govern the functioning of the civilian and military bureaucracies. Among the most flamboyant and baroque dictatorships were those that permitted the accession to power through a coup by an officer who had grown old in the military service. General Hernández Martínez in El Salvador, . . . who was responsible for the massacre of some thirty thousand peasants in 1932, governed that tiny republic of the Central American isthmus from 1931 to 1944 to the profit of the large landholders. . . . Not sparing those who opposed him, this convinced theosophist claimed that in fact it was more criminal to kill an ant than a man, since the man could become reincarnated. At the time that Roosevelt was giving his fireside chats on the goals of the New Deal, this magician general initiated programs on spiritualism in which he responded person-ally to the questions of the listeners concerning the transmigration of souls and miraculous cures for all ailments.

We do not intend to focus on these more or less extreme examples of political despotism. . . . However, . . . we seek to understand how the armed forces can support personal, and even family, dictatorships and the degree to which one can describe patrimonial tyrannies as military regimes. What are their real relations with the army? How do such dictatorships maintain themselves after having been established? What is the role of the military factor and of other power resources under their control? What is the degree of loyalty that the armed forces have to them, and how is their reliability assured? If the nation's military have become the praetorian guard of a despot, what are the causes of that transformation and what appear to be its limits?

[Here follows] an analysis [of one] of the "Sultanates" of the Caribbean where archetypal tyrannies—some of which have only recently ended—arose within the guards or the "apolitical and nonpartisan" armies established by the American marines in the course of de facto protectorates. The Somoza dynasty in Nicaragua [possessed] relatively distinct characteristics and very specific military components. . . .

Having recently become a politician in the Liberal Party, Anastasio Somoza García—"Tacho" to his friends and protectors as well as to his enemies—became Jefe Director of the National Guard that had been set up by the Yankee occupier because he spoke English perfectly and knew how to please.

Stimson, the representative of Calvin Coolidge in Nicaragua, described him as "open and friendly." Tacho was, it is true, as jovial and optimistic as his son and successor, "Tachito," was sinister and irritable. As for the son, he was a genuine military man, having graduated from West Point. One of his enemies said of him, "Khaki is like a second skin for him." In contrast, Tacho, the first Somoza, was an authentic civilian. When he received the command of the guard, the only activity of that substitute force was to hunt down the *libertador* Sandino, an action in which the first Somoza did not participate. Nevertheless, it was Sandino and the Sandinista menace that allowed him to assure himself the loyalty of that new army. With consummate ability Somoza was able to utilize the fear of the "general of free men" to unite that inglorious force behind him. And if—no doubt because of the pressure from his officers, who feared the revenge of the head of the "crazy little army"—he agreed to the traitorous assassination of Sandino without being aware of how unpopular that act would be for his future political career, it was no doubt because he understood that with the murder of the hero he signed a veritable blood pact with his officers and with the guard as a whole. By 1936 the way to power was open to him; his control of the guard was total, thanks especially to his enemies, who denounced his crime and his ambition and identified him completely with his men. President Juan B. Sacasa, a relative of Somoza's by marriage, became involved in a veritable contest with the "Jefe Director," with the National Guard as the prize. The president tried in vain to control the guard as mandated by the constitution, while Somoza took pains to deflect and undermine him by placing reliable men in all the command positions.

The result of that confrontation was that Somoza, after removing Sacasa by a judicious use of force, became the only candidate in presidential elections that were supervised by the National Guard. He won the election despite the desperate appeals of the former president and his political allies to the American authorities, who nevertheless allowed the election to take place. The Department of State and the War Department had such confidence in their creature that they were not upset by the fascist-style populism that the candidate exhibited during his campaign. As paramilitary "blue shirts" raised their fists in the streets of Managua, the Somocista campaign speeches were happy to compare the Jefe Director to Hitler or Mussolini. Rare, however, were the American diplomats such as Bliss Lane, who understood that the National Guard was not the apolitical gendarmerie that they had imagined, but rather an "American-Nicaraguan hybrid" that would henceforth constitute one of the "principal obstacles to the progress of Nicaragua."

Thus the longest-ruling Latin American dictatorship was born. (The Somoza family reigned over the country for no less than forty-three years, from 1936 until 1979.) The death of the dictator, assassinated by an opponent in 1956, did not produce the end of the dictatorship; his oldest son, Luis, took over his father's responsibilities, with the aid of his brother, Anastasio (Tachito), who commanded the guard and then assumed supreme power in his turn until he was overthrown by the Sandinista insurrection—not without the hope that his son, an officer of the guard, would take over the family business. Thus, it is a family dynasty that we are discussing, and not politics in the modern sense.

The first Somoza, the founder of the dynasty, belonged to a middle-class family and inherited a badly managed coffee plantation. He himself had made his living in different ways, including [working] as a used car salesman in the United States, as an inspector of public latrines (for the Rockefeller Foundation), and as a coffee grower. It was also said that he had tried his luck at gambling and at counterfeiting American currency. In any case, his fortune was established in 1956 at some $60 million, and the family appeared to be the largest landholder in the country: fifty-one cattle-raising ranches and forty-six coffee plantations belonged to him, as well as properties in nearby countries such as neighboring

Costa Rica and as far away as Mexico, not to mention forty-eight properties in Managua. It was rumored that 10 percent of the arable land in Nicaragua belonged to him, and his industrial interests were already very diversified. The heirs of the first Somoza did not let the family empire decline. It is estimated that the Somoza fortune in 1979 was between $500 and 600 million and included a fifth of the cultivatable land in the country, the twenty-six largest industrial companies, and interests in 120 corporations. With the eight biggest cane plantations in the country and several refineries, the Somozas were the largest producers of sugar and had a monopoly on alcohol; they had partial control of bananas, meat, salt, vegetable oils, and a monopoly on pasteurized milk. The Somozas, for whom there was no such thing as a small profit, were also the representatives of Mercedes and other European automobile companies in their fiefdom; they owned the only national airline (LANICA), the shipping companies, and had major shares in the textile and cement industries. Their holdings were in the hands of a bank that belonged to them and they controlled a savings and loan company that was concerned with building construction (CAPSA). This list is incomplete. We should emphasize that the precise and full extent of the business of the clan is not known and note that certain American business groups frequently worked with the family companies. United Fruit and the eccentric billionaire Howard Hughes were often associated with the Somoza enterprises. However, one should add that because of the Somocista domination, many foreign countries preferred to invest in Nicaragua's neighbors.

More interesting, no doubt, are the methods used to acquire these riches. It is evident that it was not unremitting labor and savings that made it possible, but rather extortion, racketeering, violence, and fraud of all kinds. The origin of the family's control of national wealth was to be found in contraband in gold and imported products, the purchase at a low price of herds that had already been endangered, or of enterprises that had been put into financial difficulty by the government or by political friends of the dictator. Intimidation and bureaucratic or physical harassment evidently played a considerable role in the amassing of the family fortune. The first Somoza also had the custom of collecting personal commissions on foreign trade and on less respectable activities: gambling, prostitution, and smuggling. The war permitted him to seize the properties of German citizens, providing the initial nucleus of his landholdings.

In addition, the weakness of capitalist development in Nicaragua facilitated the control of Somoza. It was the state or its functional equivalent that, in a period when statism did not yet have a bad name, replaced a deficient private sector in the areas of banking and public services. Electricity, hospitals, railroads, and water companies were state companies in which the clan took care to place near or distant relatives, thus furthering the business interests of the group by putting public enterprises at the service of the private interests of the dictatorship. This confusion between the state and the interests of the family gave a certain foundation to the humorous claim of the last Somoza that since the time of his father Nicaragua had been "a socialist state." In fact it was precisely the insatiable cupidity of the Somocista dynasty that produced its defeat.

The cotton boom in the 1950s and later the industrial opportunities provided by the Central American Common Market resulted in the formation of a local bourgeoisie that constituted several large groups, posing a threat to the clan. Their relations with the hydra-headed Somoza enterprises deteriorated rapidly after Tachito came to power in 1967. The bourgeoisie did not appreciate the special privileges that the Somoza businesses enjoyed or the brutal and unscrupulous "dynamism" that limited their own development. The dynasty's administration of the international aid that was given to the country after the 1972 earthquake increased that separation. Rather than dividing the bonanza and aiding private groups in difficulty, Somoza took total control of the aid and diverted the funds for his own profit, thus allowing the rewards of international solidarity to be pillaged by his friends and concealing the corruption imposed on his people. From then on the bourgeoisie joined the opposition; the dynasty no longer guaranteed the overall interests of the propertied classes. Despite its traditional capacity to maneuver, the family became isolated due to its excessive voraciousness and thus gave the Sandinista insurgents the leverage they needed to emerge from their marginal situation.

If the first Somoza had some justification for saying, "L'état, c'est moi," his personal control over the National Guard was not an inevitable result of the weakness of the organization of the Nicaraguan state. In fact the loyalty of the guard was assured by various factors that often had little to do with the military ethic. In the first place, ever since the assassination of Sandino had produced the image of the guard as a repressive and illegitimate body in national terms, the military forces and Somoza had locked themselves into a situation of reciprocal guarantees for mutual benefit. In addition, two sources of the guard's loyalty lay in its paternalism and the corruption of the officers. That army, so little statist and lacking in tradition, supported the family's power because the leadership enjoyed their privileges and benefited from the enrichment of the dynasty. There is no need to recall that since the time of the first Jefe Director family members were always at the top of the chain of command, and the Somozas never gave the direct and indirect control of the army to others. Tachito, son of the founder, did his military studies at West Point, and it could be said that he was the only cadet to receive an army as a graduation present. Once he became dictator, his half-brother, José, supervised the guard command directly, while his son, Tachito II, a graduate of American schools who had been promoted to the rank of captain for "services rendered to the country" after the 1972 earthquake, commanded the elite antiguerrilla troops.

Beginning in 1967, the year when the last Somoza actually became president, the government appeared to be simply an extension of the army. The dictatorship, faced with internal and external difficulties, became militarized, but in its own special way. As a symbol of the times, the presidential palace, which was perched on the Tiscapa Hill, became a barracks of the guard overlooking Managua in a quasi-feudal manner. The government, the army, and the family became one. Private apartments, offices, and military encampments revealed the nature of power. While denunciations and mutual espionage were abundantly utilized to prevent military conspiracies, loyalty depended on extrainstitutional factors. The Somoza who directed the guard acted more as a "godfather" than the head of the general staff. The army that was also the police force and administered the customs, borders, and prisons saw its functions multiply in the course of the years. In addition, all the commands had additional revenues that the dictator ignored. Appointments to the most lucrative posts and illegal revenues completely out of line with modest officers' salaries were common within the guard, depending on the loyalty and servility of the officers. The military command of each city had its price. The commander of Chinandega was required to collect some $20,000 a month for the protection of bars, nightclubs, gambling halls, gun permits, and various violations and fines. The head of the immigration service could make four times as much, as could the head of the central police services, a post with good connections. The officers on active service rapidly became millionaires in cordobas and in dollars—thanks to these semiofficial sources of income that were known to all. Since the dictator was able at any point to retire an officer into the reserve, the corps' economic situation was a direct function of their support for the clan. Similarly, once in retirement loyal officers could benefit from civil positions with revenues equal to those that they had had in the military. The businesses of the dynasty and the public corporations swarmed with retired senior officers who, although without particular competence, occupied the high-level positions. One observer remarked a few days before the fall of the regime that half the members of the board of directors of the national bank were retired officers, "whose knowledge of banking would no doubt fit on the head of a pin."

This complex network of military and bureaucratic factors, of economic interest and pure and simple gangsterism, all stimulated and controlled by the government, appeared to be one of the foundations of the Somoza system. The soldiers, a majority of them only semiliterate, were the first victims of the corruption of the officers: they were badly clothed and fed as a result of the "commissions" collected by their officers. An officer who deserted from the guard claims that they also had inferior military supplies because of kickbacks to those responsible for military purchases. However, for the troops military paternalism took the place of equity and served to reinforce group loyalty. During the last campaigns against the Sandinistas, the boots worn by the guard fell apart in the first rainstorm. Somoza's son, Tachito II, as a captain, distributed new jungle boots made in the United States as a Christmas present! The Somozas knew the private and family problems of the soldiers, and on their part they could ask for personal assistance in case of need. There was nothing less bureaucratic and impersonal. These soldiers were assured that Somoza "would not let them down." Enlisted men and low-level officers had easy access to the services of the presidential "bunker" and to the head of the clan in violation of military hierarchy and etiquette, because they were assigned to spy on their superiors. Institutional orders or rules had no binding power over the president. The hierarchy that counted was not that of seniority and merit, but the links between the men and the person of the dictator and his family. Officers and politicians responded by denouncing the violations of the principles of discipline. This apparently "military" dictatorship thus demilitarized the army by corrupting it and by violating the hierarchical chain of command. The Nicaraguan National Guard was not an army like the others.

Still, it would be wrong to believe because of the bloody and indiscriminate repression that accompanied the last days of the regime in 1979 that the reign of the Somozas was only maintained by the terror imposed by the praetorian guards. Whereas it is clear that the dictatorship resorted to a high level of violence, it is not likely that one could terrorize a whole people for nearly forty-five years, and besides, repression alone does not explain why the dynasty was able to survive the death of the tyrant who created the system. This is true even though in 1956, after the assassination of the elder Somoza, the wave of repression that followed was particularly intense in order to discourage any hint of opposition. It was at this time that the patrimonial character of the system appeared most crudely. Not only did the two sons of the dictator carry out military repression, but the jails in the presidential palace were filled with distinguished prisoners who were subjected to torture in long interrogation sessions in which Tacho II, the chief of the guard, personally participated. It can be said that official political violence never ceased from the time of the electoral campaign of 1967, in which the Somoza candidate (Anastasio Somoza Debayle, still in power in 1979) won a highly disputed election thanks to fraud and the utilization of paramilitary groups to massacre demonstrators who favored his opponent.

In fact, the dynasty made use of other political resources. The astuteness of the first Somoza undoubtedly played a role, but specifically political and social methods should be mentioned. Despite his common origins and his seizure of power, the elder Somoza acquired a certain social legitimacy within the Nicaraguan ruling class by marriage. He was related in that way to the Debayle and Sacasa families, that is, to the Liberal oligarchy. In these societies, where patronage plays an important role, this was a valuable asset. Those under obligation to, or unconditional supporters of, the Debayle family thus supported the dictatorship for reasons that had little to do with its politics. In addition, the dictatorship knew how to utilize the traditional two-party system. Somoza, when he took control of the Liberal party with which he was allied politically and socially, acquired a network of followers and political control that was parallel to that of the army. Paradoxically, the fact that the Conservative Party, the enemy of the Liberals, had been closely linked to the United States since Díaz helped to undermine the credibility of the opposition. That weakness, as well as the characteristics of the national ruling class, helped to produce a number of arrangements between the opposition and the dictatorship that periodically legitimized the power of Somoza. Indeed, the regime maintained a façade of constitutionality that was carefully preserved despite some problems of adjustment when the political course followed by the family was particularly irregular.

The first Somoza, who was assassinated while distributing free drinks during a workers' club festival in León, knew how to play the populist role in order to stay in power. After receiving the unexpected support of the Communist party at the end of the Second World War, after he had aligned his country docilely with the United States, Tacho overcame the serious postwar crisis that was fatal to his neighbors, Ubico and Hernández Martínez, by adopting social-welfare measures that divided his opposition. At that time the government created official trade unions and decreed a very advanced labor code that was to be applied in particular to the enterprises owned by opponents of the regime. Nevertheless, under pressure from the United States, Somoza decided to hand over power in 1947. Argüello, his carefully chosen successor, was removed four weeks later when the new president indicated that he wished to free himself of the control of his predecessor— who still commanded the guard. Argüello's puppet successor lasted three months, at which point Tacho changed the constitution and "elected" his uncle, Victor Román Reyes, who remained as president until his death in 1950. Tired of these maneuvers, the dictator again changed the constitution and had himself elected for six years by the Congress after an agreement with the Conservative Party. At his death, Luis, who seemed to have some ability for politics, was elected president. When Luis died in 1963 it seems that American pressure—under the Kennedy administration in the period of the Alliance for Progress—prevented Tachito from ascending the throne in his turn. A confederate, René Schick, occupied the presidency. Schick tried to broaden the base of the family's power, bringing the country a period of liberalization. Waiting no longer, the impetuous general who had been the favorite son, it was said, of the assassinated patriarch, had himself elected president in 1967. Although he had fewer votes than his Conservative opponent, partisan vote-counters were sufficient under the Somozas to reverse the results. In 1970 a new agreement with the Conservatives restored the façade of democracy to the system. Somoza was replaced by a provisional triumvirate without power until the December 1972 earthquake that led the general to place himself patriotically at the head of the National Disaster Committee and to use that occasion to achieve total power.

Everyone was aware of how much the clan owed to the United States. Tachito, after he was let down by his protector in 1978, said much about the services he had rendered in return for U.S. favor. Yet we should not believe that the successive dictators were puppets in the hands of the United States or simple instruments for its purposes. If this had been the case there is no doubt that a military coup d'état at the appropriate time would have deposed the unattractive U.S. partner. In fact, Somoza and the Somozas knew how to make use of the United States to maintain their power and to disarm their internal and external enemies. Besides, since relations with the great protector were a decisive political resource, the family itself made sure of the diplomatic representation in Washington. Ambassador Sevilla Sacasa, the son-in-law of Tacho and brother-in-law of Tachito, remained as the representative to the authorities of the metropole for practically the entire duration of the dynasty, and even became the dean of the diplomatic corps in Washington. In addition, to further defend their interests the Somozas maintained a lobby in Washington that was, however, more costly than effective. In 1975 the general spent an official figure of $500,000 to retain the favor of the Americans. A former congressman from Florida, N. Cramer, and the former secretary of the navy, Fred Korth, were his principal lawyers, while representatives John Murphy of New York and Charles Wilson of Texas could secure the support, when necessary, of several dozen members of Congress. The United States ambassadors, far from acting as proconsuls in Managua, often appeared to be employees or business partners of the clan that they defended at the Department of State. The famous Ambassador Whelan, "Tom" to his friend, Tacho, and a "real father" in the words of Tachito, through his unconditional support for the dictatorship acted to undermine the Good Neighbor Policy of F. D. Roosevelt. More recently, Turner Shelton, ambassador to Managua under Nixon, gave unlimited support to the Somozas in open disagreement with the more prudent analyses of the State Department and the White House.

The hereditary dictatorship of the Somozas thus seems to demonstrate more the structure and conduct of the Cosa Nostra in Sicily or New York than the values and mentality of the military. It is not without significance, however, that a certain type of armed force was able to produce this kind of regime and that it was not the only one of its kind.

22

Marysa Navarro

Is a Caudilla Possible? The Case of Evita Perón

No woman in twentieth-century Latin America has attracted more attention, more praise, and more vilification than María Eva Duarte de Perón (1919–52). Her meteoric rise to prominence, her spellbinding public role as the wife of the Argentine dictator Juan Perón, and her sudden death due to cancer at age thirty-three have contributed to elaborate myths about her life and the extent of her power. Myths about her outside Argentina have been compounded by the long running musical, *Evita!*

The essay that follows is exceptional because of its balanced appraisal of Eva Perón and the deft way in which its author penetrates the myths about her. Marysa Navarro, who teaches at Dartmouth College, was born in Spain. She brings remarkable insight into Evita's life both in this essay and in her longer study (with Nicholas Fraser), *Eva Perón* (1981).

Here Navarro skillfully explores Evita's origins in rural Argentina, her search for a career in the media in Buenos Aires as an immigrant, her political education after she met Perón, her attitude toward women in the old oligarchy, her capacity to deal effectively with Argentine labor after Perón's election in 1946, and her extraordinary power as her husband's link to the *descamisados*, or shirtless ones. While the assessment is primarily of Evita, the reader learns essential things about Perón's rise to power as well. Navarro's revisionist interpretation destroys the myth held by both admirers and enemies of Evita that she played a major role in the mass rally of October 17, 1945, which rescued Perón from prison and catapulted him into the presidency. According to Navarro, Evita was not a power independent of Perón. On the contrary she argues that there was no rivalry between Juan and Evita and that

From Marysa Navarro, "The Case of Eva Perón," *Signs: Journal of Women in Culture and Society* 3 (The University of Chicago, 1977): 229–40. Copyright © 1977 The University of Chicago. Reprinted with permission.

Evita knew her access to power was because of him. Finally, Navarro writes, "though in 1946 he could transfer power to her, her power was not transferable to anyone [when she died], least of all him."

IN 1946, when Doña María Eva Duarte de Perón began to take an active part in Argentine politics, First Ladies were expected to remain in the background, running a few charities and attending an occasional ceremonial function. Voting in national elections was restricted to male adults, which remained true until 1951. Except for a small number of activists engaged in the Socialist and Communist parties, women generally showed little concern for politics. However, three years later, she had become both Eva Perón, Argentina's widely known First Lady, and "Evita" the charismatic *abanderada de los descamisados,* the standard-bearer of the shirtless ones. By the time she died, on July 26, 1952, she was undoubtedly the second most powerful political figure in Argentina, though she held neither an elected post nor an official position in Perón's government. In the following pages, I will attempt to examine what personal and structural factors allowed her to acquire that power, what was its nature, and, finally, what were its limits.

Evita was born on May 7, 1919, in Los Toldos, a hamlet of Buenos Aires province. . . . Like her three sisters and her brother, she was the illegitimate child of Juan Duarte, a local *estanciero* (landowner) who abandoned their mother when Evita was three years old. She attended school first in Los Toldos, then in Junín, a railroad town also in Buenos Aires province, where the family moved in 1930. She was a below-average student, uninterested in schoolwork, and in 1935, after completing her primary education, at the age of fifteen she went to Buenos Aires to become an actress. Living in cheap and dirty *pensiones,* hungry and cold in winter, she made the theater rounds, never playing a better role than a maid or a silent character that disappeared too soon from the stage. In the meantime, she tried to break into films and here again only got small parts. Success did come at last, not from the stage or films but through the radio. In 1939, she headed her own soap-opera company, and when she gave up acting in October 1945, she was under contract with the top radio station in Buenos Aires and had two daily prime-time shows.

Evita may have had an exceptional goal in mind when she left Junín, but her background of poverty and her first years in Buenos Aires were not very different from those of thousands of men and women who also moved to Argentina's capital throughout the 1930s. . . . Unable to earn a living in the countryside because of the crisis that crippled agriculture since the world depression, they went to the city hoping to find work in its numerous factories. Argentine industry, forced to produce substitutes for European manufactured goods, was expanding at a rapid pace. Throughout the thirties, factories mushroomed and increased their output, reaching new peaks after World War II. While Argentina was undergoing such profound changes, the government was in the hand of a conservative landed oligarchy that managed to remain in power by rigging elections. Working and living conditions for the new urban masses were therefore understandably poor, and despite the efforts of a small, divided, weak, and bureaucratic labor movement they continued unchanged until June 4, 1943, when a bloodless military coup put an end to the landed oligarchy's rule.

Colonel Juan Domingo Perón began to emerge as a controversial figure among the group of officers that came to power on June 4 shortly after he took over the Department of Labor. Defining the role of the state as an arbiter between labor and management, he directed his office to terminate previous antilabor practices and to implement existing legislation. He then transformed the department into a secretariat with ministerial rank and proceeded to draft new laws, create labor boards, improve working conditions for rural and urban workers, expand the social-security system, and in general pursue a policy that raised the standard of living of workers and employees. A good listener, energetic and efficient, he gradually gained the trust of some important labor leaders. However, since his policies also found strong resistance among certain unions led by Communists and Socialists, he did not achieve his objectives without some degree of violence.

Evita met Perón in February 1944 during a fund-raising festival for the victims of an earthquake. He was a forty-eight-year-old widower. She was twenty-four, dark haired, and, despite her large brown eyes, not particularly beautiful. Two months after their first meeting, they were living together—a situation socially unacceptable for an Argentine woman at that time, especially if the man was a public figure and did not treat her like a mistress. Indeed, as Perón introduced Evita to his friends, went out with her, and actually behaved as if she were his wife, "the colonel's mistress" became a favorite topic of conversation in Buenos Aires salons.

Moreover, he included her in his political life. His heavy schedule generally ended with a round of daily meetings with politicians and fellow officers in his apartment. Contrary to what women were expected to do in such circumstances, Evita was usually present. She did not leave after serving coffee but sat and listened. It is not possible to ascertain whether she remained because she wanted to or because Perón urged her to do so. In these meetings as well as through her conversations with Perón, Evita discovered a very different world from her own. She found herself sharing and defending his ideas. In June 1944, she began to do a daily radio program of political propaganda in which she extolled the benefits that the Secretariat of Labor had brought to the workers.

Evita's transformation paralleled the changes taking place in Perón during this time period. Both his support among the rural and urban working-class and middle-class sectors and his influence in the military government were growing steadily. On February 26, 1944, when General Edelmiro J. Farrell became president, Perón took over the Ministry of War, and that same year he rose to the vice-presidency. However, his labor secretariat policies had continued to provoke very strong resistance, and by early 1945 he had succeeded in uniting all political parties against him. From the extreme Left to the conservative Right, they denounced him as a Nazi and a dangerous demagogue. As the months went by, the opposition mounted a campaign against Farrell and redoubled its attacks on "the colonel." Perón sought to strengthen his gains by pronouncing increasingly radical speeches, but to no avail. In October 1945, a group of military officers forced a confrontation with him. He finally agreed to resign from his three government posts on October 9, but not without making a speech in front of the Secretariat of Labor that angered his opponents and eventually led to his arrest and confinement on the Island of Martín García. While Farrell tried to rebuild his cabinet, which had resigned en masse, and while the opposition celebrated Perón's political demise, his supporters saw his jailing as a threat to the benefits they had obtained since 1943. With the help of some of Perón's collaborators in the secretariat, they began to organize demonstrations. On October 15, the sugar workers of Tucumán declared a general strike. The following day, as the General Confederation of Labor (CGT) debated whether or not to follow suit, groups of workers in several cities took to the streets. On October 17 in Buenos Aires, men and women marched from the outskirts of town to the Plaza de Mayo, stayed all day long to demand Perón's release, and did not leave until he spoke to them from the balcony of the Casa Rosada close to midnight.

Contrary to what has been stated repeatedly both in Peronists' and anti-Peronists' works, Evita did not play a major role in the events of October 17. After Perón was arrested, afraid for his life and her own, she left their apartment and slept at friends' homes. In the daytime, she tried desperately but unsuccessfully to get a writ of habeas corpus for his release. They were reunited on the night of October 17, after he addressed the delirious crowds in the Plaza de Mayo. Six days later, in a quiet civil ceremony, Perón married Evita.

After she married Perón, Evita became even more of a fascinating fixation for the Argentinian upper classes. According to most sources, her lower-class origin, illegitimacy, supposedly stormy love life before 1944, and notorious affair with Perón created an unsurmountable barrier between her and them once he was elected president in February 1946. Resentful and ambitious, the sources say, since the oligarchy refused to forget her past and snubbed her, she decided to get enough power to avenge herself. The only proof generally offered for this theory is her purported attempt to be named honorary president of the Sociedad de Beneficencia de la Capital, a position traditionally reserved for the First Lady. When the matrons of the Sociedad ignored her overtures, Evita's spite was so great that she demanded the takeover of the institution by the government and then proceeded to set up her own charitable foundation, the Fundación Eva Perón.

In her memoirs, Evita ridicules such an interpretation. She explains that she had the choice of being like any other Argentine First Lady or of doing something entirely different:

> As for the hostility of the oligarchy, I can only smile.
>
> And I wonder: why would the oligarchy have been able to reject me?
>
> Because of my humble origin? Because of my artistic career? But has that class of person ever bothered about these things here—or in any part of the world—when it was a case of the wife of a President?
>
> The oligarchy has never been hostile to anyone who could be useful to it. Power and money were never bad antecedents to a genuine oligarch.
>
> The truth is different. I, who had learned from Perón to choose unusual paths, did not wish to follow the old pattern of wife of the President.

Evita's decision was by no means as simple or as unilateral as she would like us to think, and it is hard to believe that upper-class opposition to her, particularly strong after the presidential campaign, would have disappeared easily had she chosen a less irritating path. On the whole, her statement might be questioned as a rationalization a posteriori. Yet certain facts tend to indicate that, in essence, it is more credible than most traditional interpretations of her behavior. In the case of the Sociedad de Beneficencia, for example, there is little doubt that it was taken over for reasons other than her anger, that is, poor working conditions for its employees and low salaries. As a state-financed institution, it had already undergone some degree of reorganization in 1943, before Evita met Perón. Denunciations of bad working conditions had been presented in Congress since 1939. Finally, the request for the government investigation that led to the intervention began in the Senate in July 1946, at a time when she lacked the means to influence such a move.

Whenever authors evaluate Evita's background as a barrier

she could not overcome, and present it, together with her resentment and her ambition as an explanation of her extraordinary political career, they make several assumptions. (1) She had remained untouched by the politicization and polarization that had divided Argentines since 1943. (2) She had lived with Perón for two years, at a time when his personality underwent a profound transformation, but somehow she had not been affected by that relationship. (3) She wished nothing better than to forget her past. (4) Her main goal was to become what the oligarchy had said a First Lady should be. (5) Driven either by her resentments, her hatreds, or her "insatiable ambition," her actions after 1946 were the direct result of her willpower and Perón's acquiescence.

It is true that after 1946, Evita never mentioned her premarital relationship with Perón and concealed her illegitimacy. Indeed, before she married Perón, she obtained a false birth certificate stating the name of her father. But even as an actress, Evita did not hide the facts that she came from a poor family and that she had started to work very young. There is no indication that she desired to forget all of her past. Moreover, it would have been difficult for her to become a ceremonial figurehead and be involved in old-fashioned charitable work at a time when Perón's election was acclaimed by his supporters as the end of an era dominated by the oligarchy and his inauguration as the beginning of a new society in which social justice would reign; poverty would be wiped out; and to be a worker, a descamisado, would become honorable.

In this atmosphere, Evita could hardly have sought to identify herself with the ladies of the Sociedad de Beneficencia. She may not have had a precise idea of her own role as First Lady, but it could not be what Argentines were accustomed to. She had indicated that much by her actions during the presidential campaign—she accompanied her husband in all his trips through the provinces, listened to his speeches, and even addressed a women's rally in the Luna Park stadium. In fact, a few days after Perón's inauguration, she had already begun to define a new model of First Lady by meeting with labor leaders three times a week in an office of the Post Office building, visiting factories and labor unions on her own, and . . . standing beside Perón every time he presided at a public gathering.

Furthermore, by that time Evita had realized that she was bound to Perón supporters with ties she could not possibly break. As as a result of the workers' massive demonstrations in October 1945, "the colonel's mistress," "that woman" so despised and criticized, had become overnight the respectable wife of the most important political figure in Argentina. Like a movie heroine or a character in her soap operas, she found herself metamorphosed by her marriage. Whatever her past may have been, she was now Perón's wife. As she would explain on countless occasions in her inimitable style, once again love had triumphed, and in this case, it had overcome the worst obstacles thanks to the men and women, the descamisados, who demanded Perón's release. When she had lost all hope of seeing the man she loved, the descamisados brought him back to her. On October 17, she therefore contracted with them an immense "debt of gratitude" which could only be repaid by loving them as they had loved Perón and dedicating her life to them.

By themselves, Evita's personal reasons for wanting to "pay her debt" to the descamisados and to Perón or wishing to be a different First Lady do not explain how she gained access to the political structure or the role she eventually performed in Perón's government. Neither is it sufficient to recognize that she ultimately could do so because he did not put a stop to her activities in the initial stage and later on legitimized them. Considering his relationship with Evita prior to 1946, his behavior is not really surprising. The question, therefore, is not why he did it but rather what were the structural factors that permitted Evita to play her political role.

At this point we must return once again to October 17, 1945, a date that shaped the following thirty years of Argentine history. The consequences were felt immediately insofar as the workers' mobilization ended a twelve-day-long crisis, allowed Perón to become a presidential candidate, and changed Farrell's regime into a caretaker government. But perhaps more important, it also brought forth a new type of political relationship. Built gradually by Perón after he took over the Secretariat of Labor, the charismatic relationship between "the leader" and the descamisados that revealed itself on October 17 neither destroyed existing institutions nor replaced them partially but superimposed itself upon them once he became president. His election was the culmination of the bid for power begun in 1943 and the ratification of the mandate of October 17.

Yet Perón's position in February 1946 was far from secure. Although he had obtained 52 percent of the votes and could count on a favorable Congress, he faced a number of problems. The already acute polarization that had characterized the political process since 1943 was accentuated even more by the bitterly fought presidential campaign in which almost all political parties joined in an anti-Perón front, the Unión Democrática. He entered the campaign without a solid organization. His supporters were divided into two major groups, united mainly by Perón: the Unión Cívica Radical Junta Reorganizadora, a small offshoot of the old Unión Cívica Radical, and the Partido Laborista, a party organized by labor leaders right after October 17. Of the two, the Partido Laborista was undoubtedly the more important and the more dangerous for Perón because he did not control it. The October crisis had proved that labor was the social basis of his power and his leadership. Therefore, if he was to retain them, he could not allow his charismatic relationship with the descamisados to deteriorate. On the other hand, as president Perón could no longer play the role of social agitator he had performed as secretary of labor, nor could he continue to receive workers' delegations, listen patiently to their complaints, and help them to solve their internal conflicts or their confrontations with management. The limitations imposed by Perón's new presidential functions threatened his leadership of the descamisados.

His situation was particularly troublesome because, among other reasons, the labor movement was undergoing a vast process of expansion. In 1941, the CGT had a membership of 441,412; in 1945 it rose to 528,538; in 1948 1,532,925, reaching 2,256,580 by 1954. Furthermore, there were growing signs of dissatisfaction among labor. Workers continued to strike for higher wages and better working conditions, even in the openly Peronist unions such as the one that declared the general strike on October 15. The composition of the labor movement was also changing rapidly. In 1941, only 33 percent of the CGT membership belonged to the industrial sector, while in 1948 the number had gone up to 52 percent. Perón's control of the CGT was shaky. Its performance during the October crisis had not been entirely satisfactory: after a heated debate, the central committee voted to strike on the 18th, without mentioning his name. Finally, in May 1946, when he decided to dissolve the Partido Laborista to form a more pliable organization, the Partido Peronista, some labor leaders openly resisted his orders. Others obeyed them but continued to oppose the growing identification of their movement with him.

If Perón was to maintain and strengthen his labor support, he needed a strong minister of labor, especially at a time when the ministry was unprepared to meet the demands of an expanding and aggressive labor movement. He could not appoint to the ministry a person who could use it to build his own political power—as he had done under Farrell. That is probably why he bypassed all the officers who had worked with him in the secretariat from 1943 to 1945 and named instead José María Freire, an obscure labor leader. But the workers continued to flock to Perón, looking for his advice or his help as they had done while he was only secretary of labor. They were turned back until Evita began to meet with them in her office of the Post Office building.

In September 1946, Evita abandoned her Post Office headquarters and moved to the ministry of labor itself. Her presence in the old secretariat confirmed what had gradually evolved in the previous months and what the descamisados already knew: all contact with Perón was to be channeled through his wife, his personal representative in the ministry. Perón never announced officially that Evita was his liaison with labor. In another example of his pragmatism, he let it be known by her move, after she had worked long enough for him to see positive results: workers accepted dealing with her and she proved to be quite efficient.

Perón's decision to rely on Evita for maintaining his personal contact with labor legitimized the activities she had been carrying out since his inauguration and altered their political value significantly. From then on she began to act as the extension of Perón, his substitute, his "shadow," as she described herself in her autobiography. Evita's presence in the ministry indicated to the workers that, despite his presidential functions, Perón had not ceased to be secretary of labor. His wife, the person who was closest to him, would perform some of his duties and also keep him informed of the needs and problems that the descamisados might have. She therefore could summon ministry of labor functionaries to give advice to a delegation on how to organize a union, help workers to force the compliance of a labor law, or back their requests for additional funds to build a clinic. She also began to represent Perón at union rallies. She would arrive accompanied by the presidential military aide, but while he remained silent, she spoke to the workers in the name of Perón. She acted as his delegate in ceremonies marking the signing of new labor contracts and once again made speeches in his name. Indeed, as early as 1946, one of Evita's main activities was to address the descamisados. The content of her speeches in this period indicates that her task was to impress upon them the continuity between 1943–45 and the present. Perón was always "the colonel," not the president. She also reminded her audiences how badly Argentine workers had lived before 1943, what "the colonel" had accomplished for them through the secretariat, and how his enemies had wanted to destroy him but how the decamisados had saved him on October 17.

Evita's experience as an actress proved to be an enormous asset in her work. Although unsure of herself at first, she showed none of the inhibitions and self-consciousness that might have paralyzed another woman in her place. In fact, she plunged into her life as First Lady as if it were a role, like the ones she had performed on the stage and in films. Her keen eye for theatrical effects was particularly useful in molding her public image, and she was most careful of her hair, by then bleached blonde; her jewels; extravagant hats; and elegant clothes. Although she knew that the oligarchy criticized that image, she sensed that the descamisados approved of it, and indeed they looked at her with a strong feeling of self-satisfaction and pride. Furthermore, at a time when the radio first became a powerful means of communication in Argentina, Evita found herself in possession of a very special talent. Having worked for so long in soap operas, she was comfortable in front of a microphone.

Because of that talent and the wildly enthusiastic responses it elicited, from 1946 to 1952 Evita acted as an indefatigable one-woman ministry of propaganda for Perón. The style of her public speeches reflected unmistakably the political role she played in Perón's government. Whereas he was "the leader" who elaborated the doctrine, explained it, and led the road toward social justice, she was the rabble-rouser who whipped up emotions; urged the descamisados to "offer their lives to Perón" as they had done on October 17; professed an undying love for Perón, the workers, and the poor; and lashed out violent diatribes against the oligarchy and other enemies of "the people." She never passed up the opportunity to make a speech, even when she had to interrupt most of her activities because of her illness. Too weak to carry on her heavy load in the ministry of labor, she still had the strength to do broadcasts from the presidential residence. Her highly emotional style may have been an expression of her passionate temperament, but it also reflected to a large extent the years she had played women who proclaimed their love or suffered because of it in her soap operas. The adaptation of her radio style and vocabulary to politics was facilitated by her year-long program of political propaganda, "Hacia un futuro mejor" [Toward a Better Future]. The scripts of this program were written by the authors of her radio shows, and at least one of these persons continued to write speeches for Evita throughout 1947.

Her social origin, which created so much resistance among the upper class, turned out to be another asset. When she spoke at CGT rallies or in her meetings with workers, she never failed to remind them that she was born poor, a descamisada too, and that she could therefore understand their problems and their concerns.

In the initial stage of Evita's political career, being a woman and being married to Perón proved to be crucial factors. She did not represent a threat to him or to his relationship with the descamisados precisely because she was a woman. Furthermore, as his wife, she was part of him, an extension of him, and since all her actions appeared endorsed by him, from the very first moment she had a substantial latitude to exert her influence. She strengthened her position by asserting her power to influence decisions and by contributing to the Peronization of labor unions. Her activities in the ministry of labor were the basis of the political power she accumulated from 1948 onward. In so doing she defined a new identity for herself. She gradually made herself into the indispensable link between Perón and the descamisados, the only means to reach him outside normal channels, or, as she would call herself, the intermediary between the leader and the descamisados, "the bridge between Perón and the people." While he remained "the undisputed Leader," by 1950 she had become "the standard-bearer" and even "the plenipotentiary" of the descamisados. Her titles reflected her own relationship with labor, as charismatic as his own, but subservient to his. She was Perón's complement, but to the workers she was also their leader.

By 1948, having gotten rid of the old, independent-minded labor leaders, Perón had also tightened his control of the CGT; the Partido Peronista was firmly in his hands, and he no longer had to worry about dissidents in Congress. The following year, he even managed to reform the Constitution so as to allow his reelection in 1951. As Perón pursued his policy of income redistribution and consolidated his power, Evita's position also became stronger.

Her power became visible after 1948 when she ruled over the Fundación Eva Perón (1950). She organized her own party, the Partido Peronista Femenino (1949), whose officials she named personally and whose candidates in 1951 she designated herself. Among additional sources of her power and influence was her ability to name people to jobs of all ranks. The nature of Evita's power is perhaps best explained by the Fundación Eva Perón, her own private social-aid foundation, whose funds she controlled exclusively and whose explicit objectives were to complement the social goals of Perón's government. Though part of the political structure in an informal way and consequently outside institutional limitations, in order to implement its objectives, which in certain areas such as health, education, and welfare overlapped with the policies of various ministries, Evita very frequently interfered with the plans designed by government officials.

There are no indications that Evita ever attempted to undermine Perón's power for her own purposes. Even at the height of her influence, there were no signs of rivalry or competition between them. She understood very clearly that she had become "Evita" because of him. As she explains in the preface of her autobiography, when she met Perón she was a humble sparrow and he was a mighty condor:

> If it weren't for him who lowered himself to me and taught me how to fly in a different way, I would have never known what is a condor and I would have never contemplated the marvelous and magnificent immensity of my people. That is why neither my life nor my heart belongs to me and nothing of what I am or have is mine. Everything I have, everything I think and everything I feel belongs to Perón.
>
> But I do not forget and will never forget that I was a sparrow and that I am still one. If I fly high it is because of him. If I walk among the mountain tops, it is because of him. If I sometimes almost touch the sky with my wings, it is because of him. If I see clearly what my people are and I love my people and I feel the love of my people caressing my name, it is because of him.

Her power and her leadership depended on his. Her influence, though far reaching, was not unlimited, because she was accountable to him. Perón rarely used his prerogative to restrict her, because he consistently benefited from Evita's power. Therefore within the limits that only he could establish, she was free and did as she pleased—as long as Perón's own power was enhanced. Perhaps the best example of the relationship between his ultimate authority and her freedom of action was the issue of her candidacy to the vice-presidency. Although she wanted it and allowed the Partido Peronista Femenino and the CGT to stage a massive demonstration for the proclamation of the Perón-Perón ticket, when he opposed it, she retreated and refused to accept the nomination.

Evita died on July 26, 1952, at the height of her power, but when Argentina was entering a period of serious economic difficulties. As Perón's economic troubles increased, his policy of income redistribution slowed down and his isolation from the descamisados deepened. Though he tried for a time to substitute for her in all her activities—her social work, the presidency of the Partido Femenino, and her daily meetings with workers' delegations and the CGT—he had neither the time, the patience, nor the energy to do it. Though in 1946 he could transfer power to her, her power was not transferable to anyone, least of all him.

23

Fernando N. A. Cuevillas
A Case for Caudillaje and Juan Perón

On August 20, 1948, President Juan D. Perón of Argentina made a speech in which he said, "Fortunately I am not one of those Presidents who live a life apart, but on the contrary, I live among my people, just as I have always lived; so that I share all the ups and downs, all the successes and all the disappointments of my working-class people. I feel an intimate satisfaction when I see a workman who is well dressed or taking his family to the theatre. I feel just as satisfied as I would feel if I were that workman myself."[1]

Perón was adept at projecting himself as a leader closely attuned to the emotional life of his people. In this as well as in a multitude of other ways he fitted within the frame of reference described in the following selection as "caudillaje" by Fernando N. A. Cuevillas, a sociologist on the faculty of the University of Buenos Aires during the first Perón presidency. Trained at the University of Madrid, where he completed his doctoral dissertation on the subject of caudillaje in Spanish America, Cuevillas reflects the thinking of those academicians who still remained on Argentine social-science faculties by 1953, seven years after Juan Perón became president. In this address to a gathering of Spanish American sociologists, Cuevillas provides a rationale for the caudillo by composing a mixture of political theory, social-psychological analysis, and but faintly concealed sycophancy. While Perón is mentioned only once by name, it is well to recall Perón throughout. Doubtless because of his Peninsular training Cuevillas is also conscious of another model, Francisco Franco, who proudly called himself "El Caudillo" of Spain during his long dictatorship (1939–75). It is noteworthy that Cuevillas calls caudillaje "a specific form of monarchy."

The typology Cuevillas uses to explain caudillos and his

From Fernando N. A. Cuevillas, "El Regimen del caudillaje en Hispanoamérica," *Boletin del Instituto de Sociología* 11 (1953): 59–75.

rejection of liberal democracy as a suitable political theory for Spanish American countries suggest certain aspects of the nature of caudillismo not explored in the other documents. Curiously, Juan Perón came to prefer the descriptive term *conducción* to caudillaje. As he explained it at the time of his return to power in 1973, "the difference that exists between the caudillo and the *conductor* is natural. The first does circumstantial things. The caudillo exploits disorganization and the conductor takes advantage of organization. The caudillo does not educate, rather he perverts. The conductor educates, teaches, and creates."[2] Presumably Cuevillas had no inkling of his hero's penchant for conducción and did the best he could with caudillaje!

. . . CAUDILLAJE, or the leadership of men, is a sociological institution which may be observed in all human associations and societies. It probably exists through the accidental differences which exist among individuals. Some are learned, some ignorant; some are predominently rational and others thoughtlessly willful . . . men who behave in such a way, each after his own fashion, that some govern and others follow, naturally and without violence and without the necessity of written laws. . . . In fact, these men do not reflect on the bases of their obedience. Those who do are in the minority. And perhaps then they justify such obedience as a fulfillment of natural law, . . . for in the final analysis the natural society of men is explained in terms of temperaments, affinities, and sympathies. The relationship which we call caudillaje, . . . the subordination of one and the supremacy of the other, reflects the basic order among men. . . .

The bonds of caudillaje are found in individual relationships: . . . the husband who leads his wife through life, and thanks be to God that it seems that among us the husband still commands his spouse. Among friends there is always one who insinuates his control over the other . . . the incubus and the succubus. Families also demonstrate the bonds of caudillaje. . . .

In effect all associations are interdependent and hierarchical. . . . And in a political sense I would use "caudillaje" to apply to that regime which consists of the personification or incarnation of authority, where he who governs acts with an extraordinary charismatic moral ascendency over his people: advising them, guiding them, leading them paternally. The power of the caudillo is inspired authority before it is juridical authority, . . . Caudillaje appears as a social institution full of ethical content (political and military control, the authentic totality of power, the psychic leadership of the governed, the moral magnetism of the leader's personality) which makes it most suitable for those States whose political life is determined by the integration of individual and collective traditional values. . . .

This view of the essence of what we call caudillaje may be further pursued by some reflections on the sociological institutions which might be associated with the term caudillo:

1. *The caudillo is not a public functionary.* He is not a functionary in the modern sense of the official who must confine himself to the strict fulfillment of this or that provision of such and such an article of a constitution, who is rigorously controlled by other powers, jealous of his authority and who therefore obstruct his work, and who is only able to exercise executive power. . . . The public functionary is the agent of his countrymen who consider themselves sovereign, a political concept emerging historically out of eighteenth-century England and France and which has been adopted by peoples all over the globe. The caudillo is, on the other hand, both governor and mandator who leads his people with their consent.

2. *The caudillo is not a tyrant.* A tyrant is one who governs for his own benefit or for that of his clique, without justice and, therefore, violently. What in certain Spanish countries is called caciquismo is nothing more than a special brand of tyrant. . . . There is nothing more contrary to the rule of caudillaje in spite of having in common with caciquismo the mere *external forms* of rigid coercion of social conduct. Nothing . . . can justify the tyrant's invasion of justice.

3. *The caudillo is neither despot nor dictator.* It is certainly not within the essence of caudillaje to govern without a council of state or a national representative legislature. Moreover, there ought to be active, vigorous opposition groups operating within the caudillo's regime to inspire him

to good government. Nevertheless, when a caudillo emerges to clean up an anarchic social and political state, he may feel that it does not suit his purpose to coexist with representatives in a national congress and that he must transform his government temporarily into a dictatorship. But never, not even in the most extreme cases, would he be within the spirit of caudillaje to dispense with the counsel of the wise.

4. *The caudillo is not a rightist ruler.* Rightist politics and a government of the right are modern concepts . . . which, however, suggest the old conservative monarchies. Cautious in his attitude toward revolution and the left, the rightist leader is downright fearful before the masses. Surrounded by learned men of the elite, the rightist ruler oversees a social and political reality which is profoundly divided and which he restrains more than leads. . . . He conserves the existing social order rather than provides for the common welfare. . . .

5. *The caudillo is not a leftist demagogue.* As a premise . . . I would say that a pure demagogue is incapable of ruling and that no government can be purely demagogic. . . . While it is tolerable for a leader to employ demagogic tactics in order to capture public support, it is impossible to imagine this as a permanent situation because once given over to the caprices and passions of the masses there will be no acceptance of any form of normal public order.

Caudillaje as a Sociopolitical Institution

The regime of caudillaje is an entity in what we recognize as that most complex reality, civil society. . . . In this situation the power of leadership is granted naturally to the caudillo by the consent of the community. This is what is called election, which can be either express or tacit. In the ultimate analysis, simple consent is not enough in caudillaje; rather, there must be total adherence, an adherence which is akin to the reciprocal attachment of lovers.

But what form of government or leadership is that of the caudillo? . . . In its essence, caudillaje is a *specific form of monarchy* [author's emphasis]. Its characteristics include: government by one man who possesses exceptional qualities of leadership and who governs righteously and virtuously, with love, and for life.

... Above all else, the caudillo ... is the veritable incarnation of authority. He enlivens those forms which are most conducive to order among his people according to the most cherished national values. The caudillo feels that he is heir to the men of the heroic age; he continues their work and achieves their goals. His successors in government should in turn see in him their inspiration and their teacher.

The caudillo loves his people and their customs; he rewards their services by an indestructible devotion. Celebrities and notables respect him, the humble folk love him, and he serves them both. . . . The caudillo is an authentic aristocrat who understands his social-service mission. At the head of his people he laughs with them in their fiestas as he cries with them in their sorrows and defeats.

Magnanimous in the sight of all, true to his promises; chivalrous and splendid in so far as is necessary to display the magnificence of the dignity of authority; austere in his private life so as to be above the suspicions of public opinion; liberal and kind with the poor; capable and skillful in the business of government; aware of the force of human passions; a student of the psychological qualities of his subjects so that he may be their educator.

A soft word of understanding, . . . a rough gesture of disapproval, a shout of indignation, an opportune speech, an *abrazo* [embrace] for the faithful, a special ceremony for the learned, a show of manliness for the gathered military, a gift for the diplomat, a suave display of gallantry for the politician's wife, and, above all, a capacity for work bound up in and dedicated to the public welfare which he associates with his own: these are the multiple instruments which the caudillo must use to maintain his principate. For the caudillo is, indeed, the prince, who like the Roman emperors, the medieval monarchs, the leader of the modern Spanish state [Franco], . . . enjoys an apotheosis for he is the first in work, the first in self-sacrifice, the first in glory. The last of these is, surely, the reward which the people owe in exchange for the first two. . . .

The roots of the caudillo's moral leadership and the ethical adherence of his people, which is the formal base of his regime, is without doubt based in psychology. In this regard . . . the prestige of the caudillo can only be maintained through a permanent and subtle vigilence. . . . He must always represent the incarnation of the dominant cultural principles of his society and of his times. . . .

Caudillaje in Spanish America

In order to understand the caudillo in Spanish America we might recall the poetic and politic definition coined by the Spanish youth leader, José Antonio Primo de Rivera, when he spoke of "The Hero as Father." [José Antonio Primo de Rivera was the son of Spain's dictator in the 1920s who founded the fascist Falange Party in 1933, and was tried and executed by the Republicans in November 1936, thus becoming a martyr for the Franco forces in the Spanish Civil War (1936–39).] The phrase suggests a whole theory of sociology and politics. . . . Caudillaje is a new form of leadership which must surely be a reaction against the depersonalization of power associated with liberal rationalism; while there is much to adhere to in rationalist doctrine, we cannot agree with its impersonality but must affirm instead the charismatic personality of the leader.

It is almost impossible to explain the history of Spanish American social and political institutions without understanding something of what is meant by caudillaje. There has not been a Spanish American country which has not had its Artigas, its Portales, its Santa Cruz, its García Moreno, its Solano López, its Sandino, or its Rosas. In the wise words of a great Spanish American leader, "The ideal of fortunate government should be that of the paternal autocrat who is intelligent, impartial, and indefatigable, who is energetically resolved to make his people happy. . . ."

In Spanish America nature, powerful, rich, and hostile, has imposed its norm on her governors. It has been useless for the liberal idealists to try to see social realities as they are not and as they cannot be, for Spanish America counts only among her eponymous heroes the great caudillos. They are her popular heroes, beloved by the humble people. . . . Whether we like it or not, our nations prefer and will only tolerate democratic monarchy as a form of government. . . . It was through the constant efforts of the caudillos that the political independence of our countries was secured against the will of those ideologists who sought enlightenment from foreign forces. . . .

The caudillo in our cultural world presents himself as *founder* or as *restorer* of a past splendor. Those who came first were those who set before us the collective goals and limitations. A prime example was Simón Bolívar, Liberator, Protector, Father of the Nation, and President, . . . an authentic "natural monarch" and leader of the people. . . . In his message to the Bolivian congress, explaining the political constitution which he had drawn up for that nation, Bolívar sought, in effect, to legalize caudillaje when he said:

> The President of the Republic shall come to be in our constitution like the sun, fixed in the center, giving life to the universe. This supreme authority ought to be perpetual, because in those systems without hierarchies there must be, more than in others, a fixed point around which the magistrates, the citizens, and all the elements may revolve. Give me a fixed point, says the ancient, and I will move the earth.

For Bolívar this fixed point was the life-term president; in him all our order was to be concentrated without fear that he would abuse it. . . .

Finally, in Argentina . . . caudillaje has become fact since it was legalized under the democratic forms of the Constitution of 1949. The caudillo . . . is the expression of what his country thinks and values. . . . Between caudillo and people . . . there is a mutual relationship. . . . And this has prevailed in Argentine history during the regimes of the three national caudillos: Rosas, Yrigoyen, and Perón. They, who are true reflections of the life of my people, drew close and bound themselves to us through their personal ideals, paternal power, and sense of mission in three different epochs. What has made them the more closely attached to us has been their attitudes in defense of national sovereignty, their consultation of the national will through elections, and their heartfelt attachment to the mass of citizens. . . .

Notes

1. *Peronist Doctrine* (Buenos Aires: n.p., n.d.), 87.
2. Quoted by Colin M. Winston, "Between Rosas and Sarmiento: Notes on Nationalism in Peronist Thought," *The Americas*, 39 (January 1983), 325.

291

24

Lee Lockwoood

Fidel Castro Speaks on Personal Power

No leader in Spanish American history since Simón Bolívar has attracted as much attention as Fidel Castro. His vehicle for personal power has been the Cuban Revolution, a profound social movement with global implications. Both Fidel and the Revolution have been praised, vilified, and dissected with great intensity for more than thirty years. The most articulate authority on Castro is Castro, and his frequent self-assessments are widely known to an international audience largely through the many interviews he has given to journalists, politicians, and scholars. Castro's critics, and they are legion, have argued that he has manipulated his interlocutors with enormous skill as his own public-relations agent. Among those who were best able to combine sympathy with criticism and to draw Castro into his most candid self-appraisal during the early years of the Revolution was Lee Lockwood, a renowned journalist and photographer.

In 1965 Lockwood spent more than three months in Cuba, during which time he travelled three times with Castro during the latter's impromptu tours around the island. At the end the two men carried on what Lockwood calls "a marathon seven-day conversation in a secluded house on the Isle of Pines." The following selection is edited from those parts of Lockwood's superbly illustrated book, *Castro's Cuba, Cuba's Fidel*, that best reveal Castro's assessment of himself as Cuba's caudillo. Readers will have to decide whether Fidel ultimately engages in self-delusion or correctly assesses the roots and manifestations of his personal power. Was he indeed slow to recognize, as he claims, that his power was total from the start and that he could not alienate it or share it with other Cubans? Students of the mature Cuban Revolution later in the century may find these early glimpses of Fidel useful for

From Lee Lockwood, *Castro's Cuba, Cuba's Fidel*, rev. ed. (Boulder: Westview, 1990), 147–86. Reprinted with permission.

comparison as he and his country were transformed. Castro's self-characterization and his relation to the management of the Cuban government should be compared with the critical views of Maurice Halperin in the following essay.

LOCKWOOD: It is a commonly held view in my country that you are a dictator with absolute power, that the Cuban people have no voice in their government, and that there is no sign that this is going to change.

CASTRO: I think we have to state the ideas a little more precisely. We are Marxists and look upon the state as an instrument of the ruling class to exercise power. What you people call "representative democracy" is, in our opinion, the dictatorship of the capitalists, and the North American state is an instrument of that class domination, from the domestic point of view as well as from the international point of view.

I believe that these are not simply theoretical positions. The ruling classes exercise power through the state and through all the means that they can depend on to defend their system. They depend not only on the state, its administration, and its armed forces for this purpose, but on all the rest of the instruments at the service of the system: the dominant political parties, which are completely controlled by those classes and take turns in power, and all the media of communication—the press, radio, television, newspapers, magazines, movies, publishing houses, technical and scientific societies, public education, the universities. All those media are at the service of a system that is under the control of the wealthy of the United States.

Naturally, you might tell me that in the United States it is possible to publish a book that is against the government or to write some critical articles. This doesn't at all threaten the security of the system. Anything that might threaten the system would be repressed, as has been proven. Even activities that constitute no danger at all to the United States have been persecuted; various personalities who were characterized, not by Marxist, but by progressive thought—in the movies, in television, in the universities, and in other intellectual media—have been investigated, have been imprisoned, have suffered persecution, have been required to appear before the Committee on so-called Un-American Affairs, with all the consequences that this implies. So, a real intellectual terror exists in the United States. The people who have the courage to express progressive opinions are few, out of fear of bringing down those consequences upon themselves. Criticisms are made in the United States, yes, but *within* the system, not against it. The system is something untouchable, sacred, against which only genuine exceptions dare to express themselves.

So I ask myself whether that isn't really a class dictatorship, the imposition of a system by all material and moral means? In the United States the people vote every four years for one of the candidates that the two parties choose, but that doesn't imply any change.

On the other hand, we think of the revolutionary state as an instrument of the power of the workers and peasants, that is, of the manual and intellectual workers, directed by a party that is composed of the best men from among them. We organize our party with the participation of the workers of all the centers of labor, who express their opinions in a completely free way, in assemblies, proposing and supporting those whom they believe should be members of the party or opposing those whom they believe should not be.

Our party is the representative of the workers and peasants, of the working class, in the same way that the Congress of the United States is the representative of the capitalists. So that our system is a class system too, in a period of transition. Ultimately, we will go even a little further and proclaim the nonnecessity of the state, the disappearance of the state with the disappearance of social classes. When Communism is a reality, that instrument will no longer be necessary as a coercive force by which one class maintains its domination over another, since neither exploiters nor exploited will exist. As Engels said, "The government over the people will be replaced by the administration of things and by the conduct of the processes of production."

You ask about power concentrated in one person. The truth is that, although I perform certain functions inherent to the offices that I hold within the state and the party, my authority to make decisions is really less than that of the President of the United

States. If we are going to speak about personal power, in no other country in the world, not even under absolute monarchies, has there ever been such a high degree of power concentrated in one person as is concentrated in the President of the United States. That officeholder whom you call president can even take the country into a thermonuclear war without having to consult the Congress. There is no case like it in history. [President Lyndon B. Johnson] intervened in Vietnam on his own decision. He intervened in Santo Domingo on his own decision. Thus, that functionary you call president is the most complete expression of the dictatorship of a class which on occasions exercises itself by conceding really absolute powers to one man.

Why don't you North Americans think a little about these questions, instead of accepting as an irrefutable truth your definition of democracy? Why don't you analyze the realities and the meaning of the words a little, instead of repeating them mechanically?

We honestly consider our system infinitely more democratic than that of the United States, because it is the genuine expression of the will of the vast majority of the country, made up not of the rich but of the poor.

LOCKWOOD: How do the majority express this "will"?

CASTRO: By struggling and fighting against oppression. They revealed it in the Sierra Maestra by defeating the well-equipped army of Batista. They revealed it at [The Bay of Pigs] by destroying the mercenary invaders. They revealed it in the Escambray in wiping out the counterrevolutionary bands. They reveal it constantly, in every public demonstration that the Revolution organizes with the multitudinous support of the masses. They have revealed it with their firm support of the Revolutionary Government in the face of the economic blockade, and by the fact that there are hundreds of thousands of men ready to die defending their Revolution.

LOCKWOOD: But if Cuba is not a dictatorship, in what way are your people able to effectively influence the leadership?

CASTRO: I believe that there is a mutual influence of the people over the leaders and of the leaders over the people. The first and most important thing is to have a genuine affection and respect for the people. The people can feel that and it wins them over. Sometimes the leaders have to take responsibilities on their own; sometimes they have to walk at the head of the people. The important thing is the identification of the leaders with the necessities, the aspirations, and the feelings of the people. There are many ways of establishing this identification. The best way of all is to maintain the most immediate contact possible with the masses.

LOCKWOOD: Ché Guevara, in his book, *Socialism and Man in Cuba*, characterizes the manner of communication between the leaders of the Revolution and the people as "almost intuitive." Do you agree that there is this intuitive element in your leadership of the people?

CASTRO: At certain moments, under certain circumstances, when there is a great sense of confidence between the leaders and the masses, yes. Especially in such a convulsive process as a revolution, the intuitive element can be necessary at the beginning, but not later on, when the revolution advances and is consolidated, because in such a process millions of men raise their political culture and their revolutionary conscience; thousands of capable men arise from the masses to take on the tasks of organization, of administration and of policy making; and all this creates a developed culture, a powerful and organized force. Individual men begin to have less importance to the degree that the whole social task becomes more and more a collective undertaking, the work of millions of persons and the responsibility of tens of thousands of men.

LOCKWOOD: But do you feel that a kind of intuitive communication between yourself and the masses during these first years has kept you from making bad mistakes?

CASTRO: I don't know how a leader can arise or how a revolution can be led without a great sensitivity for understanding the problems of the people and without the ability, too, of formulating the means of confronting and resolving these problems. A revolution is not an easy process. It is hard, difficult. Great errors can cost the life of the revolution. Not only the leadership of the revolution, but its very life.

There must be not only intuition, an emotional communication of the leaders with the people, but there are other requisites. One has to find solutions, one has to put them into operation, one has to go forward, one has to choose the path correctly, the way of doing what has to be done. The leaders in a revolutionary process are not infallible receptacles of what the people think. One must find out how the people think and sometimes combat certain opinions, certain ideas, certain points of view which, in the judgment of the leaders, are mistaken. One cannot conceive of the leader as a simple carrier of ideas, a simple collector of opinions and impressions. He has to be also a creator of opinions, a creator of points of view; he has to *influence* the masses. . . .

LOCKWOOD: In . . . this discussion of how your Revolution succeeded we have left out what is probably the most important single element—the effect that you as an individual have had on the whole process. What do you think might have happened to the Revolution if you had been killed while you were still in the mountains?

CASTRO: In the early moments it could have led to the defeat of the guerrilla movement. But as soon as our guerrilla force grew, and the second front in Oriente Province, directed by Raúl Castro, was established, if they had killed me then in the Sierra Maestra, Raúl would have been able to carry on the war. He was perfectly prepared to lead it. He was a very good organizer and a very capable leader of soldiers.

I don't know, of course, whether he would have been able to overcome all the political problems. Not that he isn't capable in that field. But Raúl is five years younger than I am. At that time he was twenty-six years old. He had five years less experience, and he would have had to confront serious political problems. But my opinion is that he would have been able to handle them.

Why do I believe this? Because often men show what they are really capable of only when circumstances place a task before them. For example, when he faced the military task of directing a front which he himself opened with only fifty men, he had to make on-the-spot decisions and resolve great problems. He did this masterfully.

It is unquestionable that my main contribution was the conception of the way, of the strategy, of the adequate method for making a revolution. But once this was accepted by a group of men who had the same faith that I did, who were just as convinced as I was, the victory would have come even without me.

LOCKWOOD: Very few people would agree with you, I think. A revolution requires a leader of extraordinary abilities; not only military and political abilities, but someone who has within his personality a spark which excites men, which gives flesh to the idea and keeps the idea real from day to day. No one knew anything about Raúl Castro in 1959. Certainly he had no great mass support. He was known as your brother and as a brave soldier, but not particularly as a revolutionary leader.

CASTRO: Yes, but look: when I speak to you of Raúl, I forget completely that he is my brother. But this matter has to be talked about in complete fairness.

Many people know Raúl and know what he is like, and they don't need to be convinced of the truth of what I am saying. I have the privilege of knowing him better than anybody else. Though unquestionably my presence pretty much overshadows him, I can tell you that Raúl, from the political point of view, possesses magnificent aptitudes. But, what happens? He does not make decisions, because he knows it is not his right to do so. He is extraordinarily respectful. He always consults with me about all the important questions. I know him very well, and I am not conducting a campaign in his favor. When he came to the Revolution, he did it as one soldier more. I myself wasn't even capable then of understanding all his worth, as I have had the opportunity to do during the whole process since then.

Of course, under the present circumstances the constant presence of one outstanding leader tends a little to obscure the rest. That is a natural phenomenon, here or anywhere else. You see it, for example, in your own country. Sometimes a misfortune occurs, an accident; the president dies and suddenly another president comes to the fore. Kennedy was unquestionably a man of strong personality, and yet I have read many commentaries published in the United States in which the newspapers speak about certain abilities of Johnson which they didn't recognize in Kennedy; for example, his ability to manage the Congress and his ability to deal with certain diplomatic problems. None of those talents was recognized by the press before he became president. Individual men have their influence, that is undeniable. That influence is greater or lesser depending upon the circumstances. It could be said that a group of fortuitous circumstances determines the greater or lesser influence of individuals in revolutionary processes, often factors quite external to the virtues or the qualities of a particular man.

LOCKWOOD: You don't think that there are certain men who, appearing on the scene, are able, by their special vision or by the force of their personality, to influence events significantly?

CASTRO: Certainly that has always occurred. It still happens today but it will happen less and less often as the problems of government and administration become the tasks not of groups but of millions of men. Eventually millions of men will take responsibility for public problems of all kinds. In my personal experience, I see how much easier everything is done in Cuba today on account of the numbers of men who have acquired experience, who have broadened their intelligence in coping with problems. And it will increase more and more.

When a country is in a situation of great difficulty, oppressed, with a low level of culture and political education and lacking collective experience, the importance of the men who lead it is much greater. Certain factors determine that those leaders arise. Take the case of France. If there hadn't been the Second World War, if France had not been invaded by the Germans, probably De Gaulle would never have played the role he played in the life of France. It was these factors, resulting from a series of circumstances, which made it possible for such a man to stand out. Nobody doubts that under normal circumstances this would not occur, even if you had men with the same character and talents as De Gaulle. Of course, there have been few men with the same character and talent as De Gaulle.

LOCKWOOD: Very few, and perhaps even fewer Fidel Castros.

CASTRO: I believe, yes, that there are not many such as me. Of all the boys who were born in the same year that I was, how many had the opportunity to go to school? In the place where I was born there were hundreds of children, children of the farmers and the workers, and the only one who had the social and economic opportunity to go beyond the sixth grade was me. The same thing must have happened with hundreds of thousands of children in all of Cuba. How many minds for all the branches of human activity must have been lost!

Certain circumstances favored me. First, economic circumstances allowed me to study. Second, the fact that I was born in the country, in a place close to the mountains, must have contributed to my trust in the land, to my belief in possibilities of fighting in the mountains even against a modern army. In addition, there were certain things peculiar to the geographical and social environment in which I grew up. Probably people born in the city would not have developed the same ideas.

It is not that I am trying, out of modesty, to diminish the role it has been my fortune to play. But I sincerely believe that the merits of the individual are always few, because there are always external factors which play a much more important role than his own character in determining what he does. . . .

LOCKWOOD: Apart from all that, you don't consider yourself a very unusual man?

CASTRO: *(long pause)* That is something that pertains to one's own conscience, to the opinion one has of oneself. I suppose that most men always have a good opinion of themselves. It would be hypocrisy for me to tell you that I don't have a high opinion of myself. But I say with all sincerity that I am also very self-critical.

LOCKWOOD: The Cubans consider you an exceptional man. The masses talk of you and cheer you almost like a savior—

CASTRO: Since you have got me onto this theme, I am going to tell you something, an opinion.

The masses bestow upon men a certain quality, perhaps out of necessity, perhaps because it cannot happen in any other way. There is a kind of mechanism in the human mind that tends to create symbols in which it concentrates its sentiments. By transforming men into symbols, they manifest a greater gratitude, they attribute to the individual what is not deserved by him alone but by the many. Often I think of the hundreds, even thousands of men who are working anonymously, making possible all those things for which the people are grateful. Recognition is not divided in an equitable way. It would be an error for any man—I say this sincerely—not to be conscious of this and to believe himself truly deserving of all that recognition and affection. One must have a proper appreciation of the things he has accomplished, but he should never consider himself deserving of the recognition that belongs to the many. I believe that that would be harmful to any leader.

LOCKWOOD: Do you think, then, that it was inevitable that some people who supported you earlier would become disenchanted with the Revolution after 1959, because their support was given for emotional reasons, and they didn't analyze your program?

CASTRO: I don't quite understand the question.

LOCKWOOD: Do you think that they idolized you as a savior who had beaten Batista and didn't ask themselves what it was you really stood for? What many of them really wanted and assumed you were going to give them was what you would call a petit-bourgeois democracy. Would you say that such people were blinded by emotionality as to what you really stood for?

CASTRO: Let me explain. Even in our own organization in those days there were many people who had prejudices, above all in the city. Even some of the leading officers of our movement, and very honorable people too, not at all opportunists. Nevertheless, one of the things that has given me the most satisfaction is to see how many of them have come to understand their limitations, their prejudices, their mistaken points of view, and how they have now been integrated into the Revolution in a devoted and sincere way.

. . .

LOCKWOOD: Would you say that when you took over the government you had what amounted to absolute power?

CASTRO: Look, in the first place, when the Revolution came to power, I was still full of certain illusions.

For example, as always in Cuba, there was distrust of the revolutionary leaders because personal ambition was always attributed to them, and that fact exercised on me a certain inhibiting influence. It was my wish that the things we wanted to do should be done without my occupying any fundamental office in the government or in the leadership of the country. Even when we were fighting in the Revolutionary War and making plans for a government that would replace Batista, I didn't plan to occupy the office of prime minister or president or any similar position.

However, there were many aspirants to the presidency who were in exile. We repudiated them, because there were excellent people struggling and making sacrifices within the country who were not motivated by any kind of ambition or personal vanity. Then we, who didn't yet have enough force to raise a man from our own ranks, put forward a candidate for president [Dr. Manuel Urrutia] who didn't belong to any party or organization and who didn't figure among the undisguised aspirants to the office. It was our proposal to offer the greatest support to that president so that he might fulfill his offices perfectly.

What was my hope? That this man would be able to carry things out while I remained completely separate from power. That was really an illusion. In the course of events it turned out that neither was the man capable of doing the job nor was it possible for me to keep apart. Not because I didn't want to or wasn't inclined to, but because factors conspired to place me in a position where all problems came to rest upon me, inevitably, no matter how much I tried to evade responsibility. That situation came to a head at a time when the Revolution had been in power for several weeks and not a single measure had been taken, not a single thing had been done! This was beginning to create a certain very detrimental discontent. It was exactly then that it was proposed—not on my initiative—that I assume the office of prime minister. For my part, I made it a condition that I must have real authority to carry out the revolutionary program. Believing that things could have been done any differently was one of my illusions of those early days.

LOCKWOOD: In retrospect, then, you feel that you had to have the formal power in order to move your program forward? Because it seemed in those days that you had the nearly complete support of the people. After all, you were the leader of the Revolution, while Urrutia was someone about whom very few people knew anything—besides the fact that he had been the judge at your trial who spoke in your favor.

CASTRO: I am certain that things would have been very different if, instead of Urrutia, we had had the good luck to choose a man like President Oswaldo Dorticós, a truly competent and truly revolutionary man.

Even then, of course, I would always have had to play some role in the Revolution. I would have been able to help in many ways, whenever it was necessary, without having to hold any official office.

LOCKWOOD: Yet today you hold even more official titles than you did then: prime minister, commander in chief of the armed forces, secretary of the party, and head of the National Agrarian Reform Institute [INRA]. Why is that?

CASTRO: The office of commander in chief is held by all constitutional heads of state, and most of the administrative tasks related to the armed forces here are carried out by the minister of the armed forces [Raúl Castro]. My office as chief of the Institute of Agrarian Reform is related to the emphasis that the Revolution wishes to place on agriculture. My work there is fundamentally political, a kind of policy direction, not really the administrative work, which is carried out by a very competent associate. . . . And my office as prime minister is not strictly administrative, but a political office. The general administrative responsibility belongs to the president of the Republic.

LOCKWOOD: Certainly your activities as the head of INRA go far beyond the political—

CASTRO: Well, I have participated directly in working out many of the agricultural plans. But the Institute of Agrarian Reform is responsible for administering all the governmental agricultural centers in the country and many other questions related to agriculture, which it carries out through a well-organized apparatus and an efficient group of men. . . .

LOCKWOOD: Isn't it likely . . . that a man who is placed in charge of a ministry or in some high position might feel inhibited about carrying out his own policies for fear that they won't coincide with yours, and that he might be removed?

CASTRO: No. And in addition, many problems are resolved without any participation from me, in consultation between the respective minister and the president of the republic, who is also the minister of economy. There is a very thorough division of labor among the leaders.

In some tasks of the Revolution, such as those relating to agriculture and education, I have developed a special personal interest. But there are many other important fields, and numerous revolutionary cadres are concerned with them and act with a great degree of autonomy.

LOCKWOOD: Fidel, haven't you been overmodest in the assessment of yourself which you have presented? Don't you think especially that you have understated the amount of influence and power you personally hold in Cuba?

If we consider first only your *legal* power, it seems virtually absolute. As prime minister, you are the chief of state. In that capacity you lead the country and direct the government's foreign policy, and you are not restrained by any legislature or judicial authority or even as yet by a formal constitution. As secretary of the party, whose highest echelons, including the directorate, are not elected but appointed by you, you occupy the seat of political power and you control all the means of political indoctrination of the people, including radio and TV, the press, and all other media for disseminating information. As president of the Institute of Agrarian Reform you have full responsibility for both initiating and supervising Cuba's agriculture—which is to say, Cuba's economy, since you have stated that the country's economic efforts will be devoted exclusively to agriculture through 1970. Lastly, you are the commander in chief of the armed forces. In your case this is much more than just a title, and logically so. As a revolutionary leader who came to power by fighting a military war with an army which you personally organized and led, it is natural for you to take the position of commander in chief seriously. For example, you personally commanded the military forces at the Bay of Pigs invasion, where you fought at the head of a column, and even did some shooting. This is certainly a much more literal use of the title "commander in chief" than most other heads of government exercise even though, as you say, they all hold it nominally.

In other words, in your hands are concentrated the four most potent sources of power: political, military, social, and economic. It is difficult to imagine what more legal authority one person might hold in Cuba.

Beyond all of that, you have a kind of personal power which may be even more significant: that is, the ability of your own mind and personality to inspire people, to convince them, to enthuse them, even to turn them into fanatics.

I personally have seen and heard evidences of this from people high and low, everywhere I've gone, all over Cuba. Everyone seems to agree that without the almost magnetic force of your personality there wouldn't have been any Revolution in the first place. Without you, there wouldn't have been any Moncada or any Granma, and the rebellion in the Sierra Maestra probably would have failed. Really, in January 1959, it was you who brought the Cuban people to power, not the Cuban people who carried you to power.

Furthermore, it is difficult to give credence to your implication that it was the people of Cuba who decided for themselves that they wanted to be socialists, that they wanted a Communist society. Rather, it was you who concluded that this was the road they should take, and they followed you, not out of a theoretical conviction about Marxism-Leninism—in fact, if anything, they had a strong prejudice against Communism—but out of love and trust in Fidel Castro, their *lider máximo.*

There is no question that you are still the maximum leader of this country. One simple evidence of this is that throughout Cuba one finds displayed pictures of you, always in some heroic pose—of yourself practically alone among living Cubans. They range from small photographs that one sees hanging on the walls of the huts of most peasants in the mountains to gigantic images of yourself on posters and billboards that are to be seen everywhere, sometimes in the most unlikely places. One thinks especially of that enormous and rather ferocious picture of you that covers the façade of the Ministry of the Interior headquarters building—it must be fifty feet high.

When you speak at a 26th of July or a May Day rally half a million people come to hear you. They come voluntarily, probably even happily. But it could be pointed out that Hitler and Mussolini used to get crowds of this size; they too came voluntarily and, to judge from the newsreels of those days, happily. Of course, I'm not suggesting that you are in a category with Hitler and Mussolini, though you have many enemies who would include you in that company. I think you are a man of greater vision, first, and secondly, I think you are motivated by a genuine desire for the well-being of your people. What I mean to suggest is that the ability to command the thunderous applause of huge crowds may be a sign that the masses support you, but not necessarily a sign that your policies are right.

Don't you feel that in having so much power, both real and potential, concentrated in the hands of one person, a potentially dangerous precedent is set? I wonder and worry what would happen, for example, if you were to die suddenly. It seems to me that it would leave an immense power vacuum.

Many things about you remind me of Lenin. He was also a charismatic revolutionary leader who held and exercised wide power. But Lenin died early, very suddenly. And his passing left a vacuum, into which, eventually, stepped a Stalin, and terror. Perhaps you believe that this could never happen in Cuba. But if you were to die tomorrow, whose picture would replace yours on the walls of the Ministry of the Interior, fifty feet high, and what would it signify for Cuba?

CASTRO: . . . In the first place, it seems to me that in what you establish as a basis for your question there is a somewhat distorted conception of the role of individuals in history.

I admit that individuals can certainly play a very important role in essential things, owing to a series of circumstances—some of which I referred to earlier—many of which are fortuitous and external to the wills of men. Actually your question seems to presuppose that a man can make history in a completely subjective way, or write a piece of the history of his country, and that really isn't true.

All men, whatever they do, have always acted within objective circumstances that determine the events. That is, no attitude is completely voluntary on the part of individuals, something that can come into being by the will or at the whim of men. I believe that the most a man can do is interpret the circumstances of a given moment correctly for a definite purpose, and if that purpose is not based on something false, on something unreal, it can be carried out.

Of course, the role of the individual man is important, but this does not in any way mean that one can talk about absolute power. What is meant by absolute power? Power without limits, a power exercised by one person, without obedience to any norm, to any principle, to any opinion, to any program, to any objective. And that, truly, is not my situation.

Mine is not a hereditary power, or one manufactured by a governing class which could unlawfully hold onto that power. This power was created from the very beginning for the sake of and in close relation with the great majority of the people. They are really the masters and the creators of that power, as well as those who really constitute it.

I don't seek to deny the influence I have as the leader of these people, as their representative, nor the quantity of power concentrated in one person. However, it was not deliberately created. It did not constitute part of a philosophy. It did not constitute a concept of the state or of leadership. It was a result of the characteristics of the process, beginning with the time when we were a handful of men, until the end of the struggle, when we carried the whole population with us, or at least the vast majority of it. This situation arose in the relatively brief period of a few years, during which there was a constant struggle which did not allow the possibility of creating any other kinds of institutions.

The concentration of influence or power can be used for good or used for evil. But it would be much more serious if we took that concept as a definitive form of government, as the ideal way of creating and organizing a state or of ruling a country. Actually, this is very far from being my concept or that of the other leaders. It has been a transitional form, determined by circumstances. And we have lately been taking a series of steps toward the creation of another kind of leadership. These steps tend, without the need for waiting until an accident happens to me, and not on account of that fear but out of deep conviction, toward the establishment of institutional forms of collective leadership that include guarantees against precisely what you are concerned about. I realize that they are well-founded concerns, and you can be sure that they concern us too.

I am not thinking about the immediate present, because right now there are capable and very influential leaders, but about a future time when circumstances will not exist such that a man could acquire so much influence over events and people, a time when these forms of personal influence will be replaced by forms of institutional influence.

I have explained to you the efforts I made during the early days not to take on any official duty and the illusions I fell into of thinking I could maintain my distance from any kind of official function or power. I mentioned how at the time the suggestion—I can tell you exactly—do you know who proposed the idea? Miró Cardona. The suggestion to nominate me as prime minister came from Miró Cardona, who was then prime minister. He saw clearly that the government wasn't operating and took the initiative of making that proposition in the innermost council of the government. So I made one condition, and it was so stated to all, including President Urrutia, that if they named me prime minister they had to give me the power to take the initiative in the legislative and administrative fields, in order to carry forward the revolutionary program. At that time all authority was concentrated in the president of the republic. I proposed that the authority be transferred and vested in the council of ministers and that the agreements passed by a majority of the council should have the character of law. And that promise was fulfilled when I took over the office of prime minister. At that time, the party, properly speaking, had not yet been organized. What existed was a series of organizations, each with its own leadership and its constitution as a separate organism.

That was how I took the office of prime minister.

Now, it is true, as a matter of fact, that my influence has increased during the revolutionary process. But the growth of that influence has had a material and social basis, and that basis is the series of revolutionary laws that we have adopted, each of which, in one way or another, has produced advantages for the great majority of the people. That is, ours is not a magical power, ours is not a hypnotic power, but rather, an influence derived from deeds, from the deeds that the Revolution has brought into effect. And I have not brought them about alone; nobody could have done it if his ideas did not represent the active will of the great majority of the people. It is my understanding that my influence flows from a correct interpretation of the needs and aspirations and the possibilities of the people and from a correct interpretation of what things have had to be done.

Now in leading the people, have I acted in a unipersonal manner? Never! All the decisions that have been made, absolutely all of them, have been discussed among the principal leaders of the Revolution. Never would I have felt satisfied with a single measure if it had been the result of a personal decision.

Furthermore, I have learned from experience that one must never be absolutely certain that the decision he takes or the ideas he has are always correct. Often, one can have a point of view which leaves out certain considerations or factors. And there is nothing more useful or positive or practical when a decision is going to be made on an important issue than hearing everybody else's opinion.

In the early days, decisions were taken in consultation with the different political leaders of the various organizations. Toward the end of 1960 all these revolutionary organizations were consolidated under a directorate, and never has a decision been taken without that group being in agreement.

It is true that the directorate was limited at the beginning, that it was not completely representative. And when the criticism of sectarianism was made, that directorate was enlarged and made more representative.

We are conscious that our leadership is still not sufficiently representative. We are involved at this moment in the task of organizing the party and its central committee. This is the next step, which we will take in order to establish in a real and formal way the broadest and most representative leadership possible.

So if you analyze the whole history of the revolutionary process, you see that, far from moving toward institutional forms of personal power, we have been taking more and more steps away from it: first uniting existing organizations; later, creating the organisms of leadership. And we will follow this course until we have finished creating, in a formal, institutional way, a method of collective leadership. We would not consider ourselves responsible men if these same concerns about the future were not present in all of us, and I believe that the statement you have made is, in that sense, very correct.

Concerning the question you raise about photographs, I don't know whether you are aware that one of the first laws that the revolutionary government passed, following a proposal of mine, was the prohibition against erecting statues to any living leader or putting his photographs in government offices. So you will see that in many places they have a small photograph in a little frame on a corner of the desk. In other places they don't have any photograph whatsoever. This can be seen by anybody. Furthermore, the same law prohibited giving the name of any living leader to any street, to any park, to any town. I believe that nowhere else, under circumstances such as ours, has a similar resolution been passed, and it was one of the first laws approved by the Revolution.

Also, notice that with regard to the very photographs which the people have, there is something curious. How have they been distributed? In an absolutely spontaneous way. No organism has been devoted to that activity. Where do most of the photographs come from that the peasants have? From magazines, from newspapers, from posters connected with some public meeting. There are photographs of all kinds and by all photographers, good ones and bad ones, an enormous variety.

Some people have even made a business from photographs, printing the ones they like and selling them in the street. What is absolutely true, and anybody can verify it, is that there has been no official initiative or policy regarding this situation. The fact that there are photographs in the houses has been a completely spontaneous thing among the people. We could have selected some photographs and printed hundreds of thousands of them and distributed them systematically, but this has not been done, because we are not interested in it.

LOCKWOOD: Perhaps the fact that it is done "spontaneously" on such a large scale illustrates the enormous personal influence which you hold with the masses, which in some cases takes on an almost religious aspect.

CASTRO: Yes, that is somewhat true, among the farmers principally, but in person they do not treat me like that. I visit many places, I talk a great deal with the farmers, and they treat me with great naturalness, which means that this mystical business doesn't exist. You yourself have seen how, when I visit the farmers, I talk with many of them, I go to their houses. They are somewhat accustomed to that and they treat me in a very familiar way. More than any mysticism, there is a certain feeling of familiarity.

And now, I don't believe that all the matters you raised have been answered yet.

In one of our informal conversations, I told you that generally twenty days or a month sometimes pass that I do not appear in the newspapers, when they don't publish news items or photographs or anything referring to my activities. Most of my activities are not made public. I mean that I do not have a press section organized so that people are constantly informed about everything I do, and I only appear in the newspapers when there is something important of a public nature. I carry on most of my work discreetly. You have been here for three months, and you can collect all the newspapers and can see how many times I have appeared in the press during that time. Occasionally, when I take a trip, some newspaperman goes along, but I do that very rarely.

LOCKWOOD: This is a relatively recent development, isn't it—that you can read the newspapers or watch TV for a month at a time without seeing your face or your name? How do you account for it?

CASTRO: Before, there were always a greater number of public meetings, and I generally appeared at each one of them. Today, people are much more involved in concrete work, so there is a lesser number of public meetings. Furthermore, there are now many more rallies in which other *compañeros* participate.

For any one of us, participation in these rallies is a strained and arduous duty. We have to resist many pressures, constant invitations to the meetings of each organization. They always want certain leaders there. I still have to speak at least three times a year at huge rallies.

LOCKWOOD: Do you prepare your speeches in advance?

CASTRO: Actually, I have ideas about the essential things, about

the most important things, about those things I want to emphasize, but I never make any formal preparation. I have found that
if you try to give a definite shape to your ideas, to give them a
prior form, when you begin to speak you lose one of the finest
influences that the public can exercise over the person who speaks,
that of transmitting its ardor, its enthusiasm, its force, its inspiration to him.

Often, my speeches are conversations, exchanges of impressions with the public. Often, that interchange of impressions determines the need to stick closer to a subject, to a question, to
some idea. It is much like a conversation; and really when you are
going to have a talk with somebody, you cannot plan the whole
conversation. Sometimes one doesn't know who is speaking,
whether it is oneself or the people.

LOCKWOOD: Do you mean that you have the feeling that the people
are speaking through you sometimes?

CASTRO: I remember a certain 26th of July celebration. The people
did not go simply to listen; they went to manifest an attitude, a
decisiveness, a state of mind, a happiness, a goal accomplished, a
purpose regarding tasks that are not completed. It was a presence,
a mobilization, and an action of the people in which they demonstrated their spirit, their support, their enthusiasm. The people
manifest themselves in many ways in each of these meetings,
especially in those that are not preceded by a parade.

LOCKWOOD: Many people in the crowds listening to you seem to
have an experience similar to yours; they seem to have the sensa-
tion that they are speaking through you—

CASTRO: Yes! When something is said which seems like what they
are thinking! Sometimes that happens. It is very strange. Our
public has a great perceptibility, a great agility, a great capacity
for understanding. In this, the levels of culture of the different
regions can be appraised too. In some regions they have more
capacity to understand rapidly, as if they sense what is going to
be said, and in others they react with more sluggishness, although
changes from one year to another are perceptible.

In the countryside, for example, people used to feel that they
were inferior to the people of the city. Country people were called

campesinos in a pejorative way. They were accused of being ignorant and uncivilized, and humorous stories were told about the
campesinos. For this reason, when he went to the city, the peasant
felt very timid and inhibited. That was in times before the Revolution. Today, the campesinos go to the city and feel another state
of mind, another spirit. They are changing extraordinarily.

I like very much the atmosphere of the country. I enjoy myself
very much when I go there. If it depended on me, I would always
be in the country, in the mountains. I prefer it a thousand times
to the city. The people are very healthy, very good.

It pleases me a great deal to visit the countryside, especially
the mountains, and see the incredible change that has taken place
in the spirit of the people, how universal the thirst for knowledge
is, the happiness, and the optimism with which everybody—but
especially the young people and the children—are looking to the
future. Communism is not such a horrible thing!

You will find, if you analyze my speeches, that I do not try to
create a faith among the people, but to teach them to meditate, to
think, and to reason about the problems, the why of each thing.
That is, we are trying to teach the people not to "believe," but to
think. Nobody who carefully studied my speeches would be able
to deny that there is a constant effort to get the people to reach
certain conclusions by reasoning, by analysis, by conviction. If it
were otherwise my speeches wouldn't have to be so long. You are
aware that I have a certain reputation for making long speeches?

LOCKWOOD: Yes. But they've been getting shorter, haven't they?

CASTRO: A little shorter, exactly because I believe there is a much
higher level of preparation, of understanding. Many of the things
that I used to have to explain, to justify, and to repeat are now
well known. But fundamentally, my whole style has always been
that of conversing and reasoning with the people. There is a great
difference between our multitudes and the fascist mobs which
you compared them to. Our multitudes are not fanatical. Rather,
very firmly based convictions have been created on the basis of
persuasion, of analysis, of reasoning.

The fascists brought together multitudes who seemed content. There is no doubt that those regimes had support in Italy and

Germany, but their organization and mobilization of the masses was done by typically military means. They never had the character of spontaneity and, much less, the enthusiasm and the magnitude that our public meetings have. That is, we do not mobilize all the soldiers, all the militiamen, all the organizations; but the public is called together, and all the workers and their friends come, each one on his own. We offer facilities so that they can be brought to the meeting, but absolutely nobody is required to come. That is quite evident. Those who want to, come; those who don't, do not come.

And I'll tell you something else. If you consider the size of our population, barely seven million inhabitants, our public meetings are incomparably larger than those the fascists used to hold in Italy and Germany, in spite of Germany's enormous population. They are larger not only proportionately, but in absolute numbers.

Moreover, there is no comparison between the enthusiasm and the support generated by a revolution, which awakens feelings of noble generosity in man, and the enthusiasm that fascism generates, inspired by resentment, hatred, and the hunger to exploit and dominate other nations, races, and men.

Our people have no egotistical feeling of any kind, they make no claim of superiority. The Revolution educates them in feelings of equality and brotherhood among all men and all peoples. It educates them in the ideal that one's own work, not the exploitation of others, is the just social way of earning one's living; in the idea of the right of each nation to the full enjoyment of its natural resources and the fruit of its labor, not the exploitation of some nations by others; in feelings of love, and not of hatred and discrimination between men. It awakens the faith of man in himself, the faith of peoples in a better life, the creative spirit of the masses. This is what generates the enthusiasm, this is what distinguishes our multitudes, this is what also distinguishes socialism from imperialist capitalism.

And permit me to say, finally, that I don't experience any personal satisfaction whatsoever when I read or hear some of those flattering qualities which are attributed to me in the press. I have never spent a single second of pleasure over such things. I can tell you in all sincerity that they have no importance for me. And I think this is a positive thing. Because, as a general rule, power corrupts men. It makes them egotistical; it makes them selfish. Fortunately, this has never happened to me, and I don't think it will. Very honestly, I can say that nothing satisfies me more than seeing that every day things depend less and less on me, and more and more upon a collective spirit grounded in institutions.

25
Maurice Halperin
Fidel's Power to Disrupt

Fidel Castro's own perception of his personal style emerges from the previous selection. That his role as Cuba's head of government might be part of Cuba's problem as well as its solution is explored now by an exceptionally astute observer who worked in Cuba from 1962 to 1968. Maurice Halperin, educated at Harvard and the Sorbonne, was chief of the Latin America Division of the Office of Strategic Services (OSS) during World War II. Persecuted for his political beliefs during the McCarthy era, Halperin left the United States and taught in Mexico, the Soviet Union, Havana, and, finally, at Simon Fraser University in Canada. While in Cuba he was a consultant to the Ministry of Foreign Trade, and it was this association with a part of the revolutionary bureaucracy that "undoubtedly affected [his] perceptions" of Fidel. Nevertheless, Halperin's view of Castro is as close to objective appraisal as actors in the revolutionary years were apt to come.

Halperin's evaluation of Castro in this selection and elsewhere in his highly readable book, *The Taming of Fidel Castro*, is informed by his belief that,

> Fidel's unfailing and often unfounded optimism was not only deeply engrained in his subconscious mind but was also a conscious instrument for mobilizing the population to perform the tasks which he imposed on it. Such optimism was a characteristic apparently shared by all charismatic leaders from Mohammed to Mussolini. At the same time, his appeal for [social consciousness] was something less than Ché's obsessive goal: the transformation of the Cuban worker, conditioned by the sordid values of the capitalist system, into the new "socialist" man

From Maurice Halperin, *The Taming of Fidel Castro* (Berkeley: University of California Press, 1981), 86–92. Copyright © 1981 The Regents of the University of California. Reprinted with permission.

(thus far a rare creature in any socialist society). It was rather a call for patriotism, the same patriotism which he so effectively mobilized when the country faced external danger, as at the time of the Bay of Pigs invasion in the spring of 1961 and the missile crisis in the fall of 1962. Later he was to discover that, as far as the great bulk of the population was concerned, the willingness for self-sacrifice and heroism in war could not be transferred to peacetime pursuits. There would be unconscionable abuse and neglect of equipment, slothful response to exhortation, and persistent absenteeism, which Fidel would be compelled to control with classical carrot-and-club procedures.

IT was difficult to measure the direct impact of Fidel Castro's personality on the day-to-day functioning of the Cuban economy, except to say that it was constant and enormously disruptive. No one who was even marginally associated with the economic process in the mid-sixties could doubt it. Except perhaps for the ministry of industries during Ché's tenure, there was no area affecting the economy—including, for example, the training of geographers and economists at the university—that was immune to the sudden intervention of the Maximum Leader, or to the near-paralysis that could follow when his attention veered to another project, resulting in the fear of making decisions if he could not be located or was not available for other reasons.

Fidel's compulsive urge for personal control of whatever undertaking struck his fancy, and at any level that he chose, was not motivated by a mere lust for power but by the great mission which destiny had entrusted to him and the conviction that he was especially endowed with the wisdom for fulfilling the mission. His intentions, therefore, were always the best: in this instance, to move the economy toward an efficient and abundant production with all possible speed. Among the obstacles he perceived to this objective were the low competence and the retarded learning capacity of most of his subordinates, which in turn fed bureaucratic inertia. In one of his midnight forays to the university campus, he was probably deadly serious when he told a group of students who quickly gathered around him—this was reported to me by a student of mine who was there—that in all of Cuba he could only count on twenty administrators with enough intelligence to handle the jobs they were assigned to do.

The Problems of Bureaucracy

Thus, while Marcelo Fernández, Ché Guevara, and others were debating Marxist economic theory, Fidel in his numerous speeches was excoriating bureaucracy as the great source of evil which he was determined to extirpate from the Cuban scene. In this respect, he set himself up as a model nonbureaucrat. According to conventional standards, he explained, as prime minister he should have an office occupying several floors in the biggest building in Havana. Instead, he practically had no office at all, just a couple of small rooms for handling correspondence. To the masses held spellbound by his speeches he even appeared to be outside the government, and, like his listeners, a victim of its myriad of dull, parasitic, paper-pushing and paper-storing officials. It was almost as if he were not only outside the government but against the government. Politically, this posture—probably a genuine reflection of his deepest feelings and hence convincing—was an important element of his strength, for it helped maintain the identification of the Cuban people with his personal leadership. The Revolution was Fidel, not the idiotic creatures who filled the ministries and messed everything up.

Under pressure from Fidel, who was also responding to the manpower pressure in agriculture, a considerable pruning of personnel in the ministries eventually took place, and not always in a rational manner. The stigma attached to office work and the aura of patriotism which glorified labor in the fields prompted a number of the more able and ambitious employees to volunteer for a year or two of work in the countryside, thereby earning service merits for later advancement—in the government or party bureaucracy! The result was not only a reduction in the employment rolls of the ministries, but also a higher proportion of drones among those who remained.

In any event, of the many problems that beset the Cuban bureaucracy, the question of numbers was not decisive. Bureaucracy in all modern and modernizing states, and more particularly in a socialist state, is both an indispensable part of the machinery of the government and a major source of its imperfections. In Cuba, however, there was a special if not unique problem. It was Fidel himself whose disorganized work habits and monopoly of decision-making at the top of the bureaucratic pyramid affected all layers beneath him. It was common knowledge that at the ministerial level the fear of Fidel inhibited critical thinking and initiative, which in turn dampened initiative and prevented delegation of responsibility all the way down the line. A large part of the paper-pushing that angered Fidel was merely the moving of routine matters, which could easily be disposed of at lower levels, up through the ranks for successive approval. But who was to "bell the cat," that is, explain to Fidel that a policy of delegating responsibility and decision-making to the lower echelons would work wonders in the Cuban bureaucracy, and that the greatest obstacle to such a policy was Fidel himself?

The "Special Plans"

"I'm not a farm manager and that's not my work, but I'm interested in these problems and to put my mind at ease I felt the need of undertaking a few little experiments in growing sugarcane. . . . I don't have any farmland, so I had to plow up some vacant lots out there on the outskirts of town." It was Castro speaking in the middle of his four-hour speech at the final session of the First National Sugar Forum, held in Havana on September 19, 1964. Two months earlier, he had combined the agricultural and industrial branches of sugar production into a single new ministry of the sugar industry in preparation for the projected ten-million-ton sugar harvest in 1970. The forum, at which some 1,500 representatives from the farms, sugar mills, and the new ministry were present, was the formal opening of the six-year campaign.

However, Fidel went on to explain, he had run into a "tremendous problem" with the consolidated electric enterprise because, according to an earlier plan of which he was not aware, they were going to put up a tower and run a high-voltage transmission line right through his cane field. "Over my dead body," he told the power officials. "You're not going to destroy this cane field." There was more to this amusing anecdote, but it need not detain us. The point is that this was Fidel's quaint explanation ("to put my mind at ease") for one of his early personal ventures into "scientific research," which rapidly multiplied into scores of farming and stock-raising projects scattered through the island—projects that were euphemistically referred to in official literature as "special plans" but were otherwise not explained or described. Information about what went on in Fidel's network rarely reached the press, and even the ministries that were supposedly to benefit from the "experiments" received no systematic reports.

In time, Fidel's "special plans" tended to grow both in size and scope. Early in June 1965, Fidel casually revealed in a speech that 3,200 head of cattle had been exported to Italy. This was how word reached the ministry of foreign trade that Fidel was exporting "his" beef in "his" ships to Italy. In other words, he had quietly set up a miniature foreign trade and maritime transport ministry of his own. How the financial aspects of his transactions were handled by the National Bank I never discovered, but I recall that it was impossible to incorporate any hard data from this "special plan" into Cuba's foreign-trade statistics because no such data were made available.

Little in the way of positive results was achieved in the "special plans"; otherwise Cuba and the world would have been amply informed about them. The negative results were more complex than appeared on the surface. A great deal of Fidel's time and energy were absorbed by his "special plans." This might not have mattered so much if it were not for the fact that countless decisions which depended directly on him could be delayed for days or weeks while he made the rounds. Frequently it was even a problem to locate him. A related development was "influence peddling" by those he placed in charge of his projects. These people had the inestimable privilege of dealing directly and frequently with Fidel. Depending on his mood at a given moment, he could spend a great deal of time with one or another of his managers. These in turn were courted by high-level functionaries desperately trying to get a favor from Fidel, or simply to get a message to him. Thus, a bit of corruption crept into Fidel's circuit as special "friendships" blossomed and withered, depending on the tenure of the manager who had access to Fidel's ear.

There is no available record of the turnover in the management of the "special plans," but from scattered information it appears that it could have been quite high. Fidel was a hard man to work for. He was a great champion of the people collectively, but he mistreated people as individuals. Foreign journalists who interviewed him usually found him to be, even if eccentric in some respects, a person who could be fair-minded, considerate of others, and compassionate when it came to matters of human welfare. But this was only one side, the bright side, of his character, which he shrewdly displayed to those who would report about him to the world public. The dark side was better known to those of his subordinates who had the misfortune to fall afoul of his overbearing and unrelenting ego.

The Case of Enrique Oltuski

One such case deserves mention because it deals with the experience of a onetime top-ranking and dedicated Fidelista who also had close relations with Ché Guevara. Thus, it provides insight into the subtleties of the Cuban revolutionary process during this period. Enrique Oltuski, son of post-World War I Polish-Jewish immigrants, in 1959 was the youngest minister in Castro's first cabinet. He was twenty-seven years old, had studied engineering in the United States, and on his return to Cuba became the leader of Fidel's underground movement in Las Villas, a key province in the center of the island. During this period he was an anti-Communist, along with other prominent members of the July 26 Movement who, like Oltuski, later went along with Fidel's conversion to Marxism-Leninism.

When Jean-Paul Sartre visited Cuba in 1960, he was much taken with the young Oltuski. In his book on Cuba, Sartre described how Oltuski had supplied weapons, food, and money to the guerrillas, and concluded that the bravery of those who faced the perils of the underground was "more difficult than military heroism: a lonely struggle without witnesses against an all-powerful enemy," with a fate worse than death if they were caught. One of the highlights of Sartre's book related the first meeting of Oltuski with Ché Guevara, in mid-1958, in the hills of Las Villas. It turned into a stormy all-night confrontation on tactical and ideological issues between two very different but equally stubborn personalities. They ended up, however, convinced of each other's integrity, and later on became fast friends.

Before the end of 1960, Enrique Oltuski was literally out on the street. Castro had fired him from his post as minister of communications. It was a concession to the PSP Communists, who were moving into key positions in the wake of the close ties binding Cuba to Soviet military and economic aid. It was the beginning of the dark period of what was later euphemistically labeled "sectarianism," when Oltuski and other prominent Fidelistas found themselves without jobs and friends in a political atmosphere clouded by fear and suspicion. Years later, in a moving tribute to Ché after his death, Oltuski told how, on the night his own mother died, only Ché came to the funeral home to comfort him and stay with him until dawn.

In February 1961, Ché became minister of industries, and a few months later he gave Oltuski his first job after his disgrace. It was the start of another career, as Oltuski moved up the ladder in the ministry and then, following Fidel's purge of Aníbal Escalante and the "Muscovite" Communists in late March 1962, transferred with Fidel's blessing to the central planning board as vice-minister. Oltuski's "rehabilitation" was underscored in mid-December when Fidel sent him to Moscow as a member of a four-man commercial delegation.

In the late spring of 1964, Oltuski became "fed up with the bureaucratic rat race," as a friend of his explained it. In addition, it was no secret that he and the minister (Regino Boti, fired by Fidel in July 1964) were constantly at loggerheads. No doubt, he was also influenced by Fidel's major passions of the moment: against bureaucracy and for agriculture. In any case, Oltuski resigned from the central planning board and asked Fidel to assign him to a job in production, preferably in agriculture. After a lapse of several months—not an unusual delay while awaiting Fidel's decision—he was placed in charge of a "special plan," a cattle ranch some hundred miles east of Havana in the province of Matanzas. In the capital, it was the talk of the town that a vice-minister would give up his rank and the comforts of Havana and move his family to the countryside. Soon, however, the word got around that Fidel was a frequent visitor to the ranch and that he considered Oltuski to be doing an outstanding job. In a short time, a stream of new and old friends began to show up at the ranch, and many speculated that bigger things were in store for Enrique Oltuski.

Six months or so after settling in, Oltuski received a telephone call from the manager of Fidel's experimental stockbreeding farm, another one of his "special plans" on the outskirts of Havana. Feed for the cattle was running dangerously low, Fidel was incommunicado, and no relief was in sight. The herd was threatened with starvation. Could Enrique temporarily put Fidel's cattle out to pasture on his ranch? Enrique agreed, and some 2,000 head were safely transported to Matanzas.

Crime and Punishment

Three weeks later, Oltuski was confined to a penal labor camp on the Isle of Pines, by coincidence the same island off the southwest coast of Cuba where Fidel had been imprisoned by Batista in 1953. When Fidel belatedly discovered that his prize cattle had been moved without his permission for whatever purpose, he was outraged. If he had just been an ordinary employee, Fidel explained in a verbal message relayed to Oltuski, he would merely have fired him. But as a close friend in whom he had placed his highest trust and confidence, Oltuski deserved a greater penalty. Fidel therefore offered him an opportunity for atonement by "voluntarily" accepting a six-month sentence on the Isle of Pines.

Part of the story of Oltuski's crime and punishment I learned from someone who had heard it directly from Ché Guevara. It seems that when Fidel offered Oltuski the job on his "special plan," Oltuski asked Ché whether he should accept. Ché advised him not to. "I told him," said Ché "that knowing both him and Fidel, he was bound to end up in Guanahacabibes [on the western tip of Cuba]. I was mistaken about which prison camp it would be."

Oltuski accepted his fate philosophically. He continued to receive his "special plan" salary, and his family moved back to their old residence in Havana. Life and work in the prison camp were not too grim. After all, the Isle of Pines was not Siberia, nor was Fidel a tropical Stalin. When Oltuski was released, he wrote an autobiographical novel, the first part of which he submitted for publication. Among those assigned to read the manuscript was Alejo Carpentier, Cuba's foremost novelist and one of the most distinguished in Latin America, who gave it high praise. But the responsible book editor prudently submitted it to Fidel for his approval. The novel dealt with the period prior to the triumph of the insurrection, and apparently was the first attempt to tell the story of the underground struggle, completely obscured by the mass of literature on the exploits of the guerrillas. The novel was never published. Its author, briefly surfacing among a collection of reminiscences about Ché published early in 1968 . . . , had disappeared into the rank and file of the Cuban labor force. Years later, he unpredictably emerged again in the ministry of fisheries, where, at the end of 1978, he was listed as deputy minister, a remarkable case of resiliency among those who once held and then lost favor with Fidel.

26

Genaro Arriagada Herrera
Pinochet's Route to Power in Chile

No coup d'etat in twentieth-century Spanish American history has reverberated in the Hemisphere more profoundly than that which overthrew President Salvador de Allende in Chile on September 11, 1973. The shock waves were felt inside and outside of the country in particular because of the exceptionally high degree of democratic government that had become engrained in Chile. For the next fifteen years, until the plebiscite of October 1988 marked the beginning of the end of totalitarian government, Chile was dominated by a military regime. In the essay that follows a distinguished Chilean political scientist provides a succinct and lucid explanation of how one member of the military junta, army chief of staff General Augusto Pinochet, was able to concentrate authority in himself. During that process, which Genaro Arriagada Herrera reveals step by step, Pinochet outmaneuvered the other chiefs of staff of the navy, air force, and police in part by his reliance on residual precedents from the very constitutional government which had been overthrown. By eventually manipulating himself into the position of president of the republic, Pinochet clothed himself with a semblance of "the solemnity and stability which always was part of the position of president of the republic." Pinochet's shrewd resort to legalism is very much in keeping with ancient Spanish approaches to law. Also, as the editors of the volume in which Arriagada's essay first appeared point out, Pinochet's personal power was "simply a product of the highly professional and hierarchical character of the Chilean armed forces, which allows its top officer to dictate to his subordi-

From Genaro Arriagada Herrera, "The Legal and Institutional Framework of the Armed Forces in Chile," in *Military Rule in Chile: Dictatorship and Oppositions,* edited by J. Samuel Valenzuela and Arturo Valenzuela (Baltimore: The Johns Hopkins University Press, 1986), 117–43. Reprinted with permission.

nates and which prescribes the apoliticism of the officer corps."[1]

Genaro Arriagada Herrera is an internationally respected publicist and a major figure in Chile's reemergent Christian Democratic Party. Among his many works is, *Pinochet: The Politics of Power* (1988).

THE Chilean democratic regime was obviously structured around the principle of subordination of military power to political power. That was, in the judgment of both military personnel and civilians, the fundamental basis on which the professionalism of the armed forces was built. As part of this subordination, the highest military authority within the state was the president of the republic. As stated in the Constitution, it was the president's responsibility "to provide the civilian and military jobs that the laws allow according to administrative statute, and to confer, in accordance with the Senate, the ranks of colonel, navy captain, and other superior officers of the army and navy. In the battlefield the President himself can confer these high military positions." The president of the republic was also able to "organize and distribute the army and the navy in whatever way he finds convenient" and to personally command them with the consent of the senate. In this case, the president of the republic could establish residence [in] any place occupied by the Chilean army. The text of the Constitution also assigned the president with overall responsibility for "the preservation of public order within the republic as well as the external security of the republic, in accordance with the Constitution and the laws." Among the presidential powers was that of appointing the chiefs of staff, as well as of calling them into retirement. He could not go below the ranks of division general or brigadier general to fill these positions, it being his duty automatically to retire all those with higher seniority than the generals he designated. Hence, given only these minor restrictions, the position of chief of staff in any of the branches was left to the sole discretion of the president.

The disciplinary norms of the army gave the greatest prerogatives to the president of the republic (eighth rank in disciplinary prerogatives), followed by the minister of defense (seventh rank), and the chief of staff (sixth rank). As stated in the Disciplinary Regulations of the army, "the president of the republic, functioning as generalissimo of the army, and the minister of national defense, as a member of the executive, have the highest disciplinary prerogatives over military personnel and army employees."

Two processes occurred after the military coup of 1973. The first one, to be discussed briefly, was the concentration of enormous power in the military junta, exceeding that of the presidency it replaced; and [the] second one was the development within the junta of a growing amount of power in the chief of staff of the army.

The first process is evident in the fact that the National Congress was dissolved, a state of siege was declared which suspended individual rights, and all municipal authorities—who had always been elected in Chile—were removed and replaced by mayors named by the military junta. During the same month of the military coup . . . all the decisions about qualifications, promotions, and the retirement of armed-forces personnel were given to the members of the military junta, each one of them acting with complete freedom with regard to his institution. In October of 1973, the universities were taken over, political parties of Marxist inclination were dissolved and prohibited, and all other political organizations were declared in recess.

In November 1973, the electoral registries were closed, and the government was authorized to expel people from the country for political reasons. In the same month, the military junta formally assumed constitutional power, with no limitations, which technically did away with the very concept of a Constitution. In December 1973, labor-union elections were suspended, and the government was authorized to remove and designate the union leaders. Rules that would allow the cancellation of Chilean nationality of political opponents were established, and new emergency measures affecting the career stability of armed-forces officers were dictated.

In January 1974, the measures pertaining to the recess of those political parties that did not take part in Allende's government became more stringent. These measures lasted until March 1977, at which time the parties were finally dissolved, their property confiscated. In March of 1974, the suspension of elections for intermediate organizations, thus far in effect only for the unions, was extended to all the other formally recognized organizations of the country, such as neighborhood associations, professional colleges, and centers for mothers. During this period, the rules on control and censorship of the press became progressively tighter, culminating in March 1977 in a total censorship over all printed matter and in the prohibition on forming any means of communication without the prior authorization of the government. Finally in June 1974 the National Intelligence Directorate (DINA) was created.

Parallel to this escalation of power in the military junta, the second process—the increasing concentration of power in the office of the chief of staff of the army—was underway within the junta itself. The position of the chief of staff of the army, General Pinochet, was relatively weak politically when compared with that of the chiefs of staff of the navy and the air force, since the latter two appear to have been originators of the military coup, while Pinochet made a commitment to the insurrection only forty-eight hours before the coup took place, on September 11.

The first formal announcement by the new authorities expressly noted that the military junta had assumed "supreme command of the nation" without indicating any form of differentiation within the junta itself. However, the members of the junta quickly decided that they would "designate Army General Don Augusto Pinochet Ugarte as president of the junta, who assumes on this date [11 September 1973] the said position." Despite this decision the relative standings of the chiefs of staff were at that point so equal that they even thought of rotating the presidency of the junta among each other for short periods of time. Thus, when he was before the press, . . . General Pinochet pointed out that "the junta worked like a single entity. I was elected because I was the eldest. But I will not be the only president of the junta; afterwards Admiral Merino will be too, and then General Leigh and so on. I am a man without ambitions, I do not want to appear as the only holder of power." Until then, all powers were assumed by the military junta. "The junta has assumed constituent, legislative, and executive powers."

The first substantial change in the structure of power came in mid-1974 with the enactment of the Statute of the Governmental Junta. This document reiterated the principle that executive power lay with the military junta, but it assigned the exercise of that power to the president of the junta. Moreover, it did not recognize the right of the military junta to designate its own president. From then on, the presidency of the junta was to be given "to its titular member who takes precedence according to the rules stipulated by Title IV." That order of precedence could be changed only if the chief of staff of the army were to cease being a member of the junta. This could occur only by "death, resignation, or an absolute impairment of the person" as stipulated in the statute.

In fact, the statute tied the exercise of executive power to army general Augusto Pinochet, with no time limit and without the possibility of his being recalled by the rest of the members of the junta. General Pinochet became the "supreme chief of the nation," a name that had been used only in the first constitutions following the Declaration of Independence to designate the titular holders of executive power.

By virtue of the statute, the members of the military junta did retain within the executive power certain prerogatives. They could "collaborate" with the supreme chief in "the exercise of his executive functions by assuming the directions of those activities, areas or duties which he [the supreme chief] requests of them." In addition, the naming of ministers, ambassadors, governors, and administrative officers should be made "with the agreement of the Junta, although these civil servants will keep their posts as long as they enjoy the President's trust." According to this same statute, the chief of staff of the navy should oversee the workings of the economic ministries, such as Treasury, Economy, and the Central Bank (Admiral Merino handled these), while the chief of staff of the air force would oversee the social ministries, like Education, Housing, and Health (General Gustavo Leigh was appointed for these areas). Their power, however, was more apparent than real, since General Pinochet was the one who really held it. By the middle of 1976, Merino and Leigh were hardly mentioned as being in charge of the economic and social sectors of the country.

DINA was created three days before the Statute of the Governmental Junta was issued. Since 11 September 1973, there had been a spectacular development in intelligence services in all branches of national defense. Such services had grown enormously in human and material resources and displayed a lot of activity. There was also a strong rivalry between them. As a consequence, the repressive power of the state emanated from a variety of organizations that were autonomous and difficult to control, leading to abuse and juridical and political irresponsibility by the state police. By the end of 1973 and during the first six months of 1974, it became almost impossible to discover the whereabouts of political prisoners and the cause of their detention. The Ministry of the Interior was in charge only of the civil police, and each branch of the Ministry of National Defense had its own police answerable only to their respective chiefs of staff. It was therefore common for a person to be detained, interrogated, and released by one police service, and immediately thereafter stopped again by another police service.

With the creation of DINA, this situation abruptly ended. All intelligence activity was given to a "military organization with a technical-professional character that took its orders directly from the junta." DINA was formed by personnel from all branches of the National Defense Ministry, plus specially selected civilians.

Although DINA was created to concentrate police power in the hands of the military junta, it did not happen that way, since power was concentrated solely in the supreme chief of the nation. Years later General Leigh, retired from the junta, recounted his experience as follows: "I increasingly took my air force officers out of DINA, not because they were behaving improperly, but rather because of the absolute predominance of the army within DINA. They asked for people from all branches of military service, but the result was that none of my top officers was given executive responsibility; they were assigned only administrative tasks. The organization was in fact linked directly to the president even though, legally, it should have been responsible to the governmental junta. In other words, I took away my people when I realized that I had no power to control DINA."

Until DINA was disbanded in August 1977, it was the backbone of the regime. No other organization during this period had so much influence nationally. And of course this influence in the hands of the president of the military junta destroyed any vestige of balance of power between him and those who, in the months right after the coup, had been his equals.

DINA was formally dissolved because of very strong national and international political pressure, but it was replaced by the National Information Center (CNI). The CNI was described in the law which created it, like DINA, as "a specialized military organization with a technical-professional character." However, the CNI, which remains the most important police service of the state, was from the very beginning subordinated to the head of the executive power. While DINA, formally speaking at least, "depended on the junta," the law creating CNI stipulated that it "will be linked to the Supreme Government . . . through the Secretary of the Interior"—i.e., through a ministry that enjoys the full confidence of the chief of state.

Another facet of General Pinochet's increasing affirmation of power vis-á-vis the junta was the evolution of his title as head of state. When he was appointed, in mid-1974, "supreme chief of the nation," no one expected this designation to be short-lived. And yet, exactly six months after the Statute of the Junta was approved, a new constitutional decree was introduced with a very significant modification: it changed this title to "president of the republic," the one used by democratically elected Chilean heads of state. The decree establishing this change read as follows: "Executive power is exercised by the President of the Governmental Junta who, under the title of President of the Republic of Chile, administers the State and is the Supreme Chief of the Nation."

Formally it was a minor modification. Juridically, however, it meant that General Pinochet would be able to exercise all the functions that the laws and regulations, throughout many years, had given to the president of the republic. Politically it had great significance, since the title of president of the republic was used to try to strip the regime of its de facto origins, covering it instead—or at least attempting to cover it—with the solemnity and stability which always were part of the position of president of the republic. Besides, this distinguished new title given to the president of the military junta helped distance him even more in the power pyramid from other members of the junta. With this title, General Pinochet has concentrated more power in his hands than has any other Chilean leader in this century. Nevertheless, in one sense he has had less power than the former presidents of [the] nation's democratic governments. Curiously, this relative lack of power has been in the military field and requires a brief explanation.

There is no question that in his own service, the army, the power of General Pinochet since 11 September 1973 has been enormous and has encountered no resistance. However, if we examine the other branches of national defense—the navy and the air force—and the police, the situation has been quite different, since the title of president of the republic did not give Pinochet the right to appoint or call into retirement the chiefs of staff of those institutions, which are powers that all the constitutional presidents of Chile had.

As policy differences between the chief of staff of the army (Pinochet) and the chief of staff of the air force (Leigh) developed to a breaking point, this limitation on the power of the new "president of the republic" became more apparent. The struggle between the two members of the junta was resolved by force, since it was impossible to resolve it by law. As we have seen, the chiefs of staff were to hold their posts as commanders and members of the junta until "death, resignation, or an absolute impairment of the person" removed them from office. General Leigh did not want to resign, and he was in good health. On 24 July 1978, however, he was dismissed by a simple supreme decree of the Ministry of the Interior, which declared his "absolute impairment" to continue as a member of the junta.

This resolution was totally out of line with the statute, because the "absolute impairment" that the law referred to could only be physical or mental and should have had nothing to do with political differences, however profound. As has occurred in many other instances during the last decade of Chilean political life, the "absolute impairment" clause was therefore transformed into a legal subterfuge to expel a member of the junta for political differences. This transformation relied on an article of the Statute of the Junta that pointed out that "when there is some doubt as to whether the impairment that prevents a member of the junta from exercising his duties is of such seriousness that he must be replaced . . . the titular members of the junta are entitled to resolve that doubt." Therefore, on the morning of 24 July 1978, all members of the junta except General Leigh declared that Leigh was "totally unable to go on performing his duties." This declaration is stated in a secret document that no one outside the junta, including General Leigh, has seen. Once this precedent was set, the president of the republic and his minister of the interior dictated a decree dismissing the third-ranking member of the junta. The controller-general of the republic, responsible for reviewing the legality of executive decrees, dispatched this one with a surprising statement: "It is understood that this action is juridically a law decree and not an executive decree."

Nevertheless, the subject of legality is not the key concern here: power is. In this sense, the dismissal of General Leigh meant that a new and decisive step had been taken in the concentration of power in the hands of the chief of staff of the army, and in the process of self-destruction of the military junta's power. From that moment on, General Pinochet started acting, de facto if not de jure, as generalissimo of the armed forces. In September 1979, for the first time in a presidential message, Pinochet used this title to refer to himself: "The high commanders are responsible for informing their subordinates about matters of government, an obligation that the president of the republic has made his own in his capacity as generalissimo of the armed forces and the police force."

The ceremonial protocol reflected clearly this new enhancement of General Pinochet's position. During 1979, in the most important official functions and celebrations, General Pinochet made arrangements to differentiate himself clearly from the other members of the junta. For example, for the centennial of the naval battle of Iquique on 21 May 1979, as well as for the celebration of the birthday of Bernardo O'Higgins and the transfer of his remains to the so-called "Altar of the Fatherland," five flower offerings were presented. The first one was given by General Pinochet and his minister of defense for the presidency of the republic, and the following four were presented for the army, navy, air force, and police by the vice chief of staff of the army and by the respective members of the military junta—all of the latter aided by their second-ranking officers. The ceremonies highlighted the existence of a presidential power above the chiefs of staff in all the branches of national defense and emphasized the status of the generalissimo of the armed forces. This was particularly significant in as institution such as the military, where the symbolism of rank is so important.

Note
1. J. Samuel Valenzuela and Arturo Valenzuela, eds., *Military Rule in Chile: Dictatorship and Oppositions* (Baltimore: The Johns Hopkins University Press, 1986), 7.

27

James D. Cockcroft

Paraguay's Stroessner: The Ultimate Caudillo?

ALFREDO Stroessner, known to his enemies as "El Tirano-sauro," epitomized the caudillo in many ways during his nearly thirty-five-year domination of Paraguay (1954–89). In the vivid account that follows James Cockcroft explores a regime which reflected both ancient patterns of caudillaje power manipulation and the new controls that late-twentieth-century modernization and technology provided. Stroessner was particularly adept at exploiting the traditional Colorado political party apparatus and the familiar anti-Communist pose to maintain himself in power. It is ironic that the seventy-six-year-old general was not driven from office by left-wing or even moderate revolutionaries, for their threat had been systematically frustrated by the adroit leader. Instead, it was General Andrés Rodríguez, his right-hand-man and the father-in-law of Alfredo Stroessner, Jr., who pulled off a brief but bloody palace coup on February 3, 1989. Rodríguez represented a faction within the Colorado party that resented the militant Stroessner wing's aim to place another son, Gustavo Stroessner, in his father's place when the old man faltered. It was classic personalist politics and a dramatic illustration of the problem of succession. Stroessner was exiled to Brazil, while Rodríguez handily won the presidential elections three months later. Readers may decide for themselves whether Paraguay's ancient tradition of authoritarian rulers from Francia to Solano López to Stroessner has definitively ended.

James Cockcroft, who wrote this essay while Alfredo Stroessner was still in power, is an accomplished historian and sociologist who has written extensively on Latin American affairs. He is best known for *Intellectual Precursors of*

From James D. Cockcroft, *Neighbors in Turmoil: Latin America* (New York: Harper and Row, 1989), 440–53. Copyright © 1989 by Harper and Row, Publishers, Inc. Reprinted by permission of Harper Collins Publishers.

the Mexican Revolution, 1900–1913 (1968), *Outlaws in the Promised Land* (1986), and *Neighbors in Turmoil: Latin America* (1989), in which this essay first appeared.

Here we respect human rights. Human rights are for the well-behaved people, for the workers.
—President Alfredo Stroessner, 1980

IN early September 1987 moderate opposition leaders were holding a public meeting in the local church of the town of Colonel Oviedo, eighty miles east of landlocked Paraguay's capital city of Asunción. Witnesses later said the atmosphere was subdued, tense. Out of long custom, people expected a police attack and spoke almost in whispers.

Suddenly a group of parapolice thugs shouting "Long live Stroessner!" and "Death to Communists!" stormed into the church, wielding whips and clubs. They beat up people, including the leaders of the PLRA (Authentic Radical Liberal Party) [and other political parties], and the journalists' trade union. Several persons had to be hospitalized.

The ruling Colorado party's Ramón Aquino, self-styled national "commander of the Colorado Assault Regiment," announced, "There will be wholesale beatings, we will beat them all up if they try to disrupt the peace, stability and tranquility of the Paraguayan people." Seventy-four-year-old dictator-president Alfredo Stroessner, completing his thirty-third year in office, gave Aquino a hearty abrazo, having earlier praised him as the "moderator" of the Catholic University, that is, the man in charge of silencing dissident students. Justice Minister Eugenio Jacquet, an ideologue of the Fascistic Anti-Communist Action Groups, lauded the attack as "a sign that we Colorados are walking tall."

Later in the month defiant opposition activists were on their way to a rally organized by the PLRA in Tebicuarymi, sixty miles southeast of Asunción. Police detained dozens of them, including Domingo Laino, head of the PRLA who had recently returned from exile. . . . All the detainees were later released, but the atmosphere remained unusually tense.

Many of Paraguay's 3.8 million people, most of whom spoke

both Spanish and the Indian language of Guaraní, knew nothing about these or other political events. They had lived under an almost continuous state of siege ever since the military coup that brought General Stroessner and the army to power in 1954. Among the politically knowledgeable, though, fear of kidnapping, torture, or death was a daily reality. Opposition activists tried to inform other Paraguayans of past events and convince them to act.

Leaflets, whether or not read, were quickly thrown away. To be caught with such material could mean arrest. The leaflets mentioned incidents like the following:

—In January 1985 police arrested 14 people attending a PLRA meeting in Itapua. Six of them, including a young girl, were tortured.

—In March 1980 army patrols in the economically booming frontier area of eastern Paraguay near the Brazilian border arrested 300 peasant members of the "peasant agrarian leagues." The army killed several of the detainees, including a popular peasant leader.

—In April–May 1974 police arrested 2,000 peasants and 200 students alleged to be members of the short-lived OPM (Political-Military Organization). Twenty of them, including two OPM leaders, died while in police custody. Seven Jesuit priests were expelled for their presumed support of OPM.

—In late 1975 and early 1976 some 70 people alleged to be members of the outlawed Paraguayan Communist party were detained. The party secretary-general, two central committee members and even pregnant women and children died from torture.

—In late 1974 authorities arrested 1,000 people accused of being involved with [Trotskyite] guerrillas [from] Argentina in a plot to kill Stroessner. Scores were deported and later disappeared in the neighboring military dictatorships of Argentina and Brazil.

Those old enough to remember whispered about the one-month lifting of the state of siege in 1959 that had led to founding [an opposition wing of the Colorado Party]. The army had opened fire on street demonstrators, and when the dictator's congress protested Stroessner closed it down, imprisoning and exiling hundreds of his party's dissident members. Ever since, up to half of all Paraguayans had lived in exile. Three-quarters of a million of them were peasants living in Argentina. A common saying was, "the slums of Paraguay are to be found in Argentina."

The main reason for the unusual tension of late 1987, however, was not merely that opposition movements were being subjected to severe repression. After all, that was not new. Rather, recent economic changes in Paraguay had generated energetic new social movements. The nation was in the throes of a full-scale political crisis. Ruling Colorado circles were divided on how to handle the situation. . . .

Background

A civil war in 1947 and its aftermath left Paraguay's politics in a state of factionalism and instability. Rival caudillos representing different landed and business interests of the triumphant Colorados could not agree on how to govern. People in Paraguay's tiny middle and working classes sought political democracy, better living conditions, and the right to organize—serious threats to traditional ways. The peasantry, although large, was too weak and passive to effect any change. It could be used by any Colorado faction gaining the upper hand as an ideological and organizational base for stable rule.

But since no faction could assert its hegemony, only one force remained to step into the resulting political vacuum: the army. A thirty-five-year-old veteran of the Chaco War, Alfredo Stroessner, recognized this. He mounted a successful coup d'état on May 4, 1954, less than a year after visiting the United States as the guest of Secretary of the Army Robert Stephens. His long reign guaranteed foreign economic interests in Paraguay and stopped in its tracks the often-repressed democratic movement of the middle and working classes.

"Preventive Repression" and *Stronismo*

Son of a German father and a Paraguayan mother, Stroessner started his military career at age sixteen and knew little more than barracks life. Order and discipline were the values he championed, values deeply ingrained in Paraguayan culture. During the political upheavals after World War II he sided with dictator Morínigo, who stepped down in 1948, and the victorious Colorados. In October 1951 he was appointed commander-in-chief of the armed forces under the government of President Federico Chávez (1950–54), a Colorado dictator in the Morínigo tradition whom he overthrew.

Although best known for his rule by terror, Stroessner differed from most other Latin American dictators in that he had a semblance of an organized, popular base, through the Colorado party. He used this base effectively throughout his long reign, subordinating it to the army that he controlled (he also brought the police under army control, in 1956). Traditional forms of caudillismo, *patrón*(boss)-peasant clientelism, and political patronage flourished under Stroessner, the supreme caudillo.

Stroessner used Paraguay's traditions of a strong state by peddling state recognition, favors, and business contracts in a manner so thorough that few Paraguayans escaped his influence. Public employees, teachers, doctors, and most students had to affiliate with the Colorado party. Those that objected too strenuously he imprisoned, deported, tortured, or killed. Two common torture techniques were immersion in the *pileta* (a bathtub of excrement) and electric shock to sex organs by the *picana eléctrica* (electric poker). Stroessner also ruled by dividing his opponents, currying favor with some while repressing others.

In the cities and bigger towns his Colorado followers built up the Urban Guard to terrorize dissidents and break up political meetings. They were augmented by secret police known by the Guaraní word of *pyragues* ("people with hairy feet"). Above all, Stroessner provided his army with modern weapons and lucrative land and industry handouts, hoping to assure its loyalty for as long as he lived.

After exiling his chief Colorado opponent in 1956, Stroessner implemented an IMF (International Monetary Fund)-proposed economic austerity program that drove real wages down and provoked a general strike two years later. Some 300 trade-union leaders were arrested, but social discontent did not go away. In 1959 Stroessner had to lift the state of siege briefly as a concession to his opposition. After troops and police attacked dissident Colorados demanding more democracy, Stroessner responded to congressional charges of police brutality by dissolving congress and arresting or exiling all remaining or suspected "dissidents" inside the ruling Colorado party. These numbered in the hundreds. From that point forward Stroessner did not even bother with the facade of democracy.

Stroessner's method of prolonging his rule became known as "preventive repression" and was publicly revealed at a 1972 Inter-American Defense Board meeting of U.S. and Latin American military brass. It was adopted by other dictators in the southern cone of South America, who coordinated with Stroessner the capturing or disappearing of exiled or fleeing opponents in one another's countries. Preventive repression involved "nipping in the bud" any signs of unrest by every conceivable means. As a result, Paraguay gained the reputation of having a "culture of fear" deeper than any other in Latin America, even though it clearly had rivals in each of its bordering countries and in El Salvador and Guatemala.

Brazilian and U.S. Investments: Economic Growth and Ethnocide

Stroessner's dictatorship established stable political conditions and a government-controlled labor force that attracted foreign investors. Brazil and the United States supplanted Argentina as the leading economic powers in Paraguay.

Construction of the world's largest hydroelectric project, the Itaipu dam on the eastern border with Brazil, sparked impressive economic growth rates in the 1970s—and controversy about Stroessner's giving in to Brazilian aggression. In 1964 Brazilian troops had occupied the Guaira Falls, the world's biggest waterfalls, today under water as part of the Itaipu dam. Paraguay had long claimed the falls as part of its territory. Nonetheless, Stroessner signed the treaty [which] provided for construction of the Itaipu dam with a capacity of 12,600 megawatts, six times greater than Egypt's famed Aswan dam. The two nations would share the resultant hydroelectric power 50/50. Paraguay would sell unused parts of its share to Brazil at a price fixed for the next fifty years at a level below international rates. For some time to come Paraguay's "sales" to Brazil would in fact be repayments of loans taken from Brazil to finance the $12 billion construction of the dam. Most of the construction contracts went to Brazil.

The two nations' armed forces policed the falls area, prohibiting anyone from seeing the conditions under which 25,000 workers labored to complete the dam by 1981. Official figures showed at least 43 workers died on the job, but most people believed the number of deaths was far higher. Wildcat strikes were put down, and in March 1978 some 3,000 workers rioted. Roads linking Paraguay to the Brazilian ports of Santos and Paranaguá were completed, breaking Paraguay's dependence on Argentina for its land and river trade routes.

New cities sprang up in the area around the falls, as the population quadrupled to more than 600,000. . . . With the new colonists came foreign industrialists, bankers, agribusinesses, and timber companies, mostly from Brazil and the United States.

Brazilian land companies bought up much of the land of eastern Paraguay, and the Brazilian "frontier" moved from the original eastern border deep into Paraguay, halfway to Asunción. Portuguese became the area's prevalent language and the Brazilian cruzeiro its most commonly used currency. Paraguayan nationalist dissenters were ruthlessly subdued, leading Bishop Claudio Silvero of Caaguazú Department (just west of Itaipu) to declare, "Too many have died, deaths have been concealed, and a climate of terror reigns."

To make way for the forces of "modernization," the ranks of bee-keeping and hunting and fishing Indian tribes were decimated. Less than 5 percent of Paraguay's population was Indian, but much of it faced ethnocide. Nobel Prize winner Elie Wiesel wrote, "Until now, I always forbade myself to compare the Holocaust of European Judaism to events which are foreign to it. And yet, I read the stories of the suffering and death of the Ache tribe in Paraguay and recognize familiar signs." Displacement of Paraguayan colonists and Indians generated a desperate and aggressive independent peasant movement that contributed to a political crisis in the mid-1980s.

Business favoritism from the top—the arrangement of land

sales and contracts by Stroessner and his friends in the military—was how the game was played throughout Paraguay. State investment went to infrastructure: the Itaipu dam, the Yacireta dam, the Trans-Chaco highway, telecommunications, river shipping.
. . .

Stroessner's government encouraged foreign investment in agroindustry and energy-intensive industries, including cattle-breeding, soybean production, fertilizers, and aluminum smelting. Three dollars left the country in profits and other payments for every one dollar that entered. Paraguay became the world's fifth largest exporter of soybeans. . . . Cotton, soybeans, and timber, in that order, surpassed meat products as the nation's leading exports. Paraguay's traditional "hidden economy" of smuggling boomed, particularly in timber (mostly Brazilian controlled), agricultural products, whisky, cigarettes, and narcotics.

Among U.S. firms investing in Paraguay were Coca-Cola, Exxon, Firestone, Florida Peach Corporation, Levi, and the "Big 3" of world banking—Citibank, Chase Manhattan, and Bank of America. Typical investment terms were those granted Gulf & Western in 1970 for 60,000 hectares of soybeans and wheat: all profits could be remitted to Gulf & Western's home offices tax-free.

Stimulated by the Itaipu project, Paraguay's annual GDP (gross domestic product) growth rate averaged 6 percent during the 1970s. With growth came government claims of improvements, including an "official" literacy rate of 92 percent and an increase in life expectancy from fifty-six years in 1960 to sixty-eight years in 1987. Few believed all the government's claims, however, since poverty remained extreme. For example, even by government figures, less than 7 percent of Paraguayans had sewage service and only 18 percent had indoor water supplies.

Itaipu's heating up of the economy generated runaway inflation, which officially stood at 32 percent in 1986 (44 percent in foodstuffs) and was said to be two or three times higher. The purchasing power of the average wage dropped by one-third in the 1970s and more in the 1980s. Unemployment soared, although the official figure was only 12 percent. Paraguay's terms of trade declined during the 1976–86 decade, and the foreign debt tripled to $1.8 billion, equivalent to half the GDP. Interest payments still were under 11 percent of export earnings, low by Latin American standards. According to the IDB [International Development Bank], industry stagnated in the 1980s because of a lack of internal demand for goods, contraband competition, and insufficient credits.

Politics: Strong Foreign Influences, Weak Opposition

U.S. military aid increased during the 1960s and 1970s, helping to convert the army into an efficient "high-tech" force. In 1965 the U.S. House of Representatives passed the "Selden resolution" authorizing the dispatch of U.S. troops to Paraguay in case of a threat of "international communism, directly or indirectly." More than 1,000 members of Paraguay's armed forces received U.S. training in either the Panama Canal Zone or the United States.

The United States backed Stroessner economically as well, despite U.S. criticisms of some of his government's practices (heroin smuggling, child prostitution, and human-rights violations). Prior to 1970 U.S. official aid amounted to $146 million. Larger amounts began to flow through international bodies like the World Bank and the IDB—half a billion dollars between 1961 and 1978.

Opposition to Stroessner's dictatorship initially came from banned political parties, the Church, and students. The most effective was the Church, which went so far as to excommunicate government officials accused of corruption or torture. All other groups were easily infiltrated by the one-million-member Colorado party or the government's intelligence agencies.

Liberal party elements launched unsuccessful guerrilla actions in late 1959, and Communists also failed with guerrilla warfare in 1960. Stroessner ordered that no prisoners be taken alive. Christian Democrats and radical priests practicing the theology of liberation organized peasant leagues. Troops and landlords' "hired guns" attacked them in the 1960s, when entire peasant communities were wiped out. In 1965 an independent student movement was formed but it too was crushed.

Paraguay's two universities, the National University of Asunción and the Catholic University, with 10,000 students, were centers of dissent monitored by Stroessner's secret agents.

Throughout most of the 1970s, preventive repression did its job effectively.

The human-rights proclamations of the Carter administration (1977–81) stirred new waves of opposition in Paraguay. Stroessner made only one concession to the pressure from Washington, however. He released some political prisoners who had been held for twenty years.

Then, in late 1977, Stroessner closed down the headquarters of the "loyal opposition" PLR (Radical Liberal Party) and froze its bank account. Most party members founded the illegal PLRA a year later. Stroessner also broke up newly emergent peasant leagues, organized by Christian Democrats. In 1978 the OAS (Organization of American States) condemned the Stroessner regime for its human-rights violations.

Despite the repression, Stroessner's opponents formed the tiny opposition coalition AN (National Accord) in 1979. Of its four parties, only the illegal Christian Democratic party went beyond middle-class demands for political rights to call for social and economic rights for the peasantry (nearly 60 percent of the population).

Stroessner resembled Chile's General Pinochet in his disdain for U.S. pressures on the human-rights issue. Both men prided themselves on having cleansed their nations of all Communists. Unlike Pinochet, however, Stroessner used a traditional political party (the Colorados) to legitimize his reign.

In 1979 Paraguay hosted the twelfth congress of the WACL (World Anti-Communist League), a fanatical ultraright organization known for its anti-Semitism and recruitment of Fascists, including former members of Hitler's SS and Gestapo. The WACL congress called Asunción the "capital of freedom and anticommunism" and elected a Paraguayan as WACL president. Other Paraguayan members of the WACL included the heads of the major branches of Stroessner's internal intelligence apparatuses. . . . Three other WACL members were a person who acted as Stroessner's ideological representative in repressing the prodemocracy wing of the Catholic Church, Stroessner's press secretary, and the former longtime head of the inactive Paraguayan Workers Federation. The president of the U.S. branch of WACL was John Singlaub, later famed for his role in the Iran-Contragate affair.

Stroessner cultivated close relations with the white minority government of South Africa and provided political refuge for former Nazis such as Dr. Joseph Mengele, the "Angel of Death" at Auschwitz concentration camp. Italian Fascists and right-wing terrorists also found refuge in Paraguay. To train his personal bodyguard, the "Escolta Batallion," Stroessner hired Croatian extremists (anti-Yugoslavian refugees). He also had his personal pilot fly Nicaragua's toppled dictator Somoza into Paraguay to set him up in a mansion that once had served as the South African Embassy. Somoza was later murdered by gunmen believed to be Argentine leftist guerrillas, leading to jubilant celebrations in Nicaragua.

The completion of the Itaipu dam project and ensuing economic downturn emboldened Paraguayans opposed to the dictatorship. The mid-1980s witnessed a rising tide of street protests, strikes, and peasant land occupations sparked by the newly created peasant and labor organizations. . . . All of these groups acted independently of the ineffective opposition parties.

The nation's Roman Catholic Bishops Conference publicly endorsed peasant land occupations and urged Stroessner to engage in a "national dialogue." Even big business's president of the Union Industrial Association stated, "All of us believe that democracy is best for free enterprise." But business groups, like labor groups, were weak, subject to either government favoritism or repression.

The government, refusing to [engage in] dialogue with an opposition it described as "subversive," "Communist," or "terrorist," responded with the largest number of arrests in many years. In March 1984 it shut down the nation's biggest circulating newspaper, *ABC Color*, whose publisher, Aldo Zuccolillo, had been a longtime friend of Stroessner and ran a financial empire in ranching and department stores. The paper had published an interview with a [dissident Colorado] leader who had been one of twenty prominent party members to be allowed back in the country after two decades in exile. The paper had also criticized "corruption in high places," a daring act in a *stronista* system that thrived on the parceling out of lucrative moneymaking opportunities. *ABC Color*'s journalists regrouped and launched in 1986 the opposition magazine, *Nuestro Tiempo*, directed by Bishop Mariot Melanio Medina.

One frequently arrested leader of the growing independent social movement was twenty-seven-year-old Dr. Carlos Filizzola, president of the Association of Physicians, the most popular labor leader in years. Striking hospital workers were able to mobilize bigger rallies than all the opposition parties combined. One problem the political parties and the Church seemed unaware of, according to Dr. Filizzola, was that, "You can't dialogue with a dictatorship."

Even the conservative Reagan government in Washington publicly expressed concern over Stroessner's escalating political repression. In 1985 a career diplomat named Clyde Taylor was appointed ambassador to Paraguay. Taylor established contact with the tiny opposition coalition AN. Younger rank-and-file AN members urged the older leadership to remain independent of U.S. influence. The leadership, however, cleansed the AN's youth ranks of "leftist influences," thereby losing many of its younger members and cutting the AN off from larger social movements being spurred by the younger generation.

In early 1987 Stroessner lifted the state of siege to allow the return of more political exiles. One who had returned earlier only to be beaten up by the police was Domingo Laino, an economist exiled for having written a book about Stroessner's friend, Somoza. Laino was the leader of the AN's largest party, the PLRA. He liked to compare himself to the Philippines' assassinated moderate anti-Marcos leader Aquino, who was killed when he returned from exile but whose widow became president after a mass popular uprising. On June 21, 1987, Laino was allowed to speak at a public rally attended by 30,000—the biggest crowd in decades.

But most opposition activity was restricted, and meetings were repeatedly broken up in the style of the September 1987 Colonel Oviedo incident described in this [essay's] . . . opening scene. In February 1987 police even lobbed tear gas at 300 "guests" seeking to enter a party being held for Ambassador Taylor, seen by the government as a symbol of the opposition because of his critiques of press censorship. The guests had come to declare their support for Taylor and had been organized by "Women for Democracy." In March the government silenced the independent Radio Nanduti; *ABC Color* also remained closed.

After so many years of banishment the opposition parties lacked a popular base. Laino endorsed the Church's call for a "national dialogue" and acknowledged that the opposition parties would play little, if any, role in a "democratic transition." The key actors, he said, would be the Church and military officers.

This was borne out in October 1987, when Archbishop Ismael Rolón, of Asunción, called for a protest campaign against "government-inspired violence." A Church-sponsored "silent march against repression" drew 40,000 citizens on October 30.

In response to the surprising eruption of protest movements, divisions inside the ruling Colorado party sharpened. The two main new factions were the "militantes" and the "traditionalists." Both supported Stroessner's proclaimed bid for this eighth reelection in elections scheduled for February 1988 which the opposition's AN boycotted and Stroessner predictably won.

Much of the intra-Colorado conflict revolved around politics in an anticipated post-Stroessner era. The *militantes* advocated continuation of rule by a military-civilian alliance, thereby honoring the traditions of stronismo. The traditionalists, while respecting those traditions, favored going further back in time to the tradition of Colorado party rule. In August 1987 the militantes ousted the traditionalists. The expelled faction objected but still stopped short of criticizing Stroessner, even though he approved their ouster.

A much smaller "ético," or "moralist," faction, also kicked out by the militantes, believed someone other than Stroessner should run for the presidency in 1988. Stroessner's ruling coalition further disintegrated in September 1987, when Liberal radicals, whose presence in congress had long given the appearance of a parliamentary opposition, walked out of congress. They ran a candidate against Stroessner in 1988, as did the Liberal party, but independent polls indicated 90 percent of Paraguayans did not know their names. Demonstrations against the electoral charade were broken up, and PLRA leader Laino was again arrested.

James D. Cockcroft

By everyone's testimony, indecipherable keys to Paraguay's political future rested inside the closed minds of the aging dictator and his army officers. Most often named "successors" to Stroessner were army commander General Andrés Rodríguez and Stroessner's eldest son Gustavo, an air force colonel. Some army commanders were rumored to be seeking a pact with the traditionalists to smooth a post-Stroessner transition. People whispered about a possible police/army conflict. No one, not even the AN parties, viewed the events of the 1980s as a transition to democracy. The army behind Latin America's longest-lasting dictator of the second half of the twentieth century still had things under control.

Further Reading

This list is designed to be more provocative than comprehensive and more representative than encyclopedic. I have chosen works that explore further definitions of caudillismo and offer more varieties of caudillaje experience.

Definitions, Theories, and Contexts

Alexander, Robert J. "Caudillos, Coroneis, and Political Bosses in Latin America." In *Presidential Power in Latin American Politics*, ed. Thomas V. DiBacco. New York: Praeger, 1977. Helps refine definitions.

Beezley, William H. "Caudillismo: An Interpretative Note." *Journal of Inter-American Studies* 11 (July 1969): 345–52. Argues that "while the genus is autocrat, the species, caudillo, is almost unique to nineteenth century . . . Spanish America."

Collier, David, ed. *The New Authoritarianism in Latin America*. Princeton: Princeton University Press, 1979. Explores bureaucratic-authoritarianism in the context of the 1970s through essays by Guillermo O'Donnell and others.

DiTella., Torcuato S. *Latin American Politics: A Theoretical Framework*. Austin: University of Texas Press, 1989. An Argentine scholar explores the nuances of caudillismo through sociological analysis based on many cases.

Duff, Ernest A. *Leader and Party in Latin America*. Boulder: Westview Press, 1985. Explores the relationship between caudillos and political parties in select places in the 1920s and 1930s.

Gilmore, Robert L. *Caudillism and Militarism in Venezuela, 1810–1910*. Athens: Ohio University Press, 1964. Gilmore argues that caudillismo was quite different from militarism in independent Venezuela before 1935. Personalism "with its accessory traits of violence, nepotism, extended families, oligarchy and pre-industrial economy" was at odds with the professionalism of the military.

Goldwert, Marvin. *Psychic Conflict in Spanish America: Six Essays on the Psychohistory of the Region*. Washington: University Press of America, 1982. Provocative if shallow studies from a Freudian perspective of "the lost father figure" (the king), youthful alienation of caudillos, and machismo.

Hale, Charles A. "The Reconstruction of Nineteenth-Century Politics in

Spanish America: A Case for the History of Ideas." *Latin American Research Review* 8 (Summer 1973): 53–73. Provides a critical frame of reference for the interpretative views of some selections in this book.

Humphreys, R. A. "The Caudillo Tradition." In *Tradition and Revolt in Latin America*, 216–28. New York: Columbia University Press, 1969. An Englishman's insights about the discrepancies between theory and practice. "Personalities have always mattered more than programmes."

Kern, Robert, ed. *The Caciques: Oligarchical Politics and the System of Caciquismo in the Luso-Hispanic World.* Albuquerque: University of New Mexico Press, 1973. A well-edited collection, with especially good essays on the cacique in literature.

Moreno, Francisco José. *Legitimacy and Stability in Latin America: A Study of Chilean Political Culture.* New York: New York University Press, 1969. A full-scale examination of caudillismo not only in Chile but elsewhere in Spanish America, along the lines suggested by Moreno's quote in the introduction to this book.

Morse, Richard M. *New World Soundings: Culture and Ideology in the Americas.* Baltimore: The Johns Hopkins University Press, 1989. Morse's essays, collected and recast. The broader and more recent context for Chapter 4.

Romero, José Luis. *A History of Argentine Political Thought.* Stanford: Stanford University Press, 1963. A classic analysis of the ideological climate that has often well served caudillismo and authoritarian rule.

Roniger, Luis. "Caciquismo and Coronelismo: Contextual Dimensions of Patron Brokerage in Mexico and Brazil." *Latin American Research Review* 22:2 (1987): 71–99. An extensive review of published research on the cacique.

Safford, Frank. "Politics, Ideology and Society in Post-Independence Spanish America." In *The Cambridge History of Latin America*, ed. Leslie Bethell. Vol. 3, *From Independence to c. 1870*, 347–421. Cambridge: Cambridge University Press, 1985. An especially insightful essay on the era that engendered so many caudillos.

Sater, William F. "Heroic Myths for Heroic Times." *Mexican Studies/ Estudios Mexicanos* 4:1 (Winter 1988), 151–61. Review article in which Sater asks why Latin American nations have more heroic figures than either England or the United States.

Schmidt, Steffan W., Laura Guasti, Carl H. Landé, and James C. Scott, eds. *Friends, Followers and Factions: A Reader in Political Clientelism.* Berkeley: University of California Press, 1977. Contains germane articles on ritual coparenthood *(compadrazgo)* by Sidney Mintz and Eric Wolf , cacique legitimacy by Paul Friedrich, and Mexican urban leaders by Wayne Cornelius.

Smith, Peter H. *Labyrinths of Power: Political Recruitment in 20th Cen-*

tury Mexico. Princeton: Princeton University Press, 1979. Helps illuminate the milieu in which political brokers are made. Compare
with Dealy (chapter 2).

Tannenbaum, Frank. "The Political Dilemma in Latin America." *Foreign
Affairs* 38 (April 1960): 497–515. A famous examination of caudi-
llismo. Tann enbaum included it as chapter 8 in his *Ten Keys to
Latin America.* New York: Knopf, 1962.

Wiarda, Howard J., ed. *Politics and Social Change in Latin America: The
Distinct Tradition.* 2d ed. Amherst: University of Massachusetts
Press, 1982. A valuable collection of essays on institutions, attitudes,
and values that are the context of caudillismo. Authors include Glen
Caudill Dealy, Richard M. Morse, Frederick Pike, and Howard J.
Wiarda.

Collected Caudillos

Boeker, Paul H. *Lost Illusions: Latin America's Struggle for Democracy,
As Recounted by its Leaders.* New York: Markus Wiener, 1990.
While these twenty-six exceptionally candid interviews with major
contemporary politicians by a retired U.S. diplomat are democratically inclined, the personalist characteristics of some of them are
subtly evident.

Brading, David A., ed. *Caudillo and Peasant in the Mexican Revolution.*
Cambridge: Cambridge University Press, 1980. Refinements of caudillismo and caciquismo are developed with sophistication from case
studies by Friedrich Katz on Pancho Villa, Linda Hall on Alvaro
Obregón, and Dudley Ankerson on Saturnino Cedillo, among others.

Díaz Díaz, Fernando. *Caudillos y caciques: Antonio López de Santa Anna
y Juan Alvarez.* México: El Colegio de México, 1972. Judiciously
applies Max Weber's theories to Mexico during independence and,
especially, in the generation afterwards.

Krehm, William. *Democracia y tiranías en el Caribe.* México: Unión
Democrática Centroamericana, 1949. Thoughtful reports on Caribbean caudillos in the 1940s by a former *Time* correspondent.

Labastida Martín del Campo, Julio, comp. *Dictaduras y dictadores.* México: Siglo Veintiuno, 1986. Uneven but provocative collection that
includes a study on legitimacy by Alain Rouquié and essays about
Rosas and Juan Vicente Gómez. Luis González's sketch of Díaz is to
be found here (Chapter 14).

Revista/Review Interamericana 7:3 (Fall 1977). A special issue devoted
to Caribbean dictators. Contains essays by Louis Pérez on Batista,
Luis Aguilar on Castro, Michael Malek on Trujillo, Charles Stansifer
on Zelaya, Richard Millett on Anastasio ("Tacho") Somoza and Judith
Ewell on Pérez Jiménez. The full text of Chapter 20 is to be found
here. Ends with a useful summary by Kenneth Grieb.

Wilgus, A. Curtis, ed. *South American Dictators During the First Century of Independence.* Washington: George Washington University Press, 1937. Extensive prosopography as useful for what it says about North American views of caudillo history in the 1930s as for the sketches themselves.

Williams, John Hoyt. *The Rise and Fall of the Paraguayan Republic, 1800–1870.* Austin: University of Texas Press, 1979. The best treatment of Paraguay's nineteenth-century history and its three famous caudillos: Dr. Francia ("El Supremo"), Carlos Antonio López, and his son, Francisco Solano López.

Wolfskill, George, and Douglas Richmond, eds. *Essays on the Mexican Revolution: Revisionist Views of the Leaders.* Austin: University of Texas Press, 1979. Includes William Beezley on Madero, Katz on Villa, Richmond on Carranza, David Bailey on Obregón, and Lyle Brown on Cárdenas.

Individual Caudillos

While the focus in this section is biographical, I have included only those works that help to increase an understanding of personal power. Less well known leaders appear when the authors pursue this goal. It is not, therefore, a complete list of works on all famous caudillos.

Anna, Timothy E. *The Mexican Empire of Iturbide.* Lincoln: University of Nebraska Press, 1990. A fresh view of a leader who failed to transform charisma into moral authority and thus overcome devisive regionalism.

Arriagada, Genaro. *Pinochet: The Politics of Power.* Translated by Nancy Morris. Winchester: Allen & Unwin, 1988. A full treatment of Pinochet's manipulative skills by the author of chapter 26, written before the 1988 plebiscite.

Balfour, Sebastian. *Castro.* London: Longman, 1990. A recent, brief, and remarkably balanced appraisal.

Braun, Herbert. *The Assassination of Gaitán: Public Life and Urban Violence in Colombia.* Madison: University of Wisconsin Press, 1985. Implications of the life and death of a personalist leader in the 1940s who challenged the liberal/conservative Establishment.

Castro, Fidel. *Fidel and Religion: Castro Talks on Revolution and Religion with Frei Betto.* Translation. New Brunswick: Transaction Publishers, 1989. An important insight into Castro's character through interviews with a Brazilian Dominican in 1985. Widely distributed in Latin America.

Crassweller, Robert D. *Perón and the Enigmas of Argentina.* New York: Norton, 1987. A readable attempt to explain psychological and cultural factors behind Perón's extraordinary power.

Crassweller, Robert D. *Trujillo: The Life and Times of a Caribbean Dictator.* New York: Macmillan, 1966. Well-researched, contains oral histories as well as documents. Printed soon after Trujillo's death. Filled with spicy detail.

Diedrich, Bernard. *Somoza and the Legacy of U.S. Involvement in Central America.* New York: Dutton, 1981. A perceptive journalist's view of the Somozas and especially of "Tachito," who was overthrown by the Sandinista Revolution in 1979.

Ewell, Judith. *The Indictment of a Dictator: The Extradition and Trial of Marcos Pérez Jiménez.* College Station: Texas A&M University Press, 1981. Against the background of Venezuela's caudillo, Juan Vicente Gómez, this book explores the remarkable trial of Pérez Jiménez (1948–58), who was prosecuted by the democratic government of Rómolo Betancourt.

Fagen, Richard. "Charismatic Authority and the Leadership of Fidel Castro." In *Cuba in Revolution,* eds. R. E. Bonachea and N. Valdés, 154–68. Garden City: Doubleday, 1972. Compare with Chapters 24 and 25.

Filippi, Alberto. *Instituciones e ideologías en la independencia hispanoamericana.* Buenos Aires: Alianza Editorial, 1988. An Italian-Venezuelan historian includes important historiographic treatment of Bolívar along a spectrum of opinion.

Franqui, Carlos. *Family Portrait with Fidel: A Memoir.* New York: Random House, 1984. Firsthand account of Fidel in the early years of the Revolution by his foremost journalist and editor, who went into exile in 1968.

Fraser, Nicholas, and Marysa Navarro. *Eva Perón.* New York: Norton, 1985. A full-scale biography coauthored by the author of chapter 22.

Fusi Aizpurúa, Juan P. *Franco: A Biography.* New York: Harper and Row, 1987. A succinct account of El Caudillo which—in Fusi's words—avoids "eulogy and calumny alike."

Goodsell, James Nelson, ed. *Fidel Castro's Personal Revolution in Cuba: 1959–1973.* New York: Knopf, 1974. A broad spectrum of essays and reports that helps to reveal Fidel's style.

Grieb, Kenneth J. *Guatemalan Caudillo: The Regime of Jorge Ubico, Guatemala, 1931–1944.* Athens: Ohio University Press, 1979. A solid biography and contribution to caudillaje literature. Ubico was a Man on Motorcycle.

Haigh, Roger M. *Martín Güemes: Tyrant or Tool? A Study of the Sources of Power of an Argentine Caudillo.* Fort Worth: Texas Christian University Press, 1968. A fuller treatment than that in chapter 10 with valuable charts, tables, and genealogies that demonstrate Güemes's family connections.

Hall, Linda B. *Alvaro Obregón: Power and Revolution in Mexico, 1911–*

1920. College Station: Texas A&M University Press, 1981. A meticulous study of the charismatic Mexican caudillo who came closest to creating order out of the Revolution.

Hamill, Hugh M. *The Hidalgo Revolt: Prelude to Mexican Independence.* 2d. ed. Westport: Greenwood, 1981. Includes an interpretation of the leadership of the insurgent priest examined in chapter 6.

The Hispanic American Historical Review 63:1 (February 1983). Given the vast literature on Simón Bolívar (1783–1830), one approach is to examine this 200th Anniversary issue for its valuable essays on various aspects of the Liberator's life. They include John Lynch, "Bolívar and the Caudillos," 3–35, and David Bushnell, "The Last Dictatorship: Betrayal or Consummation," 65–105.

Kinsbruner, Jay. *Diego Portales: Interpretative Essays on the Man and Times.* The Hague: Martinus Nijhoff, 1967. A brief introduction to the most important postindependence caudillo in Chile.

Lynch, John. *Argentine Dictator: Juan Manuel de Rosas, 1829–1852.* New York: Oxford University Press, 1981. Already classic biography of Argentina's most significant caudillo.

Meyer, Michael C. *Huerta: A Political Portrait.* Lincoln: University of Nebraska Press, 1972. The first scholarly evaluation of the much maligned Mexican anti-hero who was much less a reactionary than Revolutionary mythology would have it.

Miranda, Carlos R. *The Stroessner Era: Authoritarian Rule in Paraguay.* Boulder: Westview Press, 1990. The best account of Stroessner's ability to read the historical and cultural traditions of his society. Covers Stroessner's career through the Rodríguez coup of February 1989.

Montaner, Carlos Alberto. *Fidel Castro and the Cuban Revolution: Age, Position, Character, Destiny, Personality, and Ambition.* New Brunswick: Transaction Publishers, 1989. A caustic and witty treatment of Fidel by a Cuban exile who knew most of the players.

Nunn, Frederick M. "One Year in the Life of Augusto Pinochet: Gulag of the Mind." *The Americas* 42:2 (October 1985): 197–206. Helps reveal the mental world of Chile's most famous dictator.

Page, Joseph A. *Perón: A Biography.* New York: Random House, 1983. A thorough and balanced study that explores all facets of Perón's life and rule.

Park, James William. *Rafael Núñez and the Politics of Colombian Regionalism, 1863–1886.* Baton Rouge: Louisiana State University Press, 1985. Provides useful background on the life of the *costeño* leader.

Payne, Stanley G. *The Franco Regime, 1936–1975.* Madison: University of Wisconsin Press, 1987. A full-dress study that examines every aspect of Francisco Franco's career.

Pineda de Castro, Alvaro. *Pinochet: verdad y ficción.* Madrid: Vassallo de

Mumbert, 1981. A hagiographic defense, with pictures of the general as a doting grandfather.

Remmer, Karen L. *Military Rule in Latin America.* Winchester: Unwin Hyman, 1989. An exploration of the relationship between authoritarianism and the military, with some refreshing theoretical views. Chile's Pinochet is the prime case study.

Rourke, Thomas. [Daniel Joseph Clinton]. *Gómez: Tyrant of the Andes.* New York: Morrow, 1936. In spite of errors and bias against Venezuela's Juan Vicente Gómez (1908–35) this journalist's account provides a valuable portrait.

Smith, Peter H. "The Image of a Dictator: Gabriel García Moreno." *The Hispanic American Historical Review* 45:1 (February 1965): 1–24. The career of Ecuador's mid-nineteenth-century theocratic caudillo.

Szuchman, Mark D. "Household Structure and Political Crisis: Buenos Aires, 1810–1860." *Latin American Research Review* 21:3 (1986): 55–93. Uses sophisticated demographic analysis to argue that Rosas's authoritarian rule had mass support because it provided stability after twenty years (ca. 1810–30) of political chaos.

Szulc, Tad. *Fidel: A Critical Portrait.* New York: Morrow, 1986. A journalist's view based on thirty years' experience in Cuba and on many interviews with Castro, especially during 1984–85.

Taylor, Julie M. *Eva Perón: The Myths of a Woman.* Chicago: University of Chicago Press, 1979. An engaging view of "Evita" and her legacy by an anthropologist.

Turner, Frederick C., and José Enrique Miguens, eds. *Juan Perón and the Reshaping of Argentina.* Pittsburgh: University of Pittsburgh Press, 1983. A useful collection of articles that explore Perón and his impact on Argentina through both his presidencies.

Vallenilla Lanz, Laureano. *Cesarismo democrático.* Caracas, 1929. Philosophical apologia for the Gómez regime. Compare with Rourke's book and Cuevillas's essay (chapter 23).

Van Aken, Mark J. *King of the Night: Juan José Flores and Ecuador, 1824–1864.* Berkeley: University of California Press, 1989. A particularly important work because of its emphasis on the viability of monarchism in postindependence Spanish America. Flores led efforts to set up monarchies in Bolivia and Peru as well as in Ecuador.

Weston, Charles H., Jr. "The Political Legacy of Lázaro Cárdenas." *The Americas* 39:3 (January 1983): 383–405. Explores the paradox of a Mexican social reformer who turned corporatist, and whose selflessness and respect for principle made him no less a caudillo in Mexico.

Wiarda, Howard J. *Dictatorship and Development: The Methods of Control in Trujillo's Dominican Republic.* Gainesville: University of Florida Press, 1968. A richly detailed discussion of Trujillo's unique rule, with attention paid to theoretical constructs and the implications of the regime. By the coauthor of chapter 20.

Wise, George, S. *Caudillo: A Portrait of Antonio Guzmán Blanco*. New York: Columbia University Press, 1951. A case study of a late-nineteenth-century Venezuelan caudillo.

Caudillos in Literature

The colorful nature of personalist rule and the multitude of caudillos and caciques have attracted some of Spanish America's best writers. It is possible to list only a sample of their fiction here.

Allende, Isabel. *The House of Spirits*. Translated by Magda Bogin. New York: Knopf, 1985. Esteban Trueba, protagonist of this novel, is one of the memorable public men in modern Chilean fiction.

Asturias, Miguel Angel. *El Señor Presidente*. Translated by Frances Partridge. New York: Atheneum, 1975. First published in Spanish in 1946. The classic caudillo novel by a Nobel Prize laureate; based on the Guatemalan, Manuel Estrada Cabrera (1898–1920).

Azuela, Mariano. *The Underdogs [Los de abajo]*. Translated by E. Munguía, Jr. New York: New American Library, 1963. First published in Spanish in 1916. Classic novel of a rural caudillo, Demetrio Macías, caught up in the Mexican Revolution.

Roa Bastos, Augusto. *I the Supreme*. Translated by Helen Lane. New York: Knopf, 1986. A rich novel on the career of Dr. José Gaspar Rodríguez de Francia (1811–40); by a Paraguayan exile.

Brushwood, John S. *The Spanish American Novel: A Twentieth-Century Survey*. Austin: University of Texas Press, 1980. Includes critical treatment of many works on caudillaje themes.

Carpentier, Alejo. *El Recurso del método*. México: Siglo Veintiuno, 1974. In contrast to the unlettered tyrant in *The Autumn of the Patriarch*, the subject of this novel is an enlightened despot. By a Cuban.

Castellanos, Jorge, and Miguel A. Martínez. "El Dictador hispanoamericano como personaje literario." *Latin American Research Review* 16:2 (1981): 79–105. Discusses the genre selectively, with attention to the psychology of caudillos.

Fuentes, Carlos. *The Death of Artemio Cruz*. Translated by Sam Hileman. New York: Farrar, Straus & Giroux, 1964. The quintessential Mexican authoritarian personality produced by the chaos of the Revolution.

Gallegos, Rómulo. *Doña Barbara*. New York: Appleton-Century Crofts, 1961. The tale of a caudilla in the harsh world of the Venezuelan backcountry *Llanos*.

García Márquez, Gabriel. *The Autumn of the Patriarch*. Translated by Gregory Rabassa. New York: Harper and Row, 1976. A surrealist portrait of a mythical Caribbean tyrant.

García Márquez, Gabriel. *The General in His Labyrinth*. Translated by

Edith Grossman. New York: Knopf, 1990. The Nobel Prize laureate's controversial novel about the last days of Simón Bolívar.

Rama, Angel. *Los Dictadores latinoamericanos.* México: Fondo de Cultura Económica, 1976. An astute critic's assessment of the novels by García Márquez, Roa Bastos, and Carpentier.

Valle-Inclán, Ramón del. *Tirano banderas.* 8th ed. Madrid: Espasa-Calpe, 1972. First published in 1926 by a Spaniard, and considered the earliest modern novel about the Spanish American caudillo.

Index

Index

Index

Taxes: reform in Salta, 152; *see also* head tax
Taylor, Clyde: 346–47
Tebicuarymi, Para.: 336
Telecommunications, Stroessner control of: 342
Tenochtitlán, Mex.: *see* Mexico City
Tertulias, literary: 56
Theosophy, Hernández Martínez and: 259
Tineo, Bárbara: 150
Tineo family: 146
Tocqueville, Alexis de: 42, 56
Toledo, María de: 149
Toledo family: 147, 148–49
Tolima, dept. of: 163
Torture: by Paraguayan police, 23, 337, 339; Somoza use of, 266; see also *picanaelectrica*; *pileta*
Totalitarianism, and authoritarianism contrasted: 252, 256
Tourism, Trujillo encouragement of: 227
Trans-Chaco highway: 342
Troncoso, Jesús María: 243
Troncoso de la Concha, Manuel "Pipí": 237–38, 239–40, 244
Trujillista Party: 238, 239
Trujillo, Flor de Oro: 241
Trujillo, Hector: 242
Trujillo, María de: 242
Trujillo, Radamés: 242
Trujillo, Rafael: 5, 10, 11, 21, 24n.11, 208, 213, 218–56; anti-Communism used by, 245; assassination of, 8, 218, 235, 246, 247, 256; early career of, 240–41; as godfather, 36; nepotism of, 36, 54; personal life of, 241–42; self-promotion of, 218; and U.S. Marines, 240; *see also* Dominican Party
Trujillo, Rafael, Jr. "Ramfis": 242
Tucumán, Congress of: 151
Tucumán, province of: 152, 153
Tunja, Col.: 139–40
Turks, Isabella vs.: 73–74
Tyrant, and caudillo contrasted: 287

Ubico, Jorge: 213–14, 267
Unión Cívica Radical (Arg.): 278
Unión Democrática (Arg.): 278

United Fruit Company: 262
United States: anti-Communism of, 218; as "caudillo-friendly," 249; and Dominican Republic, 232, 236, 240–41, 295; and Latin America, 10, 197–98; and Mexico, 68; and Nicaragua, 214, 259–61, 267, 268, 269; and Paraguay, 340–44, 346; power of president of, 295; Trujillo stroking of, 251; *see also* Carter, Jimmy; Johnson, Lyndon B.; Kennedy, John F.; Roosevelt, Franklin D.
Universalism, and particularism contrasted: 59–60
Upper Peru: Argentinian invasion of, 146, 148–49, 150, 152–53; Güemes in, 146; as Spanish bastion, 151
Urban Guard (Para.): 339
Urdaneta, Rafael: 132, 135–37, 141, 143
Ureña, Estrella: 213, 241
Urquiza, Justo José de: 68
Urrutia, Manuel: 302, 308
Uruguay, political processes in: 59; *see also* Saravia, Aparicio
Utopianism, Bilbao and: 155

Valdivia, Pedro de: 3
Vallenilla Lanz, Laureano: 93
Vaqueros, Colombian: *see* Llaneros
Varela, Felice: 121
Vargas, Getulio: 9, 252
Vásquez, Horacio: 212, 241
Velasco Alvarado, Juan: 9
Velázquez, Diego: 29
Véliz, Claudio: 12
Vendettas: 35
Venegas, Francisco (Mexican viceroy): 106
Venezuela: Bolívar liberation of, 133; as "gendarmist" state, 208; horsemen of, 31; under Jiménez, 95; Llanero affinity for, 136; under Páez, 67, 80, 141; as "praetorian" state, 208; *see also* Bolívar, Simon; Carabobo, battle of; Gómez, Juan Vicente; Guzmán Blanco, Antonio; Gran Colombia; Llanceros; Monagas, José; Páez, José Antonio; Pérez Jiménez, Marcos

Victoria, queen of England: 175
Vietnam, U.S. in: 295
Villa, Pancho: 80
WACL (World Anti-Communist League): 344–45
Walker, William: 4
Washington, D.C.: 269
Weaver, Jerry: 60
Weber, Max: 11, 43, 80, 81, 82, 87–92, 94
Whelan, Thomas: 269
Whisky, Paraguayan smuggling of: 342
Wiarda, Howard: 11, 21, 218, 246–56
Wiesel, Elie: 341
Wilson, Charles: 269
Wise, George S.: 81
Wolf, Eric R.: 18, 62–71
Women: in Eva Perón's Argentina, 270–84; in Díaz Mexico, 177; in Dominican Republic, 223; Paraguayan police torture of, 337
World Anti-Communist League (WACL): 344–45
World Bank: 343
World War II: Dominican Republic in, 230, 238, 244; France in, 299

Yacireta dam: 342
Yrigoyen, Hipólito: 5, 291

Zaraza, Pedro: 31
Zavala, Pedro: 154
Zerda, Angel M.: 154
Zipaquirá, Col.: 132, 139
Zipas: 167
Zitácuaro, Mex.: 106
Zola, Émile: 176
Zuccolillo, Aldo: 345